Comets & Concordes

Peter Duffey

Burnt Ash Publishing

This book is dedicated to my wife, Jeane, for her love, loyalty and help throughout my career. Also to Christopher, Susan and Camilla who had to accept so many disruptions of family life.

First published in the United States by Paladwr Press in 1999
First published in Great Britain by Burnt Ash Publishing in 2020

Burnt Ash Publishing
A division of Burnt Ash Developments Limited
86-90 Paul Street
London
EC2A 4NE

Copyright © 1999 by Peter Duffey
Printed by T J International
Typeset in Bookman Old Style, titles in Impact, captions in Acumin

ISBN 978-1-9162161-6-7

A CIP Catalogue for this book is available from the British Library

Contents

Foreword

Since the Wright brothers took to the air, there have been two quantum leaps in civil aviation and Peter Duffey played a large part in both. He comes from a family that was steeped in aviation and whose father flew autogiros for fun. Inspired by the boyhood sight of the R101 airship and a joy ride in a Fox Moth, he became the only pilot to have flown the Comet 1, Comet 4, and Concorde.

For those of us who know Peter well, this is a very personal book. One can hear him speaking (and occasionally visualise him raising his eyebrows) as he recounts the story of a career that encompasses the Second World War, several airlines, and a multitude of aircraft types. There is something in it for everyone with an interest in aviation. The account covers a wealth of detail, from the 130 handle turns to raise an Anson undercarriage to the metallurgy and gauge of the Comet skin. For some it will be an insight into what really happened — the problems and the solutions. For others, it will trigger memories of times past, be they Star Girls, control of Very lights, falling chandeliers in Moscow, or flying faster than a bullet.

The one thing that comes across strongly in this book is the fact that Peter was a pilot with an independent spirit, an insatiable curiosity, and a healthy scepticism about all aspects of flying. One facet of his lateral thinking ability is highlighted in the training incident quoted when instructing a pilot who appeared to be unable to cope with asymmetric flying. Rather than recording a failure, he sent him to a doctor, who diagnosed an inner ear problem. That pilot must be very grateful to Peter Duffey.

People who ask questions are essential in aviation. They may ruffle a few feathers now and again; but there are times

4

when someone has to say that the king is not wearing any clothes. When he wanted to find something out, he did not content himself with merely reading the perceived wisdom in the manuals. He would go and look at the aeroplane stripped down in the hangar, talk to the maintenance engineers that worked on it and, if possible, speak to the designers. If he did not like what he saw, he would speak out. Two examples come to mind in the book: first, his voiced disquiet over the continued operation of the Comet 1 after the Elba crash; second, expressing his criticisms of the operation to the company chairman, when he was on the Concorde flight deck.

I have known Peter since the time, back in the 1950s, when we both flew Argonauts. I was just beginning my career, he had already flown the Comet 1. We have known each other for more than forty years, but the period when I came to know him really well and appreciate his talents was when we were part of a very small group of seven pilots and seven flight engineers carrying out the Concorde initial flying for British Airways. This was very demanding work, involving the route proving flying, followed by setting up the Concorde flying training programme. This book is an opportunity to share some delightful, and occasionally exciting, memories of a remarkable aviation career.

Tony Meadows
May 1999

Acknowledgements

This book would never have been written without an initial suggestion by Ron Davies that these events were worth recording, in the setting of my personal experiences. The development of civil aviation during the 20th century has been remarkable. It has revolutionised international relations, and I have been in a position to observe much of it, quite literally from the vantage point of the pilot's seat.

Air travel is safer today than ever, and statistics record the success of the air transport industry as a whole. By implication, the designers and engineers can measure their success by the technical excellence of the aircraft; while the economists and accountants can do likewise through the achievements of the airlines. But the part played by those who sit in the flight deck is too often taken for granted, and subject to minute inspection and critical analysis when things go wrong. Yet the aircrew have to maintain a constant and unforgiving daily interface with the policies and efforts of manufacturers, airlines, and regulators. I have been privileged to have been closely involved during many fundamental changes in these policies and efforts; and I know that many of my colleagues have contributed to the advancement and refinement of safety and operating standards. In writing this book, therefore, I wish thereby to acknowledge their professional competency and dedication.

The editorial requirement to lick my account into shape has been considerable, and I wish to thank Ron for his cheerful and persistent help in this respect, and for his constant encouragement. A fine and productive review was also prepared by Jacqueline Scott Mandeville, and this was appreciated by this writer, as well as by the publisher.

Although we both flew with BSAA and on Argonauts in BOAC, I never found myself crewed with Archie Jackson; but I must acknowledge the interesting and valuable content of his book, *Both Feet in the Air*, which describes our South American days so well. Other sources of reference included, *Wings for Victory*, by Spencer Dunmore, *Concorde and the Americas*, by Ken Owen, and, *The Seven Skies*, by John Pudney.

Peter Duffey
June 1999

Credits

The publishers are very grateful to British Airways, BAE Systems, Imperial War Museum, Ministry of Defence, NATS Holdings, BBC, Smithsonian National Air and Space Museum, and many others for their help and cooperation, as well as the use of their photographs, along with other information and data.

Publisher's note

In March 2020, I received an email from Peter Duffey enquiring about a book we published on BOAC. The name rang a bell and I asked him if he was the same Peter Duffey who had flown both Concorde and the Comet 1. 'It is he,' came the reply, and we began to exchange messages. I knew that Peter had written a book entitled *Comets and Concordes*, but I had been unable to find a copy. Peter explained that his publisher, Reg Davies of Paladwr Press, had died in 2011 after a long and successful career, and consequently the book was now out of print.

We are delighted to republish this wonderful work and bring it to a new audience. Of the many pilot biographies I have read, this is surely one of the most outstanding. Not only does Peter cover a remarkable era of aviation, taking the reader from wood and canvass biplanes through to supersonic airliners (with many fascinating aircraft in-between), but he also reminds us of the remarkable people whose paths he crossed and the many ways in which civil aviation changed the world. For anyone with an interest in the evolution of air transport, or contemporary history, this is essential reading.

Malcolm Turner
June 2020

Introduction

Aviation interests and experiences came my way at an early age. Perhaps the first time when I was conscious of the limitless possibilities of freedom that beckoned in the upper atmosphere was one afternoon walking home from school, when I heard the engines of the airship R101, and looked up to see it setting out on what was to be a fateful journey to destruction. Gleaming in the sunlight, graceful and ponderous, it somehow symbolised the vast dimensions of sky and cloud, at the same time making them seem attainable. Imagining myself to be on board was easy.

Various members of my family were in contact with aviation activity during the 1930s. My father flew Cierva autogyros (an early precursor of the helicopter) as a hobby, and had sometimes landed in a field close to my school, on one occasion to whisk me off on a flight — vertical take-offs were rather spectacular in those days. Based at Hanworth airfield off the Great West Road, (west London) where de Havilland Moths and Klemm monoplanes flew with increasing frequency, the London Aeroplane Club was the meeting place for many personalities, including Amy Johnson, Jim Mollison, and Reggie Marsh, who was a test pilot and instructor associated with the gyroplanes.

There was my uncle, Roy, who spent his career with de Havilland, for many years as an instructor in the Technical School, and my uncle Leslie, who was a Royal Flying Corps (RFC), pilot in the First World War. He had flown continuously from 1915 onwards, and possessed three albums of photographs, all studies of crashed aircraft, mainly in treetops.

While at school near Felixstowe, Suffolk, on the east coast of England, I would cycle to watch the flying at Martlesham

Heath, where various experimental aircraft could be seen, including the early version of the Handley Page Hampden, a twin-engined monoplane bomber, known as 'the flying suitcase' because of its shape. By the mouth of the River Deben, across from the first radio location (radar) station at Bawdsey, lay some derelict wooden flying boat hulls, cast away from the base near Felixstowe. We would climb all over these, imagining many scenarios. One afternoon we witnessed a separation of the Mayo composite aircraft, with the lower flying boat *Maia* breaking away from the seaplane *Mercury*. This may have been an historic event, and it certainly left a group of schoolboys with much to discuss.

First flight

My first flight was in a de Havilland Fox Moth on a five shilling pleasure flip, taking off from Croydon, then the premier civil airfield for London. Parked close to the control tower were a couple of Handley Page HP.42 four-engined biplanes belonging to Imperial Airways.

A second visit to Croydon was as an airline passenger, on a family holiday to Knokke-le-Zoute on the Belgian coast near Zeebrugge. The competitor to Imperial Airways was the original British Airways, and we flew in a four-engined de Havilland biplane belonging to that airline, crossing the Channel at low-level. This was very exciting, and perhaps was a deciding incentive steering me to an aviation career.

During the early 1930s aviation was still the subject of intense curiosity and publicity. The era of record-breaking flights was peaking with such events as the England to Australia race, the flight over Mount Everest, and many long distance solo attempts. The pioneering efforts across continents, even the Pacific Ocean, of Pan American Airways and Imperial Airways, using large flying boats, had caught the public attention. Lufthansa and Air France had pioneered air mail routes to South America, and the epitaph of the airships had yet to be written.

The Short Mayo Composite was a piggy-back long-range seaplane/ flying boat combination produced by Short Brothers to provide a reliable long-range air transport service to North America, Africa and Asia.

My first job at Hawker

When the Second World War started, my father joined the RAF as an administration officer, and was soon shipped overseas. I saw little of him until the end of the conflict as he spent his war in India and Burma, involved with many forward airfield operations. Eventually he became the personal assistant to the Inspector General of the RAF who, at that time, I think was Air Marshal 'Ugly' Barratt.

My mother died when I was eleven, from a dubious disease then euphemistically called pneumonia, which today would be called lung cancer, brought on by chain-smoking. My father remarried, but the enforced separation of five years caused that to break up. The domestic situation was rather difficult, and my support was divided between grandparents and other relatives. Funds ran out to keep me at school, and I was encouraged to enter some sort of employment. This resulted in a job as a junior draughtsman-cum-office boy, with the Hawker design office.

The author's first flight was in a de Havilland Fox Moth from Croydon Airfield.

Soon after the Luftwaffe raids began on London, Hawker had moved its design office from the factory at Kingston upon Thames, a vulnerable site, to a commandeered girls' school: Claremont, near Esher in Surrey. Sydney Camm, and a distinguished team of design staff, portioned out the classrooms into various sections dealing with project design, stressing, systems, airframes, and aerodynamics. Many draughtsmen and designers had previously been accustomed to visiting the shop floor to check on the implementation of component design, and regretted the necessity of the move, which separated them from the construction activity.

My initial function was confined to keeping a vast store of design prints in a systematic order and replenishing the store as needed. I can still smell the ammonia given off by freshly produced prints. This gave me a degree of familiarity with a range of activity that was to serve me very well. I was enrolled in the day release programme set up at a local technical school, together with a couple of other would-be designers. We were expected to qualify for the intermediate examinations on the path towards securing a BSc in aeronautical engineering. During this period I graduated to a seat in one of the section offices, and was given various layout and other less important tasks. We were engaged in design work on the Hurricane, Tornado, and Typhoon. Many projects appeared in response to Air Ministry specifications, including a four-engined bomber, which never did get approval.

Claremont was in rather grand and well-landscaped grounds, and during lunch breaks on fine days some of us would gather on the front lawns to launch model aircraft, to serve as an additional extra-mural apprenticeship.

The Air Training Corps (ATC)

As the war entered its third year the possibility arose of joining the Royal Air Force (RAF). The RAF Volunteer Reserve was a wartime addition to the cadre of permanent peacetime staff and the part-time Auxiliary Air Force. Joining the Air Training Corps, familiarly known as the ATC; a national organisation that had been formed to give young men an initial education and training to fit them for the service, I soon found that my spare time was completely absorbed.

We visited many airfields and other establishments such as the apprentice school at Halton. I was fortunate enough to become airborne on several occasions in front line aircraft on their daily air tests. One flight, in a Vickers Wellington, turned into quite an event as we had to divert because of an intruder raid on the home base. We visited Biggin Hill to see how a fighter unit was organised and witnessed the scramble of two squadrons on an interception mission. The noise and smell of the massed start-up is an enduring memory, with Coffmann cartridges blowing smoke across the parked aircraft, as they cranked the engines to life.

Joining up

After achieving the required proficiency certificates, and the dizzy rank of sergeant, it was time to apply for enlistment. I was in a reserved occupation in the design office, and could, or perhaps should, have stayed there for the duration of the war.

Two factors urged otherwise: the strongest was the call to fly, but also my personal situation at home, with the difficulties caused for myself and others. The problem was that I had not yet reached the age of eighteen, the minimum for recruitment. The world's wars are fought by the very young.

I was soon in possession of a letter giving me parental authorization to enlist and a declaration of age advanced by a year. After a month I received a letter from the RAF giving the time and place for an interview and aptitude testing. The night before this event was taken up by a boxing engagement, with our ATC squadron contesting another in the national league. I was categorized in the light heavyweight class, in fact at the bottom end of that weight bracket, against someone at the top end. The three-round amateur bout was painful, with punishment abundantly absorbed, before my loss was announced by the judges. The effects of this pounding were impossible to hide at the interview board next afternoon. My lips were swollen, one eye was blackened, and my nose had achieved a bulbous and inflamed tip.

Four officers were ranged behind some tables, as they turned over the paperwork. During the morning all the candidates had been given intelligence testing papers to complete, and had also 'flown' a device that tested coordination. This required crossed needles to be kept in position by manipulating a set of controls. When completing the initial application we had been asked which category of air crew we wished to join. I had given first choice as pilot, and second choice as navigator.

After asking why I was so bruised, the President of the board informed me that my tests had shown that I was best fitted to be a pilot, but not a navigator. Such an evaluation seemed arbitrary and fallible, for not only did I go on to qualify as an RAF navigator, but also as a civil airline navigator. A medical examination completed the process, which had taken all day.

There was one other hurdle, which I had not counted on. Four weeks later I was called in to see the personnel officer at work, who was a kindly and wise man in his mid-fifties. 'We have been asked by the RAF if we will release you from your work here, which is of national importance. I know what your age is, but don't want to stand in your way. Do you really want to fly, rather than continue here and qualify as an aeronautical engineer?'

I assured him that it was my ambition to fly and that I saw this as the only opportunity available. I was conscious of the risks and on balance had taken the decision with my eyes open. He agreed that he would return the release documents, duly approved, and wished me luck.

Late in 1942 I received the buff manilla envelope marked OHMS (On His Majesty's Service) containing instructions, together with a travel warrant, to report at the reception centre on 18 January 1943. My flying career was about to begin.

As an ATC cadet, Peter Duffey took an air familiarisation flight aboard a Vickers Wellington. The pilot was forced to divert when Luftwaffe aircraft attacked the home airfield.

Service life

L ord's Cricket Ground had seen better days. I remembered watching a memorable test match when the mighty Bradman demonstrated his mastery of the game. Now the ground was given over for use as an air crew reception centre.

London was subject to visits by the Luftwaffe and streets surrounding the Lords area were cordoned off with signs proclaiming 'unexploded bomb,' or 'land mine.' I made my way from the Underground station to the main entrance gates, to be directed by a uniformed airman towards one of the buildings behind the main grandstand. There my details were recorded and, together with a long line of others, I waited to receive kitbag, uniforms, greatcoat, cape, gas mask, boots, webbing, and various accoutrements essential to our new life. We had been sworn in to give our oath of allegiance to the King during the selection process, but were subjected to another medical examination.

Initial training

Falling into line we achieved a ragged formation and were marched off through the streets of St John's Wood, to our accommodation. Many of the large blocks of flats had been taken over as billets for the cadet population. Our immediate area contained three such buildings. Many rumours existed as to why we were initially placed in the centre of what was an intermittent target area, the most persistent being that the flats were owned by a certain member of parliament who was now in the Air Force. My rank was the lowest of the low, Aircraftsman Second Class, or AC2.

We had to scrub the wooden floors of the building each day, until they shone with bleached whiteness. Much was made of creating a deep shine on our inflexible and uncomfortable boots. These needed much walking or marching to break in.

Contact with the Air Force was through our flight (section) corporal, who was obviously chosen as a disciplinarian to lick us into shape and submission. The idea was to instil obedience, cleanliness, fitness, and uniformity. Our group was certainly diverse enough, drawn from many sections of the social strata, leavened with ethnic and national differences. We marched everywhere at a rapid pace, and rose early for sessions of physical training. The food was institutional, but adequate, at a time when civilian rations were down to bare minimum. We topped up by visiting the local British Restaurants, which existed to serve all who were in transit or itinerant with meals and snacks. These were made from ingredients of doubtful origin, but served by volunteers who always gave a cheery welcome.

On one morning, at the first inspection of the day, we were asked to volunteer for blood donation. Our blood groups were inscribed onto fireproof dog tags, which were worn round the neck. My group was in short supply, so I was 'volunteered' to march off downtown to a clinic where we lay down and waited for a nurse to tap into our arms. It was interestingly unpleasant to watch the bottle fill, as it stood on a small table beside my bed. As I watched a nurse flounced by, and knocked it over on to the floor, spilling my blood. She turned round, with no apology, and tapped my other arm, with a fresh bottle, before I could react. After this event we were offered sweet tea, and a pack of cigarettes. As a non-smoker I felt rather under-compensated. When we had all given our donation we reassembled and marched swiftly back to our billet, where we had to get down and scrub the floors yet again. The resilience of youth protected us from harm and, although sleep came easily, there were no noticeable ill effects.

For some reason I found myself conscripted to the precision drill squad. Many of the reception centres in Canada also practised this idea which was to complete a long series of drill routines in silence, without orders. After much time spent ironing out our mistakes we achieved the required standard. The next step was to attend a huge rally in support of our Soviet allies, held in the Albert Hall, London. We were quite relieved when informed that the programme of events could not fit us in, but dismayed when paraded outside the hall and made to perform for the entertainment of a visiting Air Commodore.

Cambridge

By this time we were eager to move on. The posting to our Initial Training Wing (ITW) did not come for five weeks. The pipeline was primed with trainees, and we had to wait. These training establishments were scattered around the country. Many were in holiday resorts, such as Torquay, and Newquay, where they had taken over hotels. But I was posted to Cambridge, where part of the university had been taken over.

We were accommodated in Clare College. Any idea of a soft billet was immediately dispelled by our constant activity, mixing physical activities with classroom work. At last we began to grapple with the basic elements of aviation. Many classes were in other college buildings, so we visited some ancient and historic places. We outnumbered the wartime undergraduates but in the evenings we were all outnumbered by the bomber crews from their airfields in the surrounding countryside. The loss rate at that period of the war was averaging about six percent per raid and sometimes more. The crews that we met were out for a good time, and consumed large quantities of beer, which was mainly a mild brew of doubtful strength and origin. Tepid and muddy, it was, however, always popular. We wondered at the way these crews seemed relatively unaffected by living with the daily threat to their survival. They were not much older than ourselves, but already displayed many medal ribbons testifying to their exposure.

Guard duty was part of the system devised to absorb our energy and time, to instil a sense of duty and responsibility, and to assess our ability. I was appointed guard commander one night, and had the dubious task of supervising four different sites where guards had been posted. These were separated by some distance, and were access points to the campus area. I made my rounds on the windy and cold night, retiring to the room used as a guardhouse, where a fire flickered to provide comfort. I had just made a cup of cocoa, and was toasting a bit of bread on the end of a fork, with my feet up on a chair, when the orderly officer strode in. A pedantic disciplinarian, he took an extremely dim view of my laxity, informing me that the main gate was at that time unattended, and did I know this?

I was defenceless and speechless, expecting to be charged with the crime. Somehow nothing much came of it, except increased diligence on my part, but I was not given further command of the guard. Many times since I have been faced with sudden and difficult circumstances, but that was the only time I can truthfully say that my blood seemed to run cold.

On a couple of occasions we spent the night detailed to guard the perimeter at one of the satellite airfields, while various heavy bombers departed and returned. The noise of heavy aircraft marshalling in the early evening across the East Anglian skies became so usual that any quiet period was remarkable. Patrolling around in the moonlight with a loaded 1916-vintage Lee Enfield rifle seemed a bit futile, but we were warned to look out for parachutists.

Four months elapsed before we completed the initial training course. One pleasant interlude came towards the end, when we entered a rowing eight into the university May races, and managed to do quite well. Life was a mixture of reality and dream: punting on the river, strolling around ancient streets, knowing that it could not last.

We paraded for our passing out ceremony. 'Graduation' would be a more transatlantic phrase, except that on a hot day there were some who toppled over, overcome by the occasion. When marching down the main streets to the stirring strains of a good brass band we began to feel a little military, or even patriotic. Our drill had become sharp, and we were precise, reasonably fit, and looking forward to seeing a real aeroplane.

Promoted to Leading Aircraftsman (LAC), my pay had reached seven shillings and sixpence daily, which was not much at all, but did allow the purchase of the odd luxury, or even tea and rock cakes from the Navy, Army, and Air Force Institute (NAAF1), the British equivalent of the American PX (Post Exchange).

I was granted no leave, and sent to a local airfield for what was described as 'Grading School'. This involved flying the de Havilland Tiger Moth biplane trainer for a few hours to see if it was worth an Air Force investment in any further pilot training. The failure rate ran at about thirty percent, and they wanted to cut this back. Before we could be sent overseas to one of the Commonwealth Air Training Plan stations there was this hurdle to jump. Should we not come up to standard then a transfer to another aircrew category would ensue.

Flying at Marshall's

I walked up to the guardhouse at the gate entrance to Marshall's airfield close to Cambridge, kitbag slung over one shoulder, and as the MP on guard duty referred me inside to sign the register, our attention was drawn to the unorthodox arrival of a Tiger Moth, fifty yards away. The little biplane fell from the sky in a steep nose down plunge, ending up as a smashed wreck on the side of the road. The cadet pilot was pulled away from the fuselage and laid out on the grass, and soon pronounced dead by the attending ambulance crew. This rather sharp introduction to the risks of service flying did not impress me as it should. Youth always knows that it is indestructible. I was, of course, interested in the cause of the accident, which was found to be a stall at low-level associated with flying too slowly.

The field at Marshall's was grassy and a bit bumpy. On one side was a large brick chimney that issued smoke constantly and was known to us as 'Smoky Joe.' This landmark helped us to find the place, and to judge the wind direction. Most of the flying was very elementary, although we were introduced to spinning.

The author began flying training, like thousands of others, on the DH.82 Tiger Moth.

The DH.82 Tiger Moth was powered by an inverted Gipsy Major, had a tail skid, and needed care when taxiing around on the ground in any sort of wind. Thousands of pilots learned to fly on the type. Airspeed was indicated by a device mounted on a wing strut. A plate tensioned by springs moved across a quadrant plate. Speed was indicated by gradations marked on the plate. Two switches for the magneto-ignition circuits, plus altimeter, oil pressure and revolution counters comprised the basic instrumentation, supplemented by a turn-and-bank indicator. The control column (or joystick), rudder pedals, and the throttle formed the input controls for the pilot. There was a spring tensioned elevator trim device. Fuel was fed by gravity from a tank mounted in the centre section of the top wing. Starting was achieved by manually swinging on the propeller, an art we had to master.

Handling was sensitive, and rudder input was essential to avoid slip or skid in turns. Landing needed a deft touch to make the classic three-point touchdown. Each time we flew, our progress was assessed carefully, although I was certainly given very good basic information from my Flight Sergeant instructor. Two tests were flown, one with the flight commander, and a final one with the squadron leader. By this time we had all flown about twelve hours. No one was allowed to go solo. We were then allowed to take two weeks 'leave before reporting to the air crew distribution centre at Heaton Park in Manchester, to await our fate.

By Queen Mary *to Canada*

After a carefree summer holiday at home, out of uniform, I took the train to Manchester. Then, true to form in that city, it began to rain. Hundreds of us were waiting for our name and number to be called out at the daily parade. Various drafts would be detailed to countries involved in the training plan: South Africa, Canada, Rhodesia, Australia, New Zealand, and the USA More than 130,000 aircrew were trained by this huge organization during the war. There is no place to feel more insignificant than when waiting in constant rain for something to happen, wrapped in a rubberised rain cape with no place to go.

Four weeks had elapsed before my name was called out as part of a pilot draft to Canada. The next morning saw us depart for the train journey to Greenock, on the Clyde, in Scotland. There we slept the night on double-tiered bunks in an old Scots Guards barracks, before embarking in navy tenders to our transport.

The *Queen Mary* seemed huge, grey, shabby, and impressive. She could carry 16,000 troops, and had already, with her sister ship the *Queen Elizabeth*, transported many divisions of American troops to Britain. Return journeys were not as crowded, consisting mainly of aircrew, and naval crews travelling to collect new ships, as well as wounded servicemen being repatriated. We were given a cabin with two double bunks, and detailed for various duties during the voyage. My task was to be alternately a mess waiter by day, and a lookout at night. The ship was unescorted, relying on her impressive speed to elude submarine attention.

The wooden handrails on the promenade decks were carved systematically with names from across America, and the whole ship had an atmosphere of well-worn use. When we departed that evening, our course took us down the Firth of Clyde, and our last sight of land was the tip of Northern Ireland. I soon discovered that my duty on the mess deck would be a sinecure, for many succumbed to the rigours of *mal de mer*. Rediscovering the delights of white bread, butter, and milk, with unlimited access to eggs and other food severely rationed in Britain, a few of us took full advantage of the abundance.

The weather turned windy and rainy. Seas ran high, and the huge ship plunged and tossed wildly. Trying to walk down the long corridors on our deck was hazardous, for one minute you were going downhill, and next uphill, pressed into the side wall. This continued for several days. My lookout duty was nevertheless maintained. Issued with high-powered binoculars I was told to scan a particular section of the sea and sky for any sign of activity.

The atmosphere on board was sporadically strained, for soon groups of sailors and airmen were gambling, and arguing. The weather did dampen enthusiasm. One event brought great amusement. A daily roll call followed the boat drill and on this occasion two persons were missing. We were carrying a section of nurses returning to their homeland and one of them was missing, as well as one of our draft. He was a remustered air gunner Flying Officer, having survived two tours of operations in Bomber Command, and now accepted for pilot training.

The roll call was obviously to check if any losses overboard had occurred, for absence without leave was improbable. In this case shrewd deduction led to a ship's inspection by the staff Captain, and a team of service police. Eventually the pair were discovered close together in a metal clothes closet. We did not know what action resulted from this discovery, but the reputation of the officer was certainly enhanced into folk lore.

The storms grew fiercer, with waves breaking over the complete bow of the ship. One was so strong that it smashed two of the fo'c'sle windows, cascading tons of water inside one of the dining areas. We had been zigzagging constantly since leaving port, using an irregular pattern, but soon after this event we changed course to head south. Within twelve hours we were in tranquil conditions. Fog and mist shrouded the vessel, and next day we saw our first flying fish, followed by seas covered with weed. We were in the Sargasso Sea, with the temperature rising steadily.

Ten days after leaving the Clyde we ran into New York at dawn, past the Statue of Liberty, to dock in Manhattan. Welcomed by the massed sirens of harbour shipping, it was a stirring sight. We were beginning to feel travel worn, but only had time for a brief cup of coffee and a packet of cookies from the USO women serving our arrival, before we were ushered into a waiting train. This transported us through New England to the Canadian border, and on to a holding depot in Moncton, New Brunswick.

Calgary and first solo

The thought of ever flying again seemed remote at that stage. We had to wait for a course vacancy at a suitable elementary flying school, and seventeen days later were told that our destination was to be the EFTS at De Winton, south of Calgary, in Alberta. The train journey took four days, in cars built around 1910, and heated by iron stoves. The steam locomotives threw out soot, and smoke. With windows open we accumulated smuts, and with them closed we breathed fumes. The scenery was magnificent, and I became used to waking up travelling in the opposite direction to when I had gone to sleep. This was because of changing locomotives at single line sidings. We had some opportunities to explore a few places en route when watering and coaling.

De Winton was constructed during 1941; 31 EFTS had moved there from Calgary, and was then equipped with the Fairchild Cornell, a low-winged monoplane manufactured in Canada, powered by a 200 horsepower Ranger in-line engine. The cockpit canopy was a luxury compared with the British Tiger Moth. Canadian Tigers were also fitted with canopies

In Canada, the author continued his training on the Fairchild Cornell.

and tail wheels. Apart from these two types, schools used, at various times the Fleet Finch, and Stearman biplanes. Hours flown per flying training accident for the Cornell were 2,292; for the Tiger Moth 1,197, for the Finch 494, and for the Stearman 920. Approximately ten percent of these accidents resulted in a fatality. At the EFT Schools alone this meant that approximately 400 fatalities occurred during the period from 1940 to 1945. Of the 3,366,579 total hours flown by the British Commonwealth Air Training Plan EFTS in Canada, the Tiger flew 53%, and the Cornell 33%.

The school was civilian, originally started as a flying club in Calgary, and although most of the instructors were service pilots, the atmosphere was relaxed and informal. It was refreshing to be able to concentrate on essentials, undisturbed by drill corporals.

The Canadian fall of 1943 in Alberta was a pleasant time to start my serious training. I was also lucky to have as my instructor an RAF sergeant of happy yet demanding disposition, and was soon off on a first solo flight after a test with the flight commander. The preliminary experience at grading school was a great help. Like so many would-be airmen I was afflicted with periods of motion-induced nausea, but did not actually succumb to the indignity of airsickness. The unwritten rule was that you cleaned up after any such event, so I was fortunate to escape that unpleasant chore. I soon grew out of the tendency to fear that aerobatics would induce sickness, and this freed me to enjoy the sensations.

The Air Force had introduced careful screening routines to help reduce accident rates, and refined the syllabus to ensure exposure to most practical problems. Standards were high, but the high failure rates were a mixed blessing, causing occasional tension. Resources were allocated to those who might proceed to operational status, although each failure or washout meant a waste of investment.

We were being regularly assessed by progress testing. A final recommendation would be made as to where our next training would ensue, either on single or twin-engined aircraft. We were also asked to give our preference. My instructor told me that my aerobatics were adequate enough if I wanted to go to fighters. This would mean to a school using the Harvard, similar to the AT-6. Texan. Otherwise it would mean a choice of schools using Avro Anson, Airspeed Oxford, or even the Cessna Crane, all twin-engined types. I declined to make any choice, feeling ill-equipped to weigh the pros and cons. First night flights were events that introduced a strange world of dim cockpit lighting, and a flarepath for landing lit by goose-neck oil lamps. The lighting provided by the unblacked-out Canadian landscape was not likely to be repeated when we returned to Britain, but was helpful at that stage. Our instructors were mainly pilots who had not seen any operational experience, although a few had returned from a tour and had a different attitude. The system chose a number of qualifying pilots to be trained for instructional duties and these would stay for as long as a year before being sent for operational training. Many found themselves locked in to the instructing world, unable to escape. Good instructors were valuable.

My intermediate flight commander's test nearly proved my undoing. 'Do me a spin to the left, I'll tell you when to recover.'

We were at about 7,000 feet above the Albertan plateau and below all cloud. Putting the aircraft into a couple of steep turns, left and right to look around for any other aircraft, and seeing none, I raised the nose, reduced the power, and as the stall started, kicked in left rudder. We span down in silence, and I recovered easily.

'Now do me one to the right, after climbing back to the same height.'

So when we reached the same altitude I repeated the spin, and was amazed to see the shape of an Anson rotating neatly in our line of sight as we descended. The earth rotated, and so did the Anson, as it moved through and out of the scene. I had forgotten to repeat the clearing turns. We returned to base in silence. Once on the ground nothing was said. I never heard the matter discussed, and did not raise it with my instructor.

We were living in semi-civilian conditions, eating in the airport diner, where a T-bone steak cost fifty cents, including the trimmings, and a jukebox accompanied the consumption of apple pie and ice cream. The period is forever etched in my memory as a most happy time. I think many looked on their EFTS experience similarly. The November of 1943 brought bad weather, wind and rains, but we were just about ready to ship out. I had flown just seventy hours on the Cornell, and enjoyed every minute of a busy time. When not flying we were in the classroom learning basic navigation, signals, radio, and other theory, but this was not intensive or demanding. Local hospitality was generous, and we got to know many families.

The RAF again

The posting was pinned up on a notice board. This was to 36 Service Flying Training School, (SFTS), at Penhold, near Red Deer in Alberta. Red Deer is about half way between Calgary and Edmonton, on the Canadian Pacific rail line. In those days it was a smallish town, primarily serving an agricultural area.

Penhold was constructed in 1941, to the standard design of the BCATP: three runways triangularly disposed, with wooden hangars, drill hall, messes, and accommodation. With our course including quite a spread of age and background we became surprisingly well-integrated. This was possibly because of the common aim and an intensive curriculum that left little time for dissent. Our group included two ex-Metropolitan policemen, each aged 28, making them ancient in our eyes.

The school was wholly RAF, one of the few in Canada, most others being run by the RCAF. We had returned to a strictly British environment under normal service conditions. One of only four stations to use the Airspeed Oxford, a twin-engined trainer derivative of the pre-war Airspeed Envoy civil aircraft, we were destined for multi-engined training. The Avro Anson and Cessna Crane were more forgiving and sedate, as the statistics show. Hours flown per accident were 1,194 for the Oxford, 2,614 for the Anson, and 2,847 for the Crane. The Harvard had the worst record at 1,062. Some of the problems arose from the lack of control after landing either in the Harvard or the Oxford. A ground loop was easy to achieve once the tail was down, as this tended to blank off the rudder effectiveness, and a rapid swerve could develop into complete loss of directional control with damage to undercarriage or airframe. On the Oxford, this could be opposed by a touch of engine power on one side, or a bit of differential braking and good anticipation, particularly if there was a crosswind. Without this it was easy to end up off the runway, and with a damaged aircraft.

I never regretted flying the 'Oxbox,' and had fun trying to perfect a decent three-point landing. At least it was not necessary to wind the undercarriage up and down each time, using 130 turns of a tiring handle. This chore went with the Anson 1, the original metal-tubed, fabric-covered British version. Canadian versions of wooden construction were made, powered by the Jacobs engine instead of the Cheetah, and had hydraulically powered landing gear retraction.

We started flying at the beginning of December 1943, when snow had already fallen intermittently, and temperatures were falling progressively. One chore was the start-up procedure. Each Cheetah engine required someone to kneel on the wing, insert a hand crank, and wind an inertia wheel to provide energy for turning the cold crankshaft. Once the engine fired you could be blown off a wing by the icy slipstream. This duty was always allocated to the new course, and we were pleased when replacements arrived to take over.

The aircraft initially seemed enormous, and complex. After five hours of circuits, emergency exercises, and a couple of single-engined landings I was passed on to the instructor who would be my main mentor. He was a taciturn Flight Sergeant, a Yorkshireman, who proved to be most helpful, if. uncommunicative at times. I was sent off solo after another half hour.

One of the most risky aspects was the number of other Oxfords populating the sky around the airfield and area. Mid-air collision was a major problem for the training scheme. Classes covering fourteen separate subjects absorbed our days. There was time for exercise and sporting activity, but the weather confined this mainly to the large drill hall hangar. As the weather became colder, runways were ploughed, and heaps of snow marked their edges. Sticks were inserted to show the safe surface limits. The snow was interrupted occasionally by the arrival of a Chinook. A warm air mass, peeling off the mountains would raise temperatures to above freezing. The rapid thaw would bring things to a halt for a while.

Christmas was celebrated by cancelling training for a couple of days, The local people flooded us with invitations, and three of us were picked up and driven across country to a little hamlet called Stettler, on a washboard rutted dirt road that allowed one speed only to avoid the car breaking apart. The village comprised a few houses, close to the main Canadian National rail track, where two large grain elevators stood. We noted that a sensible authority had painted the location in large letters on each roof, for the use of wandering aviators.

Hospitality was splendid, centred on the home of a local politician, and where we slept, ate, and drank. The family was large and gregarious. We were enticed to try a sample of the man's stock of Cuban cigars, with fairly disastrous results. Ice skating on a local pond proved equally hazardous.

We had official low-flying authorisation in an approved area, and flew many hours below fifty feet. My instructor was married, and his Canadian wife lived in Red Deer. He had been selected for instructional duty immediately after graduation as a pilot. After completing an eight-week course at the Central Flying School, Trenton, Ontario, he had been sent to Penhold, and was now bored out of his mind. He wanted to be transferred to active duty, but the training scheme needed to retain all qualified instructors.

This may have been the reason why he was so keen on low flying, perhaps hoping to get caught, and to be sent off overseas. As it was he managed to impress me with some very hair-raising flying. We sped at heights down the Bow River that were so low that I was sure the props were touching water. He did a lot of the flying, robbing me of some valuable handling time. We would come to a bend in the river, pull up over the steep bank, and see a house or school, then whistle round it in a steep turn to retrace our path down to the river. My nerve gradually steadied, and I began to enjoy the sensations. There was a mutual collusion. On other occasions we would venture into the foothills of the Rockies near Banff, and beat up a valley or two. Cross country, night, and formation flying were included as my hours increased. We practised bombing by using a camera-obscura system. A ground operator monitored the aircraft's position, and at the bomb release point we would fire a Very pistol loaded with a smoke puff cartridge. This would be plotted and our accuracy assessed. Instrument flying, including the use of Standard Beam Approach (SBA), became important as night flying progressed to cross-country work.

I was subjected to an involuntary change of instructors, an event that was caused by a near-catastrophe. During one of the practice bombing sessions, when at 7,000 feet above the airfield, I asked the instructor to fire off a smoke puff to simulate bomb release. The Very pistol was discharged through a metal chute which was mounted between the pilots' seats. When putting the pistol into the chute, after loading the cartridge, it was necessary to attach and screw down two clamps. This avoided the risk of backfire. I was too trusting, and should have checked that this had been done.

The sudden bang was deafening, accompanied by thick smoke, and the sight of a bright incandescent ball bouncing around all over the cockpit. My first action was to open the direct-view window just to the left of the main windscreen. This cleared the smoke quickly. The cartridge had burned out. Luckily there was no fire, but all the instruments had been obscured by a heavy sooty deposit, and needed rubbing to see what secrets lay beneath. Meanwhile we had entered a spiral dive, which involved increased speed and bank angle, with rapid descent. Opening a little direct vision window enabled the view of the ground, and helped me to level the wings and regain control. The instructor was in shock, for he had been burned by the fireball. I descended rapidly and landed, calling for an ambulance. On the ground we discovered that both parachute harnesses had been burned badly, and would not have supported us if we had jumped.

This put my instructor into hospital for a period. I was transferred to another instructor, an officer, who was rather more helpful and open-minded. Soon after this we were suitably worried by the news that various pilots would be tested by a travelling examiner. This was commonly thought of as a final wings test. We had not completed the syllabus, and perhaps this was more of a sampling than a sink or-swim effort, but it still figures in my log book as the final test.

Three-pointer (and a no-pointer)

The little flight lieutenant looked twice my age, and sized me up in friendly fashion. I was asked to take off to do various exercises away from the field, culminating with a simulated single-engined approach and landing. This involved energetic pumping of the hydraulic system hand pump to lower the wheels, as the failed engine supplied the main pump. It was hard to avoid lurching around the sky as the right hand pumped while the left hand controlled the aircraft with one foot held hard against the rudder pedals, opposing the Oxbox's wish to turn sharply towards the failed engine. We approached the final path, lined up with the runway.

'Can you do a three-pointer please.' He seemed to say this rather doubtfully, for both of us knew this was improbable, given the single-engined situation. There was also a crosswind, making further difficulty. My luck was in, however, as somehow or other the aircraft settled gently onto all three wheels as if controlled by an unseen force. He looked across at me, with a deadpan expression.

'Do you always manage them like that?'

I could only summon a grin of embarrassment. The test was over, and there were only a few items on the syllabus to tidy up. One of these was a long night cross-country solo flight.

This involved a triangular route, across farmland. The night was over cast, moonless, and pitch black. A few lights could be seen from well-scattered houses. The wind was quite strong, so drift corrections were important. Turning on to the last leg back to base and setting an estimated compass heading, I looked ahead to see if there was any sight of recognisable lighting.

Cloud was increasing to obscure the horizon. At last I saw what was obviously the airfield, with the runway lighting soon coming into view, so joining the pattern and aligning on final approach I used the short range radio to call my position for landing. The reply came from the duty pilot, who was sitting in a van alongside the active runway. He was one of our course members.

The author never regretted flying the Airspeed Oxford, nicknamed the 'Oxbox'.

'I can't see you yet, put your landing light on.' As this had already been switched on I was immediately aware of a problem. Sure enough, the aircraft was lined up with the runway at the relief field, Innisfail, about ten miles to the south of Penhold. Turning the Oxbox round and applying more power, I soon aligned on the correct runway and landed, wondering if my boob had been noted by other than my friend in the van. There was no follow up from any source, so my luck had held once again. The weather in Europe, with a blackout and so many confusing airfields, meant that newly graduated pilots from BCATP were found to need more training in England before they could adjust to the difficult conditions. This set an additional problem for many, as they had been trained on other types than the Oxford, which was the only type used in England for this purpose.

Wings

There was a formal presentation of our pilot's wings, by an anonymous Air Vice Marshal. We had lost more than a third of our course members for a variety of reasons. Often we would not know why a certain name would no longer be included in roll calls, or duty listings. We did not investigate. There was enough to do anyway.

On the wings parade we all pinned sergeant's stripes to our arms. Next day the process of sorting the sheep from the goats surfaced. The RCAF adopted a policy to commission all pilots but the RAF rule was that the individual must meet certain standards (not published to the trainees) of knowledge, character, deportment etc. The British class system, undefined, indiscernible, but nonetheless ever-present, still operated. The quota varied from time to time, but in general about half of graduating pilots would receive commissions.

Looking at the list pinned up on the notice board I saw that my name was in the top half, and that promotion to pilot officer was effective immediately. One of my close friends, who was in the bottom half, walked along with me out of the building and ruefully observed, I suppose it's because you knot your tie like that.'

A white arm band was issued to the new officers, who were told that they could now use the officers' mess. I not only felt elated at my success, but embarrassed about suddenly outranking many of the instructor pilots who had so carefully passed on their know-how to me. We eagerly awaited publication of the next list, for it would decide our operational future.

We stood before the notice board looking at the list. Most of the course had been posted temporarily to Moncton, pending allocation to their Operational Training Units. This usually meant that, for RAF pilots, they would return to Britain for that training, which would most possibly be for Bomber Command. Twenty pilots were sent to a transport OTU that used Dakotas, (Douglas C-47), and all of these would be involved in Operation Market Garden, the failed attempt to take Arnhem. Dropping parachutists and supplies, they sustained many casualties.

As a navigator

Four of us were posted to Coastal Command and were to proceed immediately to the general reconnaissance school at Summerside, on Prince Edward Island. There we would be trained as navigators and about many subjects peculiar to the anti-submarine and convoy-escort war.

This was another example of my fate being controlled by unseen forces. More than eighteen months would elapse from the time I was called up for service until the GR (General Reconnaissance) course would finish. This involved nine weeks of intensive classroom and air work. The school used Canadian-manufactured Avro Anson Vs for our navigational trips, when we were ferried across the Maritime Provinces and adjacent seas by some very bored staff pilots. The conditions were not helpful, often very bumpy. We were all troubled by air sickness, and so plotted our charts, and completed our navigation logs, with a bag close at hand. The art of astronomical navigation was practised, as was aerial photography, ship recognition, coding, signals, meteorology, compasses, and use of the Aldis signalling lamp. This last training required us to achieve a fast speed, to cope with navy signallers. Radio silence was maintained for much of the time so most communication was by light or Very pistol. Beautiful summer weather and the green fields of the island, which has lovely beaches, produced a pleasant environment. We had little time to enjoy this, for most of us had to burn the midnight oil trying to stay abreast of the course. Discussion among the 25 pilots who made up our ranks revealed common factors. None had chosen to go to Coastal. All had done well in the classroom work at their Service Flying Training Schools. Four were RCAF Flying Officers, ex-instructors, older, and experienced. They had some difficulty with the classroom work, no doubt because of their absence from that environment for some time. The others came from various SFTSs, and some lifelong friendships were established. We each flew about 45 hours as navigator, becoming airborne about every four days. The intervals included a full analysis of our mistakes.

One day we set off to take some photographs of shipping in the harbour at Saint John, New Brunswick. This proved an opportunity for our staff pilot to let loose on some really low flying in and around the enclosed anchorage at mast top heights. Perhaps he was trying to contrive a transfer. Three would be navigators tried to hold their heavy Williamson cameras up against the force of gravity, and into some sort of focus. I did manage a good shot of one cargo ship, accidentally pressing the shutter release as I shifted position. We did not hit anything, and arrived back at base feeling very fortunate, unlike the time when an Anson arrived back with half a tree embedded in the nose.

After completing the syllabus and final examinations we were awarded the RAF second-class navigation warrant, and were deemed ready for OTU. I was shipped off to the personnel depot at Moncton for another month's wait, before being transferred to 'Y' Depot at Lachine, near Montreal, for a further two weeks, most of which was spent on leave in New York and New England.

The hospitality was wonderful and the services' club on Fifth Avenue provided splendid accommodation. A register was kept so that invitations could be matched with Air Force crew on leave. I was given a rail pass, and with another course member went to Grand Central Station and took the train to Southport, Connecticut, where we were met by car, and transported to a house that overlooked Long Island Sound. The family were marvellously outgoing, and friendly, with an Atlantic class sailboat, and we were soon out on the Sound, diving off the boat which was making a good six knots in a nice breeze The days of exercise, with tennis and golf thrown in, soon made us forget that this was an interlude in our progress towards a war that still raged elsewhere.

To Nassau

A telephone call from Lachine alerted us to our posting. We were to return to Montreal, collect our kit, and take the train to Miami. On arrival in 'Y' Depot we discovered that our destination was to be Nassau in the Bahamas, where 111 OTU was equipped with B-25 Mitchell and B-24 Liberator aircraft. We did think that we were very lucky. The train journey to Miami was a first class operation, with separate bedrooms, a dining car resplendent with white linen, and black attendants, supervised by an overbearing white conductor. During dinner one of the waiters became abusive for some reason, arguing with a passenger. The conductor arrived and with scarcely a word pulled the emergency stop cord so that the brakes were applied with force, and the train came to a squealing, shuddering stop. The waiter was ushered to the rear of the car and out onto the tracks. He did not have any bag or clothing, being left as a forlorn figure by the track side as we moved off. I asked the conductor what had happened.

'They often get too uppity. That's the only way to deal with them. He'll get the next train down, and have time to cool off.'

It was my first personal experience of the bitter relationship that then existed in the south between black and white.

Miami was steamy, sunny, and crowded. I took a brief look at the palm-fringed boulevards as the taxi wound its way from station to dockside. I had purchased light trousers and shirts in New York, for the standard blues were impossibly warm. At the port I went to the departure office and showed them my travel documents and a ticket that seemed yards long, from which various segments had been detached. Directed to the pier where transport to Nassau waited, I was surprised to see that it consisted of a small steamer not much bigger than a trawler. Smoke curled from a single stack. A rusty hull was topped with superstructure surrounded by a wooden deck. Cabin portholes punctured the side, and a single mast was braced by wires in front of the smallish wheel house. The name *Jean Brillant* was displayed on the bow and stem.

This packet was the regular connection between the two ports, carrying cargo and passengers. Airline service did exist, and had been operated for a few years, but my pass did not cover an exciting trip with Pan American Airways. I was allocated the main cabin as I was the only passenger. This turned out to have a big double bed, and to be quite spacious. After the journey I discovered that on occasion the Duke and Duchess of Windsor had also used the cabin when visiting the mainland.

Sailing under a starlit sky, we were illuminated by regular flashes of lightning from all points of the compass.

Phosphorescence lit the sea, as we chugged along slowly in a dead calm. The temperature was in the upper seventies. Soon I was served a simple fish dinner, and retired for a sound sleep, untroubled by any knowledge of previous occupants.

Flying the Mitchell

We arrived just after dawn, when I was met by a corporal driving a jeep, and soon delivered to the adjutant's office at Oakes Field, quite close to the town. The sky seemed full of circling Mitchells curving in to land over the coast. I was allocated accommodation with another pupil in a hut with two beds, mosquito netting, a table, and two chairs. Toilets and washing facilities were outside. Bush and scrubby vegetation surrounded the place, which was isolated from other huts. Paths led through the bush to messes, hangars, class rooms, sick bay, etc. Aircraft were parked all over the area. It was hard to discern where bush ended and hard standing began.

The course included conversion to the Mitchell, including a solo flight after eight hours dual circuits and general handling. The spirited performance of the B-25, and excellent handling qualities were a revelation. We went on to practice low-level bombing, attacking towed rafts over aquamarine waters north of the island, together with navigational patrol exercises across most of the Bahamas. My instructor warned that one should not place fingers behind the throttle levers of the Wright Cyclone engines, as a backfire could cause the levers to be forced suddenly rearwards. Apparently this had been known to chop fingers. In my case this sort of event was not needed as I had attempted to open up a coconut shell with my Bowie knife, but managed to open up a three-inch slice on the index finger of the right hand instead: this without any help from the aircraft. From then on I flew with a splint and had to endure some very ribald comments, mostly about getting my finger out in time.

Ground school was about weapons and equipment that we would use on the B-24 squadron aircraft: bomb sights, radar, depth charges, sonobuoys, smoke floats, guns, radios, and lots of ship recognition training.

Our leisure time was taken up with swimming, sailing, squash, and tennis. Paradise Island, off the main island, was as yet not developed. Today it is covered with expensive resort hotels. I nearly missed one night-flying session, stranded on a diving raft offshore with six barracuda visible in the crystal clear water lying between me and safety until a boat rescue was organised. There was a club in one of the largest hotels to which we would repair and refuel with Tom Collins, prepared by a loquacious ebony-faced barman.

One day a bombing session led to tragedy. The usual pattern was to dive at the target flying below 50 feet at about 250 knots, dropping an eleven-pound practice bomb, then immediately pulling up into a steep climbing turn, and round again to dive and attack once more. This would sometimes inflict high G forces on the unfortunate tail gunner, who was travelling along to collect air experience. It was of course necessary to pull back on the controls before winding on the bank to turn. After about ten such attacks there was a tendency to become

At Oakes Field the author converted to the B-25 Mitchell.

pre-programmed. The Mitchell handled so responsively and precisely that a routine was easily established. On this occasion a re-mustered ex-fitter Flight Sergeant wound on the bank angle before pulling the nose up with disastrous result. A wingtip touched, and the aircraft cartwheeled into the shallow sea. All on board died instantly. The wreck lay easily visible for many years, and could still be seen when I was flying to Nassau with BOAC Four of us were detailed to act as coffin bearers, and a full military funeral honoured our friends in a sad morning ceremony.

Hurricane alert

We were not allowed to dwell on this for long as a hurricane alert was notified for the next day. Preparations were made for evacuation of all aircraft to Miami and Key West. There were not enough instructors to crew all the Mitchells so trainees from the most advanced course were selected to join the ferry operation. After two days of waiting it became apparent that winds would indeed be very strong so the aircraft departed. Those of us left behind were moved into what substantial buildings were available on the highest ground possible. Nassau is very flat and low lying, and so we were quite vulnerable. Our group, five pilots, took over a small stone building that stood about 400 yards inland. We fixed all the shutters, and laid in food and drink. We could see a lighthouse close to the shoreline.

The orders were issued that we should batten down the hatches, as the wind had increased to whip foam on a towering sea, and detach fronds from the palms. Coconuts were falling with ominous thumps all over the place, and the noise was intense. Sitting inside the hot, dark little building, we could see out through cracks in the shutters, and as the hours progressed through a darkening afternoon saw enormous waves breaking across the top of the lighthouse. The instinct for survival had spurred every local sand fly to take up residence with us and they found abundant sustenance. Hundreds of bites brought up swellings on our flesh. The storm did not abate until daybreak when we were able to obtain relief by running to the sea, flinging off clothes and immersing our tortured bodies. Deafened by the constant roar of the wind through trees and the breaking waves, we soon were corralled into working parties for a clean-up operation.

A touch of royalty

Occasionally we would see the Duke and Duchess of Windsor in the officers' mess. He had been appointed Governor of the Bahamas where he could contribute to the war effort, yet which afforded the couple close contact with the United States. The debate about his pre-war activities and relationship with the Germans will remain controversial. At a mess dance, where the permanent staff had wives and friends in attendance, we were intrigued to see that the Duchess accepted the invitation of a member of our course to take the dance floor. Whenever we saw the Duke he appeared to be preoccupied, and to give the impression of a troubled personality.

One incident that caused more than a flutter in governmental dovecotes occurred on a day when the royal couple were completing an official inspection, marking the graduation of a course. Twenty-two Mitchells were supposed to make an impressive low-level fly-past, crossing in front of the inspection dais, where the elite of Bahamas society were seated. By accident or design this deteriorated into a real beat-up, with aircraft coming from all angles, and so low that dust and wind whipped at the dresses of ladies, causing confusion and outrage. There were repercussions, with flight commanders on the mat, and a flood of paper admonition from the station commander. A high degree of amusement existed, however, and animated descriptions of the event dominated local conversation for some time.

Liberators

After about 90 hours airborne in Mitchells we were transferred to the other side of the island where Windsor Field housed the B-24 Liberators. Bomber Command had adopted a policy of using only one pilot on Lancasters and Halifaxes, supported by a flight engineer, but the US Air Force always crewed its heavy bombers with two pilots, as were Coastal Command Liberators. The length of patrols and the need to gain experience to become an effective commander dictated this policy. Many inexperienced low-time bomber pilots met their death long before they could accumulate survival know-how. A policy which placed a premium on numbers rather than effectiveness, and the huge investment of resources to that end, seemed to be debateable.

I was happy enough to be a co-pilot and crewed up with an experienced first pilot doing a refresher course. The Liberator, equipped with four splendid Pratt & Whitney Twin Wasp engines, came in several versions, all of which were represented at the field. Earlier types had no forward gun turret, and the engine superchargers were gear-driven two-speed types. Later versions had exhaust-driven turbo-superchargers. These were controlled electronically and rotated at very high rpm. The controls had to be set with care, to avoid over speeding. The possibility existed of a turbine flying off and cutting its way through wings or fuselage.

The most numerous version of the B-24 was the Liberator Mk 6, which had a large dustbin-shape retractable radar scanner mounted below the fuselage, and gun turrets in the nose, tail, and mid-upper sections. The crew usually consisted of two pilots, two navigators, a flight engineer, at least one wireless operator/mechanic, and a mix of four air gunners and wireless operator/air gunners. Weapons included depth charges, bombs, and the ubiquitous 0.50 calibre Brownings, which were better than the 0.303 Brownings used by the RAF, but not up to the standard of German cannons.

At the time we were completing our OTU course, submarine activity was intermittently sinking ships off the American coastline. We were briefed to keep a good lookout but never saw anything. Some Liberators had been fitted with rockets to meet the tactics of U-Boats which had been heavily armed, and were fighting it out on the surface, rather than being forced under sea. Night attacks were assisted by the Leigh Light, a moveable high-powered light fitted under one wing. After picking up a submarine contact on the H2S-type radar, an attack pattern would be flown, ending up at very low-level, with the searchlight switched on at very close range. Aircraft were lost because of the ease with which a submarine could fire up the beam. The angle of wind drift would need to be assessed and the light angle adjusted to match. It was essential to light up the target as soon as the light came on. One problem with the light fitted to a Mk 6 Liberator was the need to take-off with most of the available rudder trim used to compensate for the turning drag effect of the large light. In the event of an outboard engine failure on the same side before accelerating to a higher airspeed, control could be lost. Introduction of the Mk 8 variant removed the problem, as this version was fitted with revised control surfaces that were provided with balance tabs, and also compensated for the asymmetric trim.

Patrol lengths could reach sixteen hours in duration, take-off being at weights in excess of the figures prudent to allow suitable performance to cope with power failure on one engine. Sometimes the aircraft could barely lift off at the end of a standard runway. The initial part of a patrol might have to be flown with 5° of flap, until the excess fuel was consumed. Lowering of the radar dustbin was another problem, with the associated drag increase. A very fine auto pilot, manufactured by Minneapolis/Honeywell, was developed for the use of USAF bomber operations. The associated bombsight was removed from our aircraft and replaced with a low-level sight.

Later aircraft had a radio altimeter to assist very low-level attacks, with a triple light display to indicate selected height above the water. The main radar set had a similar design to that used by Bomber Command. Sir Arthur Harris had protested when some of these sets were allocated for Coastal Command, although they were eventually modified to operate on a different wavelength so that snorkel or periscope could be more easily detected. When coupled with the listening ability of sonobuoys, dropped in patterns to record a submarine's movement, the weapon combination had proved very effective. The procedures necessary to become part of the defence ring around a convoy involved ensuring that the escort ships could recognise us as friendly. There were many examples of naval and merchant ships firing at friendly aircraft. Although the long-range enemy most likely to attack a convoy in the North Atlantic was the low-winged Focke-Wulf Condor, it did have four engines, and could possibly be confused with the B-17 Flying Fortress, which equipped a few Coastal units, We had twin tails, high wings, and a much fatter fuselage. Despite this there was always an uncertain welcome until the use of Aldis lamp and colour signals, to reinforce the standing instruction to show the aircraft profile at a safe distance before approaching any convoy.

When ships approached the European land mass they could be attacked by many other types of shorter-range aircraft. The convoys to northern Soviet ports were subject to this type of threat for much of their journey. 'Shoot first and argue later' could mean survival (at least for the shooter) and such trigger happiness could be forgiven.

After 45 hours of flight time, plus more ground instruction and examinations, we reached our graduation parade. Our crew included two Canadian navigators of mature years, but of markedly differing backgrounds. One had completed a tour on Catalina flying boats; the other was fresh from training school. The former had been the manager of a burlesque theatre in Toronto and the latter was a mining engineer. He had managed to wangle his wife onto the island, and lived off base, close to town.

The course lasted ten weeks and after a week's leave I found myself once more in Moncton, waiting for a ship home. Only a week elapsed before I was on a train to Halifax, Nova Scotia, where together with an assortment of army, Air Force, and nursing shipmates was allocated a cabin on the *Nieuw Amsterdam*. As we sailed, it was early January. I noted that my RAF Volunteer Reserve service had now extended to two full years and yet training was still incomplete. A Heavy

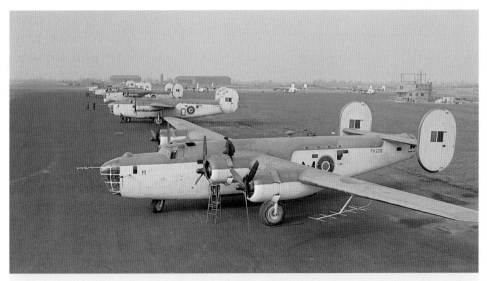

The author was trained to fly anti-submarine patrols in the B-24 Liberator.

Conversion Unit (HCU), course in Britain would be the place where we would meet the crew with whom we would proceed to operational squadron service and work up latest procedures and equipment.

The last morning of our voyage was marked by an unusual event. Rounding the north of Ireland, and entering the North Channel between the Mull of Kintyre and Ballycastle, the ship heeled over at an alarming angle. There was an extremely strong westerly wind and as the turn southwards progressed the ship listed to such a degree that it was difficult to keep a footing. Orders were given for all on deck to move to the upwind side. After about ten minutes the ship slowly began to recover level sailing. Many of us were convinced that a few more degrees of list would have been disastrous. We were told later that some of the hold cargo had shifted, which had added to the problems of wind, current, and turn. We were relieved later that day to see the busy port of Liverpool where we docked to board our train.

Back home

In January 1945, the war in Europe was reaching its final five months as I stepped from the train in Harrogate, Yorkshire, where yet another holding unit existed. The spa town was uncustomarily shabby, for England was showing the effects of five years of strife and deprivation. Two months elapsed before my posting to a Heavy Conversion Unit (HCU) was activated. This involved a transfer to Aldergrove in Northern Ireland, on the eastern shores of Lough Neagh. There we completed a re-familiarisation with the latest mark of Liberator, and spent most of 50 flying hours practising radar homing attacks and bombing.

   Each afternoon much of the station activity came to a focal point where a long line would stand outside a low stone cottage, close to the airfield boundary. Everyone carried jugs, bottles, or other containers. The mystery was soon revealed. They were waiting to collect freshly-brewed Guinness stout from the entrepreneurial establishment. The product was without doubt possessed of a smoothness unrivalled in any of the local pubs. We never did find out where the water supply was.

   After four weeks of leisurely activity there was apparently no urgency attached to our training, and we were granted a fortnight's leave. I managed to cycle across to the base at Nutt's Corner, where USAF B-17s of the Eighth Air Force landed on their navigational cross-country exercises. They were unfamiliar with Gee (the standard RAF navigation aid), and had to work up competency before becoming fully operational. The commander of one aircraft was in the operations hut, and readily agreed to give me a lift to their base at Bedford, north of London. My fare would be paid by agreeing to show the navigator something about Gee. Having successfully completed one leg of the triangular route I was asked to take the pilot's seat. Shortly afterwards, the commander, a young lieutenant, feathered first one, then two, and finally three engines. I hoped that the demonstration was over, for we had an incident in Nassau when a brave soul had decided to stop all four engines. His excuse was that he was developing a silent attack procedure, but it came nearly unstuck when the electrical power for unfeathering the propeller of the first engine proved initially inadequate, but this B-17 stayed nicely level at 8,000 feet, at a slow but safe speed, remaining pleasant to handle. No problems in restarting this time.

On arrival at Bedford I was invited into the USAF mess for a meal, and was amazed at the quantity and quality of the food. We had become accustomed to a much lower standard, although provided with many additional rations that the civilian population would have wished to have. Our preflight meals included eggs, bars of chocolate were issued individually, and milk was on tap for aircrews but not for ground staff. A visit to the American PX was also an eye-opener for the range of goods on offer which included many items that had not been seen in Britain's shops for five years, if ever.

On return from leave in a train still blacked-out, and full of service personnel, the talk was all about impending victory in Europe. We took the ferry from Stranraer to Lame after dark, and in a rough sea. I spent the time on deck, wondering about the future, and perhaps a transfer to the Far East and the Japanese war. We still had no inkling as to when and where we would be utilised.

Three weeks later, after a few more flying exercises, mainly at very low-level up and down Lough Neagh and off the coast, all activity ceased. VE day had arrived, and I was still under training, after two years and five months. When compared with the fate of so many who were my course mates at Penhold this must have been a lucky chance. To know that much effort and accumulated knowledge would probably never be used was frustrating and somewhat disillusioning.

Belfast on VE day was a delirious place, with massed crowds, rejoicing happily. No ethnic or religious problems were on the surface, only a spirit of goodwill, expressed in many ways by the older inhabitants towards those of us who were in uniform. My personal transport system was a bicycle and this was used to visit Portrush, the seaside resort, where a series of celebrations were organised.

A week later we were back in Aldergrove to complete the conversion course. Three weeks later I received a squadron posting to Leuchars, near Dundee, in Scotland. My arrival coincided with a period of uncertainty and it was soon clear that there would be no duties for me. I received a transfer to another squadron, this time back in Northern Ireland at Ballykelly, close to Londonderry.

It was rather disturbing to be arriving as a newly qualified person at the very time when the war in Europe had ended, and when most pilots were concerned about transition to civilian life and their release groups. This concern was soon answered by an edict which changed the function of the squadron from coastal to transport. The Liberators would have their front gun-turrets removed, and seats fitted in the bomb bays. We were to run a regular transport route to India.

Although still summer, the weather was appalling. Ballykelly was located so that rain was incessant, irrespective of the wind direction. The layout of buildings was typical of wartime dispersal, and long treks were made from mess to operations to billets. Bicycles were issued to each person, but for a station complement of 1,100 there seemed to be 1,099 machines. This meant that an unattended bike would vanish. We then found the nearest replacement and acquired it. Convention tolerated this solution, which somehow seemed to work, not unlike the custom, so I understand, that used to prevail and possibly still does, at Oxford and Cambridge Universities.

Transport Command to India

After some local flying, we set off early in July on a trip to Karachi Our crew from Aldergrove was augmented by an experienced commander and we flew to Tripoli, North Africa, landing at Castel Benito, the old Italian air base, where buildings and hangars were pocked with shell and bullet holes. A night stop accommodated in tents was accompanied by beer brewed from onions served in glasses made from the bottom half of old bottles. The local staff advised us to moderate our beer consumption, as a common symptom of excess was blood in the urine. This did not seem to deter the locals.

Next day was spent following the North African coastline, at about 8,000 feet, to Lydda, near Tel Aviv. We flew above the land fought over by Italian, German and Allied armies The coast road was littered with derelict vehicles,and tanks, easily picked out in the bright lighting.

Tel Aviv was hot, crowded, and busy. We visited the officer's club in town, walked round the shops, and along the beach front without feeling threatened. However, a warning was issued to all service personnel to be aware of activities that could erupt because of the Haganah and Irgun Zwei Leumi factions. These organisations were armed and ready to challenge British rule. There was a contradictory atmosphere. We could utilise the city facilities, yet be liable to murderous attack in certain circumstances. These included any period spent on the base at Lydda. Twice when night-stopping en route to India we were forced to spend a part of the night in a slit trench, avoiding bullets which buzzed overhead. On one occasion a couple of aircraft were destroyed.

Sometimes we would land at Cairo West instead of Lydda, with a bumpy and dusty trip by army truck to reach the sights and the delights of the city. The place was redolent with ancient history, and basted with many smells, under a powerful sun. Plagued by the inevitable hordes of small boys, offering everything for sale, including their sisters and mothers, we found solace at Gezireh or Shepheards, and watched the sunset as feluccas sailed downstream making graceful reflections. Cairo was still under the rule of King Farouk, and an unpopular government. Service personnel of many nations populated the main areas. Traffic was light and mostly military.

Our next call for refuelling and rest was Habbaniya, near Baghdad, where many of the living quarters and other facilities were underground to avoid the heat. This peacetime RAF station had seen the adoption of the so called 'Air Method' in the Twenties, when a large scale rebellion had been effectively controlled by the use of minimal air power, something that does not seem to work these days, even with maximized air strikes.

Alternately we used Shaibah, near Basra, as the stopover point before Karachi. Flying from there over the Tigris at a relatively low-level, we climbed to traverse the Persian Gulf at high altitude, crossing the mountainous Oman peninsula close to the Straits of Hormuz. Mauripur airfield in Karachi was a meeting place for aircraft from points farther east. We could carry 26 passengers in some discomfort, seated in an area converted from the bomb bay. Initially, before the Japanese surrender, we were homeward bound with repatriated service personnel, compassionate cases or those needed for urgent tasks elsewhere. There was a period when several squadrons were routed through the Brussels Melsbroek airfield to collect British airborne troops to move them east. Some were intended to reinforce the garrison in Palestine and others to build up the Far Eastern strength.

One of the night departures was memorable. There was trouble persuading the troops to embark. They had not received any home leave since the regiment left England, and had fought their way across France, Holland, and Germany. There was some unrest, and boarding had to be ensured by the use of military police. We positioned our aircraft in a long line of departing Liberators, unhappy with the thought of a load consisting of disgruntled soldiers. We were second in turn to depart. Watching the previous aircraft become airborne, we moved into the take-off position, and as we lined up saw the departing Liberator explode into a ball of flames and disintegrate from about 500 feet above the city. I was never able to discover the reason for this event. We were cleared to depart immediately afterwards, becoming distracted by our immediate tasks. I have often wondered how our passengers would have reacted had they known. As it was, we chose not to tell them.

We carried a substantial number of the returning British ex-prisoners of war, many of whom had spent a long time in terrible conditions, and who were emaciated, physically weak, but fantastically buoyant at being rescued. They were mostly uncommunicative about their many harrowing experiences which had so obviously flouted in the extreme the clauses of the Geneva Convention concerning captured troops.

The squadron was transferred from Ballykelly to Waterbeach, near Cambridge, at the end of September. We continued to fly the route to India for the rest of my service period, with an occasional flight to other destinations in Europe and the Mediterranean regions.

Opportunity knocks

BOAC had several Liberators, and was expanding its operations during 1946. The airline offered some secondment vacancies to Liberator pilots who were suitably qualified. My accumulated experience at that time was not sufficient to meet the BOAC criteria. Release from the wartime volunteer reserve was arranged in rotation basis, depending on the individual's 'release group.' I could expect to be demobilised (demobbed) some time in 1947. Society could not absorb the immediate influx of too many young men. This system caused the wasteful misemployment of many who wished to start a civilian life, and who chafed at the continuing restrictions of service life. The RAF offered extended-service commissions for applicants who met their requirements, this being a gamble for those successful, who mostly hoped for a permanent commission at a later date. A few permanent commissions were granted to some outstanding officers.

My long-term aim was unchanged: to take up a career in civil aviation. I set about obtaining my civilian pilot's and navigator's licences, purchasing the help of a correspondence course to steer me through the syllabus and subject matter. By July 1946 I had been through the arduous processing mill constructed by the Ministry of Civil Aviation, attending many examination sessions, tests, and medical examinations, submitting fees and forms. Many other would-be civil pilots accompanied me to the crowded and closely invigilated examination rooms. At the time when I was the possessor of a civil pilot's B licence, and a second class navigation licence, a letter arrived from the proprietor of the correspondence 'college'. This enquired if I would be at all interested in joining a small charter company, Portsmouth Aviation Ltd, as its resident pilot, and if so then they could arrange my early release from the service under the category 'work of national importance.' The salary offered was £1,000 per annum, which seemed attractive, but the main attraction was a way into the civil aviation world, and out of the Air Force. The types of aircraft used by the company were the de Havilland DH-89A Rapide, the Airspeed Consul, and the Percival Proctor. The company also proposed to buy an Avro Lancastrian, a civil conversion of the Lancaster bomber.

I lost no time in accepting their offer, reasoning that I should gain more experience before making a bid to join an airline. A few weeks passed before the official notification of my release arrived through the squadron adjutant. I was assigned to a special release unit in Yorkshire and, after a week of processing, was issued with a rail pass to the demobilisation centre in Harrow, north-west London. Three years and eight months of Air Force service were terminated by the acceptance of a demob suit, a hat, various other items of clothing, a ration book, a national insurance card, and a small sum of money called a gratuity. I was on my own, and it felt good.

This DH-89A Dragon Rapide is preserved in flying condition.

Civil aviation

I found some accommodation with a view of the naval dockyard in Portsmouth, but before I could fly the de Havilland Rapide I had to obtain an endorsement on my B licence, as it was a twin-engined type. The Proctor was considered a simple type, although the propeller was a constant speed version unlike those on the Rapide, or Airspeed Consul, which were fixed pitch. The pilot sat alone in the pointed nose of a Rapide. Drift could be measured through a small window in the floor, allowing alignment of sighting lines to read off sideways movement.

The examination of my technical knowledge took the form of an oral test by an Air Registration Board (ARB) surveyor based at Croydon Airport. At the time I had not seen a Rapide and based my knowledge on the pilots' notes and a small technical manual. Seated in front of the shirt-sleeved ARB surveyor, a few questions satisfied him that my knowledge was very insecure.

'Go downstairs to the back of the hangar and introduce yourself to the Olley Air Services engineers. They have a Rapide down there. Tell them I sent you to have a good look around it. Come back up here and we can complete the necessary forms.'

I spent an interesting period complying with this enlightened request, and acquired some valuable tips from a knowledgeable maintenance crew, particularly about starting the engines in cold or damp weather. All that remained was to complete the required six landings on both Proctor and Rapide, and have these certified in my log-book. Then the Ministry would issue me an endorsement to carry passengers 'for hire or reward' using all three types.

Next morning, I went to the airport and met the charter operation manager, a man in his fifties. His status in the company was a trifle anomalous, for he lacked any real knowledge of aviation, but possessed a substantial background in the pre-war travel agency business. He was usually to be seen with a pipe, lit or unlit, in his mouth, giving an impression of taciturn wisdom. We established an avuncular relationship. There was also an assistant, who was responsible for procuring work from travel agencies, and for securing the necessary permits, carnets, and documentation that were required for overseas flights

Portsmouth Airport was a grass field of irregular shape. The Airspeed Company was then producing a small number of Consuls, a civil version of the Oxford. I was introduced to their test pilot, Alan Jones, who also flew occasional charters for our company. The company was developing a light twin called the Portsmouth Aerocar, and he was also involved in this project, which, however, never came to fruition, It could carry either a reasonable load, or fuel, but not both.

'Would you like to come along on an acceptance flight?'

Alan Jones pointed to a new Consul that was parked outside, and I accepted, being interested in the differences that marked the civil version of the old Oxbox. We were soon over the centre of the airfield at about 8,000 feet. I was in the right seat, and nicely strapped in with a full Sutton harness which was a good thing for he nosed the aircraft down to begin a loop. This was not a certificated manoeuvre for the type, but I reasoned that, as the company test pilot, he should know what was safe or otherwise. We went round pleasantly enough, with little applied G force, but a lot of noise from the props. I should have been impressed but the event only reminded me of an unsuccessful attempt by one instructor to make me airsick during initial training. We went on to fly some more useful test sequences, landing at Christchurch for lunch.

Conversion to the Rapide was initiated by a ten-minute demonstration flight with the other company pilot, a Maltese who had decided to return to his homeland. This was followed with six landings solo, three empty, and three with a full load of willing, but unsuspecting company passengers. After lunch, the procedure was repeated, this time in the company Percival Proctor. For this flight I did not have the benefit of a demonstration, and found out that this single-engined type had some interesting characteristics. These included a good old torque swing as power was applied on take-off, and a tendency to lose directional control on landing when the tail was lowered. The added complexity of the constant speed prop control was no problem, but the view when taxiing was limited by the nose. Loading had to be carefully watched to avoid weight and balance problems.

Portsmouth Aviation

My initial civil passenger-carrying flights were all made carrying journalists on local trips around various naval installations, the Solent, and along the south coast of England.

A journey to an airfield near Gloucester for collection of an ex-RAF Dominie, the service version of the Rapide, proved interesting. Our party included two fitters, and the manager, who acted as chauffeur in his car. We spent a couple of hours examining log books, structure, equipment, and engines. The smell of leather seating, dope (treatment applied to fabric surfaces for protection and tautening), petrol, and oil remains as a special memory of that particular type. We had brought our own wheel chocks, and when the time came to start the Gipsy Six engines, one man was on fire-guard outside, and one inside, leaning over my shoulder. Both had been fitters in the RAF, a designation that marked those who had served their apprenticeship, and who were well qualified to maintain airframes, instruments, and/or engines. They viewed me with a mixture of kindness and suspicion.

I started both engines, signalled chocks to be removed and for the outside man to come aboard. He joined the other in the forward seats, and I released the brakes to move forward, only to be distracted by one of the men who asked, 'Did you see that pole on the left side as you moved out? Well, I think we might have hit something.'

I brought the Rapide to a halt, set the brakes and asked one of them to have a look. We had indeed made a small tear in the under-wing fabric. I felt foolish, and irresponsible for not noticing the obstruction, and very grateful for his suggestion. The small tear was soon patched and a bond was forged between the fitters and myself. Their support was very encouraging.

The remainder of the delivery flight was uneventful. There was a single short-range radio-telephony set, and I was able to use this for communication with a couple of airfields en route, although using light signals from the tower at home base for permission to land.

The other Rapide was fitted out with Morse key and CW radio. A wireless operator was employed to operate this. He was a small, tubby, cheerful, and experienced individual, helpful and friendly. We were flying under virtually pre-war rules and conditions. Instrument approaches were flown by a method called QDL–QDMs, where the radio officer transmitted a signal with his Morse key, and the ground station on, or close, to an airport measured the bearing of the aircraft and transmitted the QDM for the pilot to use. This was the magnetic compass heading to steer to reach the ground station, assuming zero wind. A series of these headings would allow the pilot to revise his handling to compensate for wind and to approach on any specific path over the ground. A descent would not be started until the 'motors overhead' advice was received, or until the headings reversed, indicating that overhead passage had been achieved. A degree of skill was needed, but the slow speed of the aircraft helped.

I was expected to fly in most weather conditions although the aircraft were not certified for flight in icing. Night operations out of Portsmouth depended on the provision of a flare path and advance notice, but the civil airports at Bournemouth (Hurn), and Southampton (Eastleigh) were available and close enough to provide alternate facilities.

Most of the charter flights were to the Channel Islands, involving quite a long spell over water. The single-engined performance of the Rapide was generally in a downwards direction if carrying anything but a very light load, engine condition, good inspection, and careful handling contributed to my peace of mind.

We also flew to Paris (Le Bourget). On one of these trips, carrying four well-dressed passengers and a lot of baggage, we met an example of what could have been mistaken as chauvinistic preference when the radio man handed me a signal from Le Bourget control advising us to hold clear of the circuit. We were flying in good visual conditions below the overcast and could see that there were no aircraft on the airfield, or in the circuit pattern. After a long delay during which the passengers were becoming restive, I decided to position for a visual approach, only to be warned off by a red Very light fired from the ground.

The cause of all the fuss soon appeared on final approach. A four engined Air France Languedoc appeared low on the horizon. After it had landed we received a green light from the tower, and at last managed to land. I rang the traffic control office and asked with some trepidation if there was any problem with our approach. The duty officer was quite forthcoming. 'No, the fact is that we don't have too many aircraft these days that are not equipped with R/T, and our light in the tower had to be fixed in a hurry when you arrived. In any case we expected the Languedoc to arrive before you. I am sorry for the inconvenience.'

Long-distance charter

Few aircraft were on the ground at Le Bourget as we strolled out to begin the return journey. A man ran across to meet us. He was carrying a suitcase, and wore a black overcoat of excessive length. His appearance was a mixture of opulence and untidiness, topped off by a luxurious moustache. In good English, flavoured with a central European accent, he asked a leading question.

'Can you take me to Johannesburg? I will give you five hundred pounds now and another five hundred when we arrive, and pay for all the fuel and accommodation.' The prospect of taking the little Rapide on such a journey was to say the least rather impractical at such short notice. Arrangements for the necessary overflight and landing permits would take several days to arrange, and then there was insurance, company permission, and a host of other considerations. I was attracted by the idea, and the sum offered was considerable in those days. After a brief conversation it appeared that he had been at the airport for five days, accosting the pilot of each charter aircraft with his proposition. Few airline seats were available to South Africa, and the waiting list was a long one. We bade goodbye to him with our regrets, departing for Portsmouth with a last sight of his somewhat forlorn figure standing by the building in an attitude of dejection. On arriving home I told the manager about the request.

'Actually we have just arranged to lease a Consul for the very purpose of running charters to South Africa. Alan Jones is going to take the first one out soon. I expect that you will be involved in this too.'

The itinerary for this long journey in a small twin, seating a maximum of four people, was interesting. From Eastleigh it went to Marseille (Marignane Airport), Malta, Benina (in Libya), Cairo, Luxor, Wadi Haifa, Entebbe, Nairobi, Dar es Salaam, Blantyre, Salisbury, and Johannesburg (Palmietfontein Airport). After a couple of trips the lease ceased, because the aircraft was destroyed. Engine failure, caused by a broken rocker mechanism on one of the Armstrong-Siddeley Cheetahs, forced Alan to make a precautionary landing close to the main Salisbury-Johannesburg road, which was successful until collision with a large tree stump on the roll-out.

Charter work continued to be offered, and on one occasion involved a flight to Eastleigh from Guernsey late in the evening. Thick fog formed and I was forced to tum back from overhead Bournemouth. The forecast had been optimistic, and on returning I just managed to scrape back to Guernsey with enough fuel, landing after dark. During this period after the war, information was hard to secure in flight and caution was required. Our manager did not appreciate the niceties of aviation safety if they led to disruption of utilisation. This was amply demonstrated when returning to Eastleigh the next morning. After arrival in thick mist, and picking up the approach lights at a low height to make a successful landing to clear customs and discharge passengers, I saw that the visibility had fallen substantially. It was possible to taxi, and see about a hundred yards. The Meteorological Office said that there was little hope of an improvement. I rang the company to explain that it would not be prudent to return to Portsmouth, only to be advised in strong terms that the airfield there was in good visibility and that I should get back there as soon as possible. The aircraft had been booked to go to Croydon, on another charter.

Against my better judgment I agreed, making a take-off with the sides of the runway barely visible. After arrival the manager was unsympathetic when I explained that I had only complied with his request as there were no passengers on board. I knew that he would have expected the same performance as a standard routine, and began to realise a potential conflict between my inexperienced judgment and the economic need of the company.

Scottish Airlines

The winter months of 1946 elapsed without much intensive flying. The company did not seem able to secure enough work. The Lancastrian project was no longer mentioned as it had been dropped. I began to recognise that the future lay with obtaining work flying larger aircraft, and that this would mean a change. Answering an advertisement by Scottish Aviation Ltd, asking for pilots with experience of the Liberator, I was pleasantly surprised to receive a letter from the operations manager, Wing Commander Dobson, and an invitation for interview. This proved positive, and I was offered a position with Scottish Airlines after a short check flight in a DC-3 with Tim Hope, a senior Captain.

I had met my future wife rather by accident, thanks to a last minute invitation and a change of holiday location during the previous summer. After some months we agreed that an early marriage would be possible, once I had achieved some sort of financial security. I had saved most of my salary from Portsmouth, and with the RAF money had what looked like a reasonable balance in the bank. Looking back on that time I can only wonder at how so many post-war marriages were made in poor economic circumstances. The nation was recovering from so much. We made plans to marry a few weeks after I took up the job with Scottish Airlines, and at the interview I asked for some time off for that purpose. This was a surprise to the operations manager, but he was most gracious. This set the pattern followed by the company, which treated their staff in an exemplary way.

The airline had been formed by Scottish Aviation Limited (SAL), and was based at Prestwick Airport near Ayr. Prestwick had been a wartime maintenance base and ferry terminal and activity had been constant since the beginning of the war years when SAL had been running a wireless operators' school. Since then a widening number of activities had included a large maintenance organization that inspected and modified many of the American lend-lease aircraft as well as routine work for the RAF. As the terminus for many ferry flights from North America, Prestwick was now used by most of the postwar trans-Atlantic airlines. Trans Canada Airlines (TCA) used Lancastrians, KLM, and SAS used DC-4s. BOAC was retiring its Liberators, and introducing its first Constellation L-049s.

Scottish Aviation was now intensively engaged in the conversion of many ex-RAF Douglas Dakotas to civilian DC-3s. Many of these were for British European Airways (BEA), and formed a substantial part of that airline's fleet until the Vickers Viking appeared on the scene. Scottish had also designed and manufactured a short take-off and landing aircraft called the Prestwick Pioneer, later produced as a twin-engined version. Its own fleet included ten DC-3s and three Liberators, converted for civilian use, which were quite luxuriously trimmed. A four-engined high winged Fokker XXII was used for air cruises up

A B-24 Liberator of Scottish Airlines.

and down the Clyde. This had been used for wireless operator training and was fitted with four Wasp Junior engines with the same propeller installation as the Harvard. The noise of this aircraft on take-off was enough to wake up the dead. There was also a Percival Proctor, a Tiger Moth, an Airspeed Consul, and a converted Dominie/Rapide would soon arrive.

I was qualified to fly this complete fleet with the exception of the Fokker and the DC-3, so once again had to study the manuals of the Douglas twin so that the local ARB surveyor could grill me before approving my application for licence endorsement. Luckily this time I was able to get at the actual aircraft, which helped, and was also able to obtain aircraft handling in advance of the test.

Scottish Airlines had a route network of scheduled services that covered many points in the British Isles and overseas. The airline was flying many of these routes when BEA possessed only a few ex-German Junkers Ju 52s.

Scottish Airways, not to be confused with SAL, was based in Renfrew, near Glasgow, and flew a fleet of Rapides, on a network of services to many destinations in Scotland. These pre-war aircraft still used the QDL QDM instrument letdown procedure to land at Renfrew, around the cranes on the River Clyde, and in the fog and rain.

SAL used the Liberators for a regular service to the city airport at Reykjavik, Iceland, and to Copenhagen (Kastrup). They also flew from Northolt to Athens, with one of the aircraft carrying Greek registration as part of Hellenic Airlines, which had been formed in a co-operative venture with SAL.

At various times DC-3s were based in Greece to fly internal services to several of the Grecian airfields in areas that were cut off by the civil war in 1947. Some very large passenger loads were carried during this period. One DC-3 was involved in emergency evacuations and once uplifted more than eighty people, including women and children. Their transit at Larissa was exposed to small arms fire but fortunately from long-range. The bullets could only just reach the perimeter of the field.

The internal services included Renfrew, Sumburgh (in the Shetland Isles), Aberdeen (Dyce), Belfast (Nutt's Corner), Inverness (Dalcross), Northolt, and Manchester (Ringway). Charter flights were also made to a variety of places, including Montreal, Lagens in the Azores, and many French destinations. A specialist navigator was carried on the Liberator's long-haul flights, and a flight engineer on all DC-3 and Liberator flights.

The chief pilot was Alastair Cormack, a competent but rather remote character. The Duke of Hamilton and his brother the Earl of Selkirk were closely associated with the firm, which employed well-qualified and experienced aircraft commanders. I was most impressed with the company's maintenance, operational training, and general efficiency. This was shown by much attention to detail in all aspects. Regular practise of instrument procedures, using a Link trainer, kept us current with the latest requirements. Documentation was handled sensibly, with a section providing up-to-date information. Conditions of service were good, with a superannuation (retirement annuity) scheme, and medical cover. Insurance was part of the package. Even the uniforms were of a high quality, from good marine tailors in Glasgow. Loyalty among the staff was manifest, and a very pleasant co operative spirit existed at all levels.

Flying with the Duke

I was called to fly each of the types on a random basis, spreading the time between the larger and the smaller aircraft in almost equal proportion. As the only pilot who had endorsement for the Consul, I was tagged to act as the ferry pilot to take the Duke or the Earl to their weekend retreat on the island of North Uist in the Outer Hebrides. We would usually land at Benbecula on South Uist, whence they would be driven to the north if the tide allowed, on the shallow sands between the two islands. When the tide cut off the two islands, we could land on the little field at Sollas. I would occasionally wait overnight for their return, and spend the time touring the local farms or cottages to obtain eggs and butter, which were in very short supply in 1947.

The journey from Prestwick to Benbecula passes close to the isle of Iona, and the whirlpool of the Corryvreckan. Flying at about 3,000 feet on a day with good visibility it is easy to spot the disturbed water, where legend has it that many a small boat has vanished into the abyss. On one such day I was happily musing along, with the Earl in the right hand seat, reading The *Times*. We were also carrying two boys of school age, sons of the Duke. As we drew close to Iona the aircraft began to weave from left to right in a strange way. I felt the rudder pedals moving, and looked back to find that the boys had taken up the carpet, and a floor section of the rear cabin. They were pulling on the control runs, and causing the problem. The Earl looked at me, rolled his *Times* into a baton, undid his seat belt, and went aft. I could see that he was laying about both culprits with a great deal of energy. Soon he took his seat again, and smiled at me.

'Sorry about that. They are devils at times you know.'

He was soon immersed in the crossword. We had no more troubles that trip, and they both came to me after we had disembarked. One said, in a fine Inverness accent, 'Pilot. I want to apologise for what we did. We won't do it again.'

That said, they turned and left me wondering at the eccentricities of the ruling classes.

The supply of ex-RAF Dakotas came mostly from a holding unit at Silloth, on the north east coast of Cumberland, west of Carlisle. One of my tasks was to ferry the collection crews in the Proctor down from Prestwick. This involved a choice of two routes; one via the Nith valley and Dumfries across land, and the other following the coastline all the way, the last part crossing the Solway Firth for about ten miles to reach the airfield. The valley route was often impractical for visual contact flight because of fog, or low cloud, and the Proctor had no navigational aids. Often I would need to fly at under 500 feet, with a quarter-million-scale topographical map on my lap, and follow each bay and inlet carefully against compass headings to ensure accurate identification. My colleagues, unused to this, were justifiably nervous when the visibility was reduced in the rain and mist. I was also asked to fly a few charters to the London area. On one occasion we were supposed to land at a grass field near Broxbourne. I map-read to the exact vicinity of the field, but could not recognise it as a landing area. Luckily one of my two businessmen passengers identified it for me, and we successfully made our landing. His partner decided to return by train.

Stranded in the Shetlands

Proctor flying was a change from the scheduled work on the Liberator and DC-3, and sometimes I was expected to fly in some bad weather. One of the DC-3s was stranded at Sumburgh in the Shetland Islands, needing spares and engineers to fix the snag. I was asked to fly up two maintenance fitters and the spare parts. Low cloud, rain, and fog covered the western part of Scotland, although the east coast was relatively clear. I planned to fly across to the Firth of Forth via valleys well known to me, under the overcast. Near Barrhead, the valley narrowed to about a mile in width before we could break out to the low ground and wider valleys over Glasgow, Falkirk, and the Forth Bridge. Flying at about 700 feet above the ground, and 500 feet below the overcast, I saw that the narrow part of the valley ahead was covered with mist and cloud, and would be impassable. Immediately reversing course I was appalled to see that my return path was blocked by advancing cloud. There was little option. Climbing above 4,000 feet on a westerly heading, breaking out on top of the lowest cloud below another layer, I timed my westerly heading with an allowance for the strong wind, and flew on for some time. My companions were not impressed with this process, but were reassured when we descended and broke out of cloud over the Firth of Clyde. We were soon on the ground at Prestwick, where a DC-3 was ready to complete the task, with me as the co-pilot.

DC-3 baptism

This particular aircraft was a true DC-3, manufactured in 1938, and differed in some respects from our other aircraft, which were converted C-47s. The heating system was based on a hot water design. Steam could be generated in sufficient quantity to alarm the crew. However on this particular occasion it was not the heating that caused a problem. After levelling off at 7,000 feet, and with the Sperry autopilot engaged, I was busy tuning in radio beacons and plotting bearings to find a position. This was done on a chart clipped to a board balanced across my knees. All pilots who have ever flown DC-3s in rain will know about leaks from the windscreen. These could require a raincoat, or at least something protective across the knees.

I was a little surprised to note that the dampness arriving on my chart was tinted red this time. This was soon explained by the flight engineer announcing that we had a leak from the hydraulics. Many of the hydraulic system components were mounted in a small compartment behind the co pilot, and the flight engineer emerged from this area covered in red fluid. His hair and shirt were quite lurid, and his eyes seemed to match. Apparently we had lost all the fluid because of a pipe rupture. This left us without braking, or flaps, but with an emergency method of lowering the undercarriage. The runway at Sumburgh was long, and the weather good for our arrival, so we continued towards the Shetlands. On landing we managed to stop well before the end of the runway, and disappointed the single and rather ancient fire truck that was standing by. Our two fitters soon did the repair, and with the system replenished, a clean shirt for the engineer, and a sandwich or two, we were on our way back to Prestwick.

Liberator procedures

North Atlantic aviation in the Liberator was interesting. Westbound to Iceland or Montreal would be planned at lower levels because of the prevailing winds, although this placed us squarely into the temperature range when airframe and engine icing could be expected as a normal occurrence. Intermittent use of the leading edge inflatable boots would succeed in breaking up most of the wing ice, if done carefully at the right time. Propellers threw ice as it was discarded when heat was applied. Sometimes this made a lot of noise as bits flew onto the fuselage with a thump. The engines were unaffected, and well-protected when handled correctly. Navigation was primarily by the use of wartime type LORAN receiver and sextant, backed up by radio range and radio beacons. High blower (supercharger) operation was necessary at high altitude, but was generally avoided if possible to reduce maintenance problems. As the aircraft was unpressurised the stress of putting passengers on the available oxygen system was also undesirable. By the standards of those days flight times were long, as the Liberator cruised slowly. A trip on 1 November 1947 from Prestwick to Gander (Newfoundland) took 11 hours and forty minutes. My fastest time on Concorde from London (Heathrow) to Gander was just over two hours.

Medevac

We were occasionally asked to fly medical evacuation flights from the more remote Scottish airfields. This led to a rather scary night in January 1948. The airfield at Machrihanish on the Mull of Kintyre, near Campbeltown, is only about 50 miles west of Prestwick. The small grass field has since been expanded into a NATO and RAF base, and is now deactivated. Situated on the west side of the Kintyre peninsula, the ground slopes upwards sharply on each side. An urgent stretcher case for immediate operation in a local hospital had to be collected. Notification of the requirement was telephoned through to me in the late afternoon, and it was dark by the time I was picked up by the company transport. Wind howled round the Bedford van, with heavy rain beating on the windscreen as we made our way to the company headquarters.

After a consultation with the weather office, who told me that the cloud base would remain at about 2,000 feet despite the 40 knot wind, and moderate rain, I reluctantly filed a flight plan for the trip. The Airspeed Consul had been chosen, and its endurance was over four hours. A medical attendant was waiting in the large hangar, where the aircraft was fully prepared. At the last minute the operations manager decided that I should be accompanied by one of the DC-3 commanders, although he did not have the Consul on his licence. I was very grateful for his presence, as it promised to be a demanding little trip. Taking off into a very turbulent and dark sky, we were battered by heavy rain. The Prestwick radio range west leg, giving on-course guidance, was a help in ensuring a good track towards the southern tip of the Mull. The lights of Arran slid by on the right, and slowly we moved on westwards to round the peninsula and fly up the western shore. The turbulence was less severe, but the wind drift was stronger. The airfield lights were difficult to identify in the rain, and the terrain was shrouded in darkness. To land into or close to the wind direction I would have to fly inland towards the higher ground, and turn in an area where the turbulence could be dangerous, close to the hills. I decided to fly back east to the Campbeltown area, and see if an approach to the field could be made through the valley. When positioned on a run in to the coast the visibility was not good enough. Darkness, rain, and turbulence all contributed to my decision. Throughout this uncomfortable session my co-pilot had sat silently, offering no advice. When I announced my intention to return to Prestwick he merely nodded assent. The patient died two days later, and I have often wondered if my judgement was faulty in attempting the trip, or in trying the alternative approach.

When we called the Prestwick approach controller on our return we realised that we had been out of radio contact for nearly an hour. There was no radio at Machrihanish, and our non-arrival had triggered an air-sea rescue alert. Journalists picked this up, and the details were luridly covered in the local papers. Despite all this there was never any query from the management after I had filed my report. Scottish Airlines always backed their pilots, who consequently felt able to exercise their experience and discretion. There was never any attempt to encourage a 'press-on' mentality, an attitude which has sometimes led to catastrophes involving considerable loss of life.

Bonnie football charter

One of the funniest charters involved two DC-3s in a trip to Morlaix in Brittany. We were carrying the Glasgow Police Pipe Band and a football team, in celebration of a visit made by Bonnie Prince Charlie. Lovely August weather in 1947 greeted our arrival at the ex-Luftwaffe base, situated on high ground overlooking the coast. Morlaix is a small provincial town, with a viaduct across the centre, and had not been damaged too much. On arrival we were transported to the mairie (town or city hall) to be met by the city council and the mayor. Long tables were set with an abundant supply of food and wine. We were stopping for two days, until all the events had been completed. These included parades, a concert involving the police and local pipe bands, and a football match. Kilted locals paraded around with bagpipes held aloft.

The town party developed intensively, and spread along the streets. Many of our passengers were seen departing to various destinations, carrying bagpipes, and already a little worse for wear. We found our hotel, and the advice to attend the local opera house for a special performance of *La bohème* that evening.

The opera house was small and intimate. Inside seating was for about 500, with four rows of balcony seating, facing a few boxes, above a pit stall seating about 150. The music was well done, with an orchestra attired in the local dress. The performance was at times moving, but the singing lacked volume to compete with the incessant chattering of the audience who seemed most intent to punctuate all events on stage with their own comments. A sprinkling of our passengers could be seen, easily recognised by size, conversation, and physique. Many had been partaking of the local libations. This was confirmed by the sight of one 220 pound six-foot, six-inch individual standing up at the edge of the lowest balcony and slowly toppling over, to fall amongst the assembled audience below. This did not cause more than a few bruises, although it may have contributed to the problem next morning.

The parade ground was a running track surrounding the football ground. At the appointed and civilised time of 11 o'clock the viewing areas were full. A march around the track was initiated by the local pipers, dressed in black and white, and making noises remarkably familiar to the tone deaf like myself, who were still hoping to acquire a taste for Scottish laments. As the dying squeal of expiring breath cut through the morning air, we looked for the next set of pipers. After a few minutes it was clear that there had been a serious shortfall, and that our passengers had disappeared to the farther recesses of Morlaix. A search party was appointed from the few attendees, it also being apparent that any hope of a football match would depend upon a successful result.

The football match was postponed for a few hours, and it started with five substitutes on the Glasgow team recruited from the local club. By half time there were enough Glaswegians to take over, but they were unable to defeat the Breton team, who had the advantage of much experience with the local vintages.

Naval encounter

The company Tiger Moth was used mainly for instruction associated with a local club, but one day I was asked to take a photographer from the Glasgow Herald newspaper on a journey from Prestwick up and down the Clyde. The Royal Navy had the complete Home Fleet in the area and was about to depart down the Firth in line astern. More than four years had passed since I had last flown the little biplane. I seated the photographer in the rear seat of the Tiger. His camera was large, with a big telephoto attachment. Communication was to be by signs, or in written form, as he was unable to use the Gosport-type intercommunication tube without restricting his movement.

I obtained clearance to use the grass surface next to the main runway for take-off, after receiving assistance from club members who walked out holding the wingtips. The wind was luckily quite gentle, so we avoided the problems that a strong breeze might have caused. It was a lovely sensation as we purred into the sky over Troon to set course at 1,500 feet towards the fleet, which was soon seen moving in stately line ahead, at about ten knots. The newspaper had received permission from the RN to make several low passes. The only restriction was that we should not fly over any warship.

My ship recognition was still of some use, identifying a King George V class battleship heading the long line of grey ships, followed by cruisers, destroyers, an aircraft carrier, and many other smaller vessels. As we flew alongside the flagship at about 300 feet, I was alarmed by the aircraft turning involuntarily towards the ship. The photographer had leaned out of his seat, holding his large camera, and this had produced an effect as if rudder had been applied. My gesticulations to him were acknowledged by a cheery wave in reply, but no adjustment of his position, as he focussed on the targets. I gave up, and concentrated on trying to keep the Tiger in trim. Looking at the ships I saw to my horror that all the anti-aircraft guns on the flagship were tracking us as we flew past. This procedure was repeated as we went down the long line of warships, so that we looked down at a succession of gun muzzles. I am not sure what sort of medal would have been awarded for downing us. Perhaps the journalist was fair game? The session lasted for an hour before we returned to Prestwick, to receive clearance to land on the grass. I was almost as anxious about landing the lovely little trainer as if it was my first solo, as we were being watched by quite an audience by this time. I avoided the disgrace of a bounce, and did not attempt a full three pointer, easing onto the ground as I took the power off, but the rumble of wheels on grass distracted me and I had to apply coarse rudder input to stop losing directional control as the tail lowered. The photographs figured next day in a special supplement of the paper.

Marriage

In April 1947 I went south to London, having been given a few days off for my wedding. Jeane had served as a Land Army girl on a farm in Surrey, where she introduced me to the delights of pig swill, and mucking out. She was a talented artist, from a family with a long history of artistic achievement. Her father was a career army officer, Charles Shearman, retiring as a Brigadier, with distinction for his service in two wars. The wedding took place in the little Christ Church, Down Street, Mayfair, and the reception was at the Connaught Hotel. I was introduced to many family members for the first time, in a whirl of activity. That evening we left for Scotland on the night sleeper train, en route to Pitlochry for our honeymoon. As this was early in the season we were one of only two couples in the huge hotel, and danced alone in the ballroom to an amused orchestra. All too soon we caught the train to Troon, on the west coast north of Prestwick and Ayr, where we had rented rooms in a shared house.

My married status at the age of 22 did not seem inappropriate, as so many young marriages were contracted in the immediate post-war period. The company staff accepted Jeane as a welcome addition to the corporate family, and her Celtic red hair fitted in well.

Navigation

I had decided to work for the full civilian first class navigator's licence as this would bring a rise in salary, but the main reason was to protect me in future should there be difficulty in maintaining employment in the industry. International air routes were being opened, and the specialist navigator was still in demand. Pilots who could also navigate might be more productive and efficient crew members, and the additional training and knowledge would load the odds towards economic survival.

After much help from friends and colleagues, and months of spare time study, the day arrived for the examination, at Edinburgh. The main University hall was a huge room, with marble flooring under a copper clad dome. Four other candidates were seated at each corner, with about fifty yards separating each table. The invigilator sat on a raised dais when he was not pacing around with disconcerting clicking of his heels on the hard flooring. During the lunch interval I was given what may have been a lucky break. One of the other applicants asked me what I knew about polar stereographic charts. I admitted that I was relatively ignorant on that subject, only to be told that there would probably be a question covering it on the next paper. He then gave me a 20-minute crash course from his personal notes. Sure enough the second question turned out to be about the polar projections, and was worth a lot of marks. I have never had any occasion to use this knowledge in my aviation career, and indeed much of what we were required to learn at that time of transition from pre-to post-war requirements was superfluous.

Passing the examination led to issue of the First Class Licence by the Ministry. I was the proud possessor of another piece of pasteboard, and immediately a candidate for use as a navigator on the longer Liberator flights.

Greece

Athens (Ellinikon) airport was a hubbub of disorganised, almost chaotic activity. The heat was oppressive, the customs and immigration officials uninterested and officious. Our passengers were variously of many eastern origins, sprinkled with the occasional British businessman. The flight time from Northolt was usually about nine hours. We would night stop at the Grand Hotel, in sight of the Parthenon. Inflation was rife at the time, and wads of drachma notes were needed to purchase anything. The shops did not have much stock except a superabundance of tinned goods, all labelled 'UNRRA. Planters Peanuts.' The widespread availability of this commodity testified either to a Grecian aversion, or perhaps a doubtful deal struck by the relief agency.

The return trip across the Gulf of Corinth to the French Riviera and over France usually took more than nine and a half hours, avoiding the Alps. Over the Massif Central, north of Marseille, the weather can be quite severe, triggered by the high ground. In later years a Handley Page Hermes belonging to Airwork picked up so much ice on the wings that it stalled and fell several thousand feet before recovery, and this led to a detailed investigation of the wing profile and de-icing systems of that type. On one of my trips we were struck by lightning twice, and found several small holes in the structure as a result.

Danish and Icelandic smells

The trip between Iceland and Copenhagen involved a night stop in each place, allowing a little relaxation and shopping. I was able to buy margarine, made from whale oil, in Reykjavik. We were very short of cooking fats so this was a welcome help. This regular purchase was thwarted on one flight when we heard that visibility was low over the airport because of smoke. The whale oil refinery factory had caught fire, and the smell was appalling, permeating everywhere in the town. My clothing carried the smell back to Troon.

In Copenhagen dairy produce was obviously a preferred buy. I thought that at Christmas it would be a good idea to buy a whole Danish Blue round for distribution among friends. This scheme came to a sticky end, as the parcel was positioned in error next to a heater unit in the flight deck, providing a very rapid meltdown followed by an incredible change in the atmosphere.

Bishop's move

An interesting diversion was granted one day when I was required to carry the Bishop of Dublin from Prestwick to the Collinstown Airport of that city, flying the Proctor. He arrived in his ecclesiastical purple, and brought enough baggage to cause a stowage, weight, and centre of gravity dilemma. This was juggled to arrive at a safe result, and we set off, following the coastlines. The Mourne Mountains, in Northern Ireland, were on the right-hand side after a while, and he reminded me that they rightfully belonged to Eire. I was diplomatically silent. When we had arrived at the peaceful Collinstown Airport he invited me to the restaurant, bought me lunch, and produced a five pound note as a tip. I explained that it was company policy for us not to accept such offerings. In those days the sum was equivalent to a week's wage for a working man. I did not explain my religious allegiances. This little trip had involved crossing about 25 miles of open sea in the single-engined Proctor, so I had climbed to 9,000 feet for peace of mind, not entirely sure as to what degree of life insurance the carriage of a Bishop would ensure.

Dakota ferry

During these immediately post-war years, air traffic control (ATC) was in its infancy. London had a Control Zone based on a circle drawn round the city, entry to which was prohibited unless certain rules were respected. Aircraft were required to inform ATC by radio before entry to the zone. This rule was not observed on one November night.

In 1947 a few Dakotas had to be collected from various parts of France. On this occasion we were flown down to Villacoublay, a military airfield near Paris, where we found our aircraft sitting forlornly at the edge of a perimeter track next to a wartime Quonset hut. The grass had not been cut, and had grown through the asphalt over the parking spot. An aura of decay was confirmed by a brief look inside the hut. Our flight engineer speculated that it would probably take several days to ensure that we could have an airworthy departure.

The handling agents who were supposed to smooth the paperwork came from a local operator called Aigle Azur. We did not see much of them. The various contacts that we had with French Air Force personnel were less than informative. Accommodation had been arranged in a small hotel close to Montmartre, not too far from the Place Pigalle. Paris was short of food, and heating. Power cuts were expected each day, and warm clothing was essential. Restaurants served horsemeat steak, which seemed plentiful, but other things were limited. The coffee was ersatz, and mainly chicory. A major crisis had occurred for the local sex trade, for a government edict had banned all street soliciting. The result was that all the hotels were full of prostitutes (and their clients), to the disadvantage of residents. An overall impression of chaotic post-war poverty and deprivation was countered by the essential beauty of the city. We walked for miles looking at everything from Notre Dame, and the Tuileries, to the Champs-Élysées, where luxury shops were displaying expensive haute couture, and exotic scents. Since this visit I have always had a passion for fresh French bread.

After a couple of visits to the airfield, for equipment checks and engine run-ups, we were ready to depart late in the afternoon of the fourth day. I was asked to prepare a flight plan which would just skirt the London zone to the west, and then direct to Prestwick. As usual, navigation would be conducted from the right-hand seat by using bearings from radio beacons. I did, however, have a sextant, and the aircraft had an astrodome from which to take star shots, but for an overland and shortish flight I did not expect to use it. I had also brought the Air Almanac, and Hughes Tables, so that the astro could be used.

We took off in the failing light of a grey and overcast afternoon, climbing to 8,000 feet, where we battled along in cloud, getting wet, predictably, from the leaking windshield. The condition of our Dakota was imperfect in a number of respects, and it would certainly not have met the requirements for commercial service. The permit to fly, issued by the French authorities, covered us only for this journey. The aircraft still carried French registration, and we were using a French radio call sign, having filed the flight plan as that nationality. This arrangement was decided by consultation between our management and Aigle Azur, no doubt to avoid trouble with the UK authorities. I was not confident of the radio compass accuracy, having had minimal opportunity to check it from local beacons, and unable to convince anyone that it should be calibrated before use.

Fixing position was made more difficult by the constant static generated in the cloud. St Elmo's Fire played sparkling phosphorescent patterns on the windshield, and our VHF reception included noise from the storms. By now it was dark, and I began to realise that we could be far from our intended route. The westerly wind had been forecast as strong, and we were flying a heading that included a substantial compensation for drift. At last we broke out of the cloud, on top of low stratus, which obscured the ground below. I was able to tune in a couple of radio beacons, and plot a quick fix of position. To my horror we were right in the middle of the London Control Zone. A position report was necessary, and it was useless, and dangerous, to misreport it as if we were maintaining our filed routeing. There was also the probability that a bearing could be taken of our transmission which would give the game away.

At this point the captain showed great presence of mind. He transmitted the position report in a guttural and Gallic accent, using, of course, our French call sign. The reply from London control was to the effect that we had just flown through their zone and did we know this? Assuming ignorance the captain replied that he did not know anything about that. The response was to pass us on to another radio frequency, and controller. We never did have any further comment or feedback from this event. I have always assumed that we were written off as crazy continentals.

Thoughts of a move

As the anniversary of my joining Scottish Airlines occurred, the company dream of becoming Scotland's national airline was impeded by political considerations centred in Westminster, where policy was firmly behind the 'chosen instruments' of three nationalised airline corporations, BOAC, BEA, and BSAA. Our flying began to decrease, and some pilots left for other companies. We had moved to rather better accommodation, but Jeane was now pregnant, and felt that she would rather be closer to her family in England. The climate did not suit her either, for Troon is remarkable for its exposed position to coastal gales. The winter had made a lasting impression on her, despite visits to the surrounding islands such as Arran, and exploration of the countryside.

I had recently joined the pilots' union, the British Airline Pilots' Association, (BALPA) after realising that they ran an employment contact listing, and also because I had heard that there was a wide variation in contractual terms of employment amongst the aircraft companies. After discovering that Airwork Ltd, a company based at Blackbushe Airport, near Camberley in Surrey, was recruiting pilots, I wrote to offer my services. Airwork operated a scheduled service to East Africa, using Vickers Vikings, and later used Handley Page Hermes aircraft. Apart from that, they were a firm of long-standing, with much contract work for the services and government. I was offered a job to fly Douglas C-54s for a contract flying immigrants to Canada. The terms of employment were harsher than those offered by SAL although the salary was identical.

We decided that I should give my month 's notice to SAL. This was received with genuine regret, and their subsequent actions confirmed that they were the most enlightened employers. During my working life I have never discovered such interest by personnel officers in my individual well-being, although one firm in Canada came close. I was repaid my superannuation contributions, and also theirs.

Much of the last month was spent flying the Rapide. I checked out several of the other pilots by sitting behind them in a passenger seat to offer advice if needed, and flew many pleasure flights around the locality for an inexhaustible series of families.

An excursion to the games

One trip with the Earl of Selkirk and a party of friends was memorable. This was to attend the Highland Games at Inverness. On the way up from Prestwick the cloud was broken and I took the scenic route following the Caledonian Canal, noting the topography carefully against the map, as the weather was slowly deteriorating with the advance of a warm front from the west. After spending the day at the show watching the games and hi jinks, I was increasingly worried that we might not be able to beat the weather and nightfall. The party arrived back late at the aircraft full of bonhomie and other sustenances. I advised the Earl that we would be flying quite low, beneath the cloud, and in sight of the canal, land, and coastline.

The route was along Loch Ness, which is quite wide, but which has a saddle of land at the southern end connecting to Loch Lochy, and then another saddle of land passing Fort William, before reaching Loch Linnhe, the Firth of Lorn and open sea. The cloud base lowered steadily as we flew southwards, so that we had about 300 feet to spare as we crossed the saddles.

Visibility was good, and I was aiming to turn left to aim for the Crinan Canal, where there was a nice wide gap to give entry to the Firth of Clyde and on home.

The point to tum left had to be identified by recognising the island of Scarba, and as we approached I could not be sure which of the islands on the left side was in fact Scarba, because of the different perspective caused by flying so low. I did know from previous experience that the whirlpool of Corryvreckan could be seen on the south side of the island. As we passed by it was apparent that I had gone too far, as the pool came into sight. I needed to reverse course to fly past the north side. We were at about 500 feet above the sea as I turned back. Soon we were across into the Clyde area, and able to climb under a clearing sky, landing as the sun set.

I was eating lunch next day in the management restaurant, where we were permitted to meet the executives over our meal times. This improved communication remarkably, and was responsible for sustaining mutual confidence. The Operations Manager came across and seated himself at my table. He addressed me in a friendly tone.

'I was rung by the Earl this morning to say that he and his party were worried at the way you flew so low, and obviously lost yourself on the way back last night. What actually happened?'

I explained all the circumstances, and recommended that a radio compass would be a prudent installation, and a better radio telephony set. The alternative would, and perhaps should, have been a night stop, but they appeared very eager to return. This was accepted without demur or criticism, and once again was an example of the support received from this closely knit company, run by practical and intelligent people.

The last trip with SAL was in a Liberator on a positioning flight to Northolt, with my wife carrying her white cat in a shoe bag, head free, and horrified as he saw the ground recede on take-off. Our worldly goods were in the hold.

COMETS AND CONCORDES

Airwork

We had rented a flat in Camberley, part of a house owned by a doctor, and not too far from the airport at Blackbushe. Jeane was familiar with the area, as her father had spent time as an instructor at the army Staff College, when her family lived in Farnham. Summer was warm and we felt that the move was beneficial.

Airwork offices at the airport were in the usual temporary ex-wartime buildings, and I soon met some of the other recruits, as we completed the usual formalities. We were given sundry paperwork, and detailed for instrument practice on a Link Trainer involving the North Atlantic airports. Naturally we were interested in when and where we would be receiving our conversion training on the C-54. This was originally planned to occur under the auspices of KLM in Amsterdam. Meanwhile we studied the technical manuals, reporting to the airport daily. We saw the Vikings come and go on the regular African service, and a variety of other aircraft. Westminster Airways had a base, operating DC-3s, and there was a fair amount of smaller traffic. However, Blackbushe seemed quite sleepy compared with the activities at Prestwick.

I soon sensed that there was something wrong. This was confirmed by a chat with the local manager, who seemed unable to say the same thing twice. He constantly referred to the latest pronouncements of the manager of the special charter department, which were very equivocal. We never did become airborne, and began to consider what jobs were available elsewhere. I had been with the firm for five weeks when the situation was clarified.

Westwards to Santiago

The letter, from Sir Archibald Hope, Manager, Special Charter Department, Airwork Ltd, came as no surprise. Dated 9th August 1948, it gave me one month's notice of contract termination. The plan to use Douglas C-54 Skymasters for the International Refugee Organisation was in abeyance, and in fact never did revive. The Canadian authorities would not grant a landing permit, and there was no route to fly. I was told, helpfully, by the assistant manager at Blackbushe, Geoffrey Ford, that British South American Airways was looking for pilots, and given a contact to arrange an interview.

The prospect of unemployment was disturbing, particularly as I had given up a reasonable job with Scottish Aviation. This was my first experience of the instability affecting pilots who were outside the state airline corporations, and who were at the mercy of political factors unrelated to their professional experience or qualifications. Fortunately I had provided some degree of self-protection by obtaining that full 'peacetime' first class navigator's licence during the time with Scottish Airlines.

Introduction to BSAA

British Latin American Airlines, formed in 1945 by five shipping companies, was soon renamed British South American Airways and Air Vice Marshal DCT (Don) Bennett was appointed Chief Executive. After the Labour government was elected to power, it nationalised the company, and made it one of three nationalised airline Corporations: Overseas, European, and South American.

BOAC had a core of very experienced pre-war veterans, and many seconded pilots from the RAF who had gained invaluable

An Avro Tudor of British South American Airways.

exposure to scheduled long-haul routes, often on flying boats, but also using Yorks, Lancastrians, and other types. Most of the original group of BSAA captains were recruited from RAF Bomber Command, many of these from the Pathfinder Force. They included a good proportion of those who had held higher rank, and had been successful as leaders.

I had little knowledge of this background when attending the headquarters office in central London for interview. In August 1948 there were few vacancies. Expansion outside the corporations was halted by the uncertainty of the world economy, and by the vagaries of the world of politics. I was not informed in any detail about the poor accident record that had been accumulated by the airline, and was even ignorant of the route network, crewing philosophy, and future planning.

The selection board was led by Captain Gordon Store, one of several ex-BOAC pilots who had been brought in to strengthen operational standards. I was seated opposite three inquisitors, who seemed to ignore my presence as they studied the details on the application form. The office was hot, stuffy, and dark, in contrast with the brilliant summer afternoon outside. Gordon Store was the spokesman.

'I see that you have been flying Liberators into Iceland. Was this into Keflavik?'

'No, we used the field at Reykjavik.'

He went on to ask about the various hazards around that destination, perhaps to confirm that I was truthful. That concluded the session. They did not ask to see my pilot's B (commercial) licence, and navigator's licence, or to show my log book. I soon found myself outside the office, on the hot pavement in King Street, St James, wondering about the future, and if I had passed muster.

Training and teething

The uncertainty was soon resolved, for a letter from the staff superintendent at Starways House dated 16 August 1948 confirmed the offer of an 'appointment,' and a salary of £600 per annum from 30 August, rising to £750 after one month. This was a significant reduction in money from my previous jobs, and I wondered if the improved security of working for a nationalised corporation was worthwhile. My confidence was not improved by the appointment Letter which made employment subject to obtaining a second class navigator's licence within three months, and a first class licence within six to eight month's service. As I had informed them that I already had a first class licence on the application form, this confirmed my initial impression about that sleepy interview.

I do not think that either of us realised how far-reaching the decision would prove, or of the effect on our personal lives, but we agreed that I should accept the offer.

My initial job with the airline was to be used as an assistant in the navigation office, which was in a hut at the north side of London's Heathrow airport. Development of the central area had not started, and a variety of temporary and rudimentary buildings was in use to serve passengers, crew, and catering. All the aircraft used by BSAA were four-engined. The Avro Lancastrian was a converted civilian version of the Lancaster bomber, fitted with up to thirteen seats, and also used as a freight carrier. The Avro York was a transport aircraft fitted with 21 seats, and had been developed during the war, using the Lancaster wing and engines. The Avro Tudor bad been designed for BOAC, which rejected the Tudor 1 as being unsuitable.

BSAA took the Tudor 1s and used them for crew training. The Tudor 4, with a longer fuselage, was produced in two versions, one with a flight engineer's station, and one without. The airline policy was to use three-pilot crewing when possible, so the majority of the Tudors on order, reputedly 45, were of the later type, without a flight engineer's station.

I was initially under the tutelage of an ex-accountant, Captain Maurice Aries who, at that time, was running the navigation department. Time was spent preparing instrument letdown sheets to the company specifications. Paddy Cormican, whom I was to meet again 27 years later in Toulouse, was part of the office staff, waiting a turn to become involved in the flying side.

Our small group of new recruits was given a week of classroom lectures by Tony Nelson, a line First Officer. These covered the technical details of all three aircraft types in sufficient depth for us to take the required examinations for licence endorsement.

We had been recruited from other airlines, or civil operators, and had experience of aircraft which were equipped with more advanced navigational instrumentation and were not impressed with the minimum information that the course provided nor the obvious speed with which we were being rushed through the system. Some flight training was provided, but not to a standard suitable for licence endorsement.

At that time the Ministry of Transport and Civil Aviation allowed transport aircraft to be crewed with co-pilots who did not possess type endorsement. The International Civil Aviation Organisation (ICAO) had not yet introduced the recommended changes which would lead to a different licensing system. There was no such thing as an instrument flying rating, unless it was an internal rating administered by an individual company.

In BSAA the aircraft were fitted with ex-service radio and navigational equipment. American aircraft, supplied under

Lend-Lease, arrived in Britain equipped with SCS 51, an instrument landing system similar to today's ILS, and always with at least one ADF set (automatic direction finding, where a needle pointed towards a ground radio beacon). These valuable navigational aids were disconnected or removed by the RAF maintenance centres before delivery to squadron service.

Post-war navigational aids

By the end of the war the RAF was using Gee and LORAN systems to aid long-range navigation and to assist the use of astro-navigation. These were based on time-lapse measurement of received radio signals from several ground stations. There was also a German-developed system, Consol, transmitting segmented signals which could be interpreted to give a position line. Visual devices were fitted to see the ground or sea, and measure aircraft wind drift. For landing in poor conditions there was a system called BABS (Blind Approach Beacon System) based on a radar pulse return interpretation from a ground station transponder. This required an operator on the aircraft other than the pilot, and a dialogue talk-down procedure. At some airfields a ground team provided radar-based talk-down approaches in bad weather. This was called GCA (Ground Controlled Approach). The wartime SBA (Standard Beam Approach) was being progressively withdrawn from civil airports in Britain, and was not available elsewhere.

BSAA aircraft were fitted with Marconi radio sets that could receive ground beacon transmissions. The bearing to or from the ground beacon was displayed by the intersection of two needles on an instrument, commonly known as 'Twitchers.' It was difficult to establish an accurate overhead position, and instrument descents or 'letdowns' were completed by flying a box pattern around the beacon.

Most of this worked well enough in Britain, where there was also still a wartime system called FIDO for those winter days when fog covered the English countryside. This involved burning large quantities of fuel to heat the air and disperse the fog sufficiently to allow sight of a runway. Today's environmentalists would have had a case to make, but Heathrow maintained this system for some years. I am not sure when a similar system, based on using a line-up of jet engines, was withdrawn in France, but it was available for the initial Concorde commercial operation at Paris (Charles de Gaulle).

In the Western Hemisphere where BSAA flew, holding and letdowns were usually accomplished by using ADF and ILS American influence was dominant. An additional problem for pilots occurred when communicating with Spanish or Portuguese-speaking controllers, who sometimes seemed mystified by the patterns flown by BSAA Starliners.

The radio-range system was still used extensively in North America, and although there were a few of these in Britain, they too had a limited future, based, like SBA, on the dot-dash or steady signal alignment principle, in this case defining four separate guidance paths. Subject to inaccuracies, static interference, and interpretation ambiguity, they still provided essential navigational guidance. The simple non-directional radio beacon was the primary location aid in South America, and even today provides many of the world's minor airports with their only system.

Communication with airports was usually by VHF, but in some cases had to be made using MF. En route the use of the Morse key was still required, and so a radio officer was part of the basic crew on BSAA aircraft. Many of these crew members were very experienced, and competent, but contact with the controlling ground stations could be intermittent. In particular the provision of weather reports could not be guaranteed to coincide with the time when they were needed. Difficulty was often experienced when entering Brazilian airspace.

Yorks and Lancs

Four sessions of flight training followed, all completed at Cranfield. This gave me a total of 14 landings on the York, under the circumstances a reasonable introduction to the type. In typical economy mode, so well established by AVM Don Bennett, the instructor was a line first officer. Qualified captains were too much in demand to be spared. The first officer had held an RAF Category B instructor rating on the York, so it was a logical economy. Captains were all required to possess first class navigator's licences, and would usually navigate the most critical route segment of a day's work. Much responsibility was passed to these men.

The York was roomy for the crew, as opposed to the Lancastrian, and had a nice navigator's station. Perhaps its worst aspect was poor three-engined performance on approach. One learned never to lower the wheels too soon, to avoid drag. Noise level in the front passenger cabin was unpleasant for those travelling long distances. As an interim type it was no match for a C-54/ DC-4. The use of any such US types seemed impossible, either economically or politically, at that time, as there was great shortage of dollar currency.

BSAA had commenced service on 1 January 1946, and had gone through many trials and tribulations before I joined the airline. A large expansion was planned because of the number of Tudors on order, and we were intended to become part of a much larger outfit. Plans were already being discussed that included using the first jet airliner, although I could never see how it would fit into the long-segment requirement of South American routes. When I joined, the route pattern was split into two: east and west coast.

The east coast of South America was served by the Yorks, The west coast used a mixture of Lancastrians and Tudors. Because of the distances involved, both these types were short on range for the longest segments. This caused many headaches for the crews. Routeing would vary with the weather, particularly the headwinds. Two freighter Lancs had long-range belly tanks, and were a little easier to plan. The limiting sector was from Santa Maria, in the Azores, to Bermuda, a distance of about 2,000 nautical miles.

My first route trip was as the third pilot on a Lancastrian. On the first day we flew via Lisbon (Portela) to Santa Maria.

I had never been in the type before. The Captain was very competent and helpful. He had been an actuary before the war and had earned several decorations during his service with RAF Bomber Command. He was quite an extrovert, and was a sight as he sat in the seat wearing his headset over his hat, which was usually set at a rakish angle. At that time flags were displayed from the cockpit when on the ground. One would be that of the local nation, the other was the British Civil Air Ensign. My duties included providing the correct national flag, and installing the flagpoles in sockets at each side window. I cannot tell up from down on some of these national emblems to this day and wonder if we amused or offended anyone. I do know that a very dim view was taken if one flew the wrong flag. Some of the nations in South America were very sensitive if they saw a rival nation's flag at our masthead.

Stargirls

Contact with the passengers was possible on the Lancastrian although it meant the squeezing and minor athleticisms familiar to the Stargirls, as our stewardesses were known. Our aircraft were fitted with quite comfortable forward-facing seats, allowing just enough space in the narrow fuselage for passage. We carried a variety of people, including members of the Foreign Office, businessmen, and a few well-dressed women. The era of mass tourist and economy air travel was yet to come, and the then habitually more formal standard of dress and deportment would make a startling contrast to what passes for *de rigeur* today. This required a certain discretion in treatment of these passengers to be exercised by crews, for many of those carried were influential in politics or business. Most people were friendly, and resigned to the noise, and journey length. When compared to weeks on a ship, they felt privileged.

Flight time to Lisbon was about four and a half hours, cruising at 8,000 feet. I was given the dubious privilege of navigating, which was easy enough on that segment. This enabled me to become familiar with the documentation, and of the navigator's station, which was behind the pilot, and on the left side. Tucked in there by a wing spar that crossed the floor and made passage difficult, I was served drinks and snacks by our Stargirls. The agility to surmount a metal obstacle course was a qualification that these ladies had to acquire. They had some difficulty in maintaining modesty, and ran through many pairs of nylon stockings, which, although scarcely obtainable in Britain, could easily be replaced in Bermuda. Many of the Stargirls came from upper reaches of the social order, and were well organised at each port of call. World travel seemed to be the attraction. They did do a very good job with the passengers, who were usually very complimentary. Food on board was usually cold, and often boxed, with hot drinks. The Lancastrian was unpressurised and so oxygen masks were fitted for all on board. This meant we could climb high to obtain better winds or to avoid high ground.

Atlantic hazards

An hour' s transit at Portela allowed time for a snatched meal in the airport restaurant, and then there was a similar flight time to Santa Maria, this time with the First Officer navigating. I was impressed to see a very steep cliff close to the runway end, with the sea about 200 feet below. The wreck of an aircraft lay between the runway and the cliff edge, on sloping ground, and had obviously been slewed sideways just in time to avoid precipitous descent.

After four days of uncomfortable accommodation, with time to kill exploring the wildernesses of the island, acquiring a taste of the local goat, and goat cheese, we met the next incoming Lancastrian, and set off for Bermuda just after sunset. This was good timing, for some of the schedules involved day flight, and made navigation difficult. Fuel was carried for a minimum holding time of 90 minutes after arrival over Bermuda, called 'Island Reserve,' a practice still in use. In fact, the tanks were usually filled, and nominally this would ensure the endurance required. However it all depended on the headwind component that would be actually experienced. The weather forecasters had little to go on, and were usually optimistic. In mid-winter an error could add more than a hour or even two to a flight plan, and the wind direction was often different from that forecast. Navigation was mainly by the use of a Mark 9A bubble sextant, using star or sun shots. Both required a clear sky for the period of sighting, each shot taking about two minutes. For an accurate fix of position three shots from different stars, planets or the moon would be needed. The ocean was visible during the day to allow drift to be measured, but unless the moon was also up only single sun shot position lines could be used. The combination of 'dead reckoning' and sun shots could be combined to deduce a 'most probable position (MPP).' This inspired guesswork, if continued for several hours, would widen the 'circle of uncertainty' to produce a phenomenon best described as seat itch.

By this time I was well informed on the demise of the Tudor *Star Tiger* which had recently disappeared on the same route. Many assumed that this was caused by running out of fuel, for there were too many cases recorded of BSAA aircraft arriving in Bermuda with little fuel remaining. The fallout from this accident led to the dismissal of AVM Bennett, after he issued public statements uncleared with the Board, and Air Commodore Brackley, (Brackers) from BOAC was appointed as replacement. This was to last but a short time, as he was drowned while swimming from a dangerous beach in Rio de Janeiro during his first route inspection tour.

The flight to Bermuda, on this occasion, proved uneventful, with good star sightings, and excellent navigation by the captain. Ten hours and twenty five minutes elapsed before we established beacon and voice radio contact with the US Air Force at Kindley Field, the base granted to the US under the wartime Churchill-Roosevelt 5O-destroyer exchange agreement. Twenty minutes later we were on the ground, and soon on our way to the little island of St George's, connected to the main island by a small bridge. There by the waterside was our inn, a cosy little place run by two friendly people plus a small and dedicated staff. I was amused to see that they kept one room entirely stocked with nylon stockings so that crews could purchase enough to supply family and friends, or replace the wear and tear of flight.

Bermuda

Bermuda has not changed too much in all these years but in those days there were fewer tourists or hotels. The pink and white houses, small roads, and absence of traffic, joined with the profusion of bright sub-tropical flowers, trees and vegetation, came as a welcome contrast to the drabness of post-war Britain. The small shops were full of goods that we had not seen for a long time. The other crew members, familiar with things, soon began to show me around. A two mile run in the prevailing eighty-degree temperature ended up on a beautiful white sand beach, to immerse my tired body into the warm water.

The climate during winter months could be very wet and windy. A tropical storm would pass overhead occasionally, and things could be pretty vicious. The single runway was laid out to take advantage of the available land, and inevitably seemed to be misaligned with the prevailing wind direction. The prospect of a crosswind landing was always present. The Lancastrian was relatively simple to land in a strong crosswind, having a small fuselage side area, and enough rudder and fin surfaces to help control. The touchdown attitude was reasonable, when compared to the Tudor, which had a big fuselage fitted with a tailwheel, unlike the DC-4 series that had a nose wheel and landed in a more level attitude. BSAA pilots had some interesting times with Tudors when landing in crosswind conditions, as once the tail was lowered the nose-up attitude diverted airflow from much of the fin and rudder, and control was reduced. The innate instability of a tailwheel configuration accentuated any turning tendency, so that a touch of brake on one side, or even a burst of power from the appropriate outboard engine might be needed to persuade the aircraft to run straight. To counter some of this effect the Tudor had a very tall and rather ugly fin and rudder. But this did improve the handling control if an outboard engine failed at high power on take-off. On icy, snowy, or slippery runways, and even taxiways, things began to get really hairy. Many runways in Canada accumulated so much snow during the long winter that banks of icy snow could exist on each side of the cleared landing strip.

Nassau and Havana

After a pleasant stay of three days we took the next Lancastrian on to Nassau (Oakes Field), and then to Havana. This was a day spent avoiding heavy cumulus cloud, weaving around each group of build-ups. We had no weather radar, and relied on developed knowledge and sometimes best guesses to keep out of trouble. The Lancastrian gave a very solid firm ride in turbulence, and inspired confidence, but such is the power of storm cell development that we knew enough to stay as far away as possible. Inevitably we sometimes did get into heavy cloud, if the sky was covered with masking altostratus, or at night without moonlight. Then it was a matter of careful handling to keep within recommended structural airspeed limits, and to avoid pitch attitude variations, even at the expense of altitude gain or loss.

Arrival in pre-Castro Cuba was interesting, initiated by the broken English of the control tower operator, as we completed an instrument approach, breaking out of cloud at 600 feet and in sight of the runway. The rain was heavy, but soon vanished with the storm, and hot sunshine replaced it as we drove into town.

The Hotel Presidente had echoes of 'Grand Hotel' evidenced by the size of the lobby, the caged lifts, elegant furnishings, and smartly uniformed doorman. Soon we were involved in a tour of the largest cigar factory, and possessors of boxes containing Romeo y Julieta, and Upmann No. I torpedoes. At that time Havana had a reputation as the Paris of the Caribbean, but we had no time to confirm this. Things seemed to me rather rundown when compared to my previous visit in wartime, and the street people seemed rather sullen and depressed, despite the lovely beaches and climate.

Next morning we returned to Nassau where we were held up for five hours sorting out an engine control problem that developed on the pre-take-off run-up. Our passengers included a cheerful Bishop, who readily agreed to the suggestion that they all went for a swim. Unfortunately it proved impossible to find a swimsuit to fit him.

By this time I was being entrusted with the navigation of alternative route segments. When not navigating I sat on a folding seat beside the captain, did the radio-telephony, raised the undercarriage, operated the flaps, and watched with interest, monitoring and learning.

We arrived in Bermuda four hours after nightfall, and I was able to use the sextant to take about ten star shots, and gain some confidence in my ability to discover our position. This trip retraced the outbound route, ending in London fourteen days after departure.

My return home after what seemed a prolonged absence was welcomed by my wife, who being six months pregnant, was beginning to feel very lonely.

Lancastrian to Santiago

Six days later I was given some more York flying, this time night circuits, again at Cranfield. I wondered if the York flew like the Lancastrian, and also wondered if I was planned to go to the east coast route. This was soon answered by another Lancastrian trip which was to last 22 days, all the way to Santiago, Chile. This time we avoided the Azores-Bermuda problem by routeing from Santa Maria to Gander, Newfoundland, and then to Bermuda. This involved nearly sixteen hours of flight time, and about nineteen hours of on-duty time, starting at 4 pm local Azores time, and ending at 9 am next day in Bermuda. This was very tiring, and it was quite challenging to remain fully concentrated when navigating from Gander to Bermuda, for I had woken up at 8 am, and had thus gone a full 25 hours without sleep. Being young, and not used to this, it did not make much of a lasting impression at that time, but a pattern of 'pressing on' did still exist in the airline, despite the introduction of more rules and regulations.

After Bermuda we called at Kingston, Jamaica, and then Barranquilla, the port on the north coast of Colombia, where we night-stopped. I was told to taxi the Lancastrian to a hangar area for overnight parking. This, naturally, involved starting the engines. As I had never sat in the captain's seat till then, and certainly had no training in the operation of such things as brakes or systems, the task should have been deferred to the first officer, but by the time I had realised my dilemma the rest of the crew had disappeared to the terminal building. Rationalising that the engines were the same as the York-Merlin T24s, and that the brake gauge was the same old standard RAe/RAF thing, I looked for the start buttons, which I had seen the captain use on previous sectors. Fuel selector controls were also obvious, so engaging the attention of our ground engineer, and checking that chocks were under the main wheels, I set the throttle on the left inboard engine, switched mags and booster pumps on, and pushed the button. It started with that sweet gurgle you hear from all Merlins. I decided to use all four engines, unsure about the supply of air, hydraulics, or electrics. The ground engineer had told me where to go, which was along a portion of the taxi track, and not close to the runway. The tower did not reply to my calls, so after consulting with our engineer it was decided that he would lead me in his car. The journey accomplished, I joined the others who were waiting in a taxi. They wanted to know what had kept me.

We checked into a hot, dusty, and third-rate hotel close to the town centre, changed quickly into slacks and open necked shirts, and met in the lobby. We had been invited to attend the local bullfight, as it was Saturday night. I was quite hungry, but was told that we could get something there. On arrival at the bullring the affair had obviously started, as there was a crowd of maybe 3,000 roaring and waving energetically, while a band played raucous music. Seats were arranged in four tiers, and a special guest area provided shade. Opposite that was the pen from which bulls would appear. After witnessing the fate of one bull, our Stargirl announced that she would prefer to go and eat, which was endorsed by all. The following meal, in a little restaurant by the ring, exceeded the outside heat by a considerable margin, containing numerous pieces of potent chilli. This led to a thirst for the local brew, and when I woke next morning at 4.30 am, responding to hammering on the door, I seemed still to be breathing fire.

We were off for Lima, Peru, before 7.30 am. The aircraft had been brought onto the departure ramp by our first officer, after a quiet word from me. It was my navigational segment anyway. We prepared our own flight plan and filed it with the tower control after visiting the meteorological office. The flight time was just under eight hours, and our route paralleled the Andes, along the coastline to Guayaquil, and then directly to Lima. On the left throughout the flight the mountains displayed their size in snow-covered magnificence, covered with heavy cloud for part of the time. Flying below 10,000 feet, we looked up at their impressive bulk for hours, also noting the minimal amount of flat land close to the coast. For much of the year Lima's airport at Callao is covered each night by very low cloud. Sometimes this is so very low that landing is impossible without the most modern landing aids. We did not possess these. We could not use ILS, so flights were arranged to arrive in the afternoon to avoid the problem. The route was flown regularly by several airlines, including Panagra, Faucett, and LAN-Chile which would occasionally provide us with information and support. A diversion to Antofagasta, in northern Chile, was one alternate. Return to Guayaquil was impracticable because of the distance, but could be used en route.

After another brief night stop with the same Lancastrian, we were becoming very familiar with this particular aircraft and its small foibles. This time we were accommodated in the Hotel

Crillon, on the top floor, in some style and comfort. I always wondered about the background behind the local selection of crew accommodation by BSAA. In general, perhaps, the main aim was economy, and it was some time before they stopped the practice of 'doubling up' male crew members in the same room. The Crillon was a first class hotel, and was still in use for British Airways crews in the Seventies. We did not see much of Lima though, as departure was at 7 am for a seven hour flight to Santiago, Chile. By this time we had been away from home for ten days and had begun to feel very far away. I was not used to this length of trip, and began to have doubts about the probable effects of years spent apart from my wife and incipient family.

We continued to follow the coast and the Andes, landing at the inland Santiago airport of Los Cerillos on a nice clear afternoon, taking the time inbound to show the passengers a large Inca city carved in terracing at the summit of a local mountain. It was not difficult to imagine a sacrificial ceremony with victims being cast off the peak.

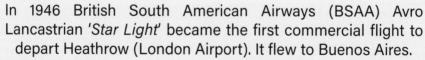

In 1946 British South American Airways (BSAA) Avro Lancastrian 'Star Light' became the first commercial flight to depart Heathrow (London Airport). It flew to Buenos Aires.

The mass of mountains that serve as a dramatic backdrop to this attractive city made a lasting impression. I continued to fly in to the area for another four years, and made many crossings of the Andes from Buenos Aires. Those who fly in this part of the world on a year-round basis have my respect. Despite jet aircraft, GPS, and other modern aids to navigation, the potential for trouble is ever present.

Accommodation was in Santiago. Meanwhile our aircraft was flown across to Buenos Aires by a crew based in Santiago and who were locally experienced. There had been an accident when the Lancastrian *Star Dust* had vanished on the crossing from Buenos Aires to Santiago. The captain was on his first command trip. After this accident it was decided to base an experienced captain and radio officer in Santiago to minimise the risk. Exhaustive air searches and ground expeditions have never found the crash site.[1]

After the return of our aircraft we began to retrace our route to London, this time routeing from Bermuda to Santa Maria nonstop with tailwind help. On arrival at Heathrow I was amazed to find that London had gone from the last vestiges of autumn to the depths of winter cold.

The Tudor

My wife had begun to recognise the problems we now faced in dealing with her lonely existence. We lived in a small rented bungalow, in a damp low-lying area near the river Thames and the place was vulnerable to thieves and other security risks. Relatives provided occasional visits, but for a young woman facing her first delivery this was not a happy situation. Economics demanded that employment should continue, and so it was not long before I was scheduled out on a first Tudor trip. I had not set foot in the type until that morning, when

---

1   The wreckage of *Star Dust* was discovered by mountaineers in 1998. The crew may have overestimated their ground speed and descended too soon. In 2000, an Argentine Air Force investigation cleared the captain of any blame, concluding that the crash resulted from 'a heavy snowstorm' and 'very cloudy weather', as a result of which the crew were 'unable to correct their positioning.'

I walked out to climb up to the crew entrance, and take my seat in a shiny Tudor 4B. This variant was without a flight engineer's station, and I was to navigate the first segment, to Keflavik, in Iceland.

BSAA had fitted some aircraft with radio compasses (ADFs) bought second-hand from various sources, but had not yet calibrated them, nor trained anyone in their use. The navigational aids on the Tudor were inferior to the Lancastrian's because there was no optically correct window through which to take star or sun shots. The old Perspex dome had been replaced with a flat panel because of the pressurised fuselage. Two types of periscope sextant were currently available that could be used through a pressure hull, but the designers of the Tudor, or those who wrote the equipment requirement, had ignored the need.

As I sat at the navigator's position, readying charts and flight plan, a shape appeared by my side. It was Captain Gordon Store, dressed informally, clad in Burberry and trilby.

'Will you show me your navigational licence?'

I rattled around in my briefcase, and came up with the pasteboard document. He inspected it with care, and gave it back without comment, then moved forward to the pilots. I wondered if he was asking them similar questions. It seemed a bit late in the day to be rectifying the error made at my initial interview, but I had now ceased to wonder at the strange ways that things were being organised.

Anyway, we departed on our way to Bermuda, via Keflavik, avoiding the Azores, as winds were forecast to be strong. The Tudor 4B had controls for Godfrey cabin air compressors, placed above the navigator's station. Take-off was made unpressurised, and then blower input was selected by inching forward the controls, feeding pressurised air progressively into the cabin. Practice makes perfect, and I was certainly practising on that departure, for there were wild swings in the cabin pressure, ears popping, and ribald remarks from the radio officer close to my position. As we reached cruising altitude the flight deck heater failed, and the long freight compartment behind my seat soon became encrusted with inches of hoar frost. I put on fingerless mittens (carried thanks to warnings from a colleague), and tried to write in the navigation log. The sextant window was frosted over, so there was no hope of astro. The best way of checking on our progress was to listen to the numbers of dots or dashes transmitted by the Consol stations at Stavanger and Bushmills until we came close to the Westmann Islands.

There was a radio beacon on one of the islands and we did have an ADF, so could use that as a check. This was received and we managed to arrive in Keflavik more or less on our planned route, but chilled to the bone. The petrol-fuelled flight deck heater was of a type that had seen extensive and troublesome service in many aircraft. This was activated by a cut-out switch that responded to the head-of-air pressure caused by the speed of the aircraft, designed to protect against ground operation. This switch was often faulty, and it became the practice for ground engineers at route stations to short it out from the ignition lockout circuit by one means or other. A favourite method was to insert a small screwdriver or other metal rod to compress the switch into contact to allow heater operation. This heater was directly under the navigator's position beneath the cabin flooring, which sometimes became quite hot. A hydraulic pressure pipe ran close to this unit and the type of hydraulic fluid used was inflammable. This leads to one theory for the disappearance of Tudor *Star Ariel* on climb-out from Bermuda.

On arrival at Keflavik we were met with the news that weather was extremely bad at all the Canadian maritime airfields. Two aircraft were delayed, one of which was a BOAC Lockheed Constellation 049, with Captain O P Jones in command. They had only recently received the aircraft, which although a well-developed type with longer range than anything else currently in airline service, was still short of endurance for westbound crossing of the Atlantic. A KLM DC-4 was the third parked aircraft. We were all accommodated in a heated hangar, with ex-forces iron beds laid out in line abreast. The ladies were spirited off elsewhere. Snow could be seen gently falling as a mist in front of the airport lights. We ate in relays at tables set at the end of hangar, bedding down for a fitful sleep. Regular checks on the weather showed no improvement. Twenty-four hours later we saw that the BOAC crew was departing. This cue did not go unnoticed by our captain, and we soon followed suit, walking across to the weather office. The latest forecasts had just arrived, and they showed an improvement, although cloud bases and visibilities were still poor. We prepared a flight plan for Gander, and about forty minutes later were running up the engines at the holding point as the snow still drifted gently down. The Constellation had departed some fifteen minutes before us, and the DC-4 was following us.

We climbed up through continuous cloud, with periods of ice accumulation accompanied by turbulence. The de-icing and anti-icing systems were given a workout until we broke out on top of bubbly dense cloud in starlit and smooth conditions. After a couple of hours the radio officer delivered a set of weather reports and forecasts that showed conditions to be very marginal throughout the Maritimes. The conditions at Gander and Stephenville could often be expected to differ; when one was poor the other would be reasonable, but this time they were both socked in.

As we studied this information, and calculated the point-of-no-return to Keflavik, the radio officer handed us another message. The BOAC 'Connie' had turned back and our captain reacted immediately. 'Tell ATC that we are returning to Keflavik, and ask for a clearance.' He turned the aircraft to reverse course. 'We might be able to get back before O P and get some accommodation.' I was never quite sure if he had taken the action of the very experienced BOAC Captain as a guide to his timely decision.

We landed at Keflavik after six hours of fruitless endeavour and expense, to be again accommodated in the hangar. The DC-4 had also returned. Our passengers were very understanding, with exception of one portly and floridly-complexioned man, who approached us with the statement: 'I'm Lord Strabolgi,[2] and I have a most pressing need to complete this journey. This delay is most unfortunate, and I must warn you that this matter will be brought to the attention of your Chairman. Can't you find any better place for me to stay than here?'

He loomed pompously over the seated captain.

'I don't care if you inform the Prime Minister himself, we are stuck here until the weather improves, and the only other rooms are being used by the ladies from all three aircraft.'

Slightly deflated, but unmollified, the complainer moved off to discuss his plight with a group of unsympathetic passengers, who by now were quite phlegmatic about their predicament.

We managed to get going again by the next afternoon, this time to Stephenville, where arrival was at 10 pm local time. The flight took ten hours, against formidable head-winds. When attempting to refuel, handled by US Air Force base personnel, we discovered that we had no connecting hose adapter, so the Tudor's pioneering under-wing central refuelling points could not be used. The alternative was fuel delivery into over-wing tank receptacles. The problem was that there should also have been a special tool to hold down the spring loaded valves in each tank receiver. This could not be found so refuelling was accomplished by one man using a large screwdriver to hold the valve down, as another put the hose in to the tank. Spurts of aviation petrol sprayed over the operatives. The temperature was just on freezing. This process took three hours before we had enough in the tanks to set off for Bermuda, and we left behind some very disillusioned US enlisted men One fellow surveyed me and the aircraft with amazement, wide-eyed, as fuel ran down from his uniform onto the wing and ground. I don't think they had seen anything like us, or the Tudor, and probably hoped that we would not return.

Bermuda was a welcome sight, but we stopped only briefly on the way to Kingston, Jamaica. After a night stop there we were off to Barranquilla, and Lima, another night stop, and then Santiago.

---

2   David Montague de Burgh Kenworthy, 11th Baron Strabolgi (1914–2010), was a Labour Party peer.

Next day we were up early to depart at 7 am for Buenos Aires, crossing the Andes well south of the mountain Aconcagua which is 22,800 feet high. The pressurised Tudor could climb to about 29,000 feet, but we would often still be in and out of cloud. Weather fronts stagnated over the Andes until pressure changed and then a mass of unpleasantly active cloud could race across the pampas towards the east coast and Buenos Aires.

On this occasion we took only three and a half hours to reach Ezeiza airport, situated close to La Plata, a large suburb of Buenos Aires, and after a brief lunch went back to Santiago. The same crew had been using the same aircraft since London. This involved night stops for both crew and aircraft, in contrast with modern-day practice, which emphasizes maximum aircraft utilization, with crew changes to comply with flying-hour limitations, in the interests of safety.

The direct route crosses close to Mendoza, which is about 80 miles east of Aconcagua. Tupungato, 22,300 feet high, is to the south-west. When the weather was too bad for crossing the Andes, aircraft could land at Mendoza, and wait until things improved.

In good weather, with light winds, it is possible to follow the road and railway through the central pass. An altitude of about 14,000 feet is needed to cross the ridge that connects the main divide. If you are not careful, it is possible to take a blind alley pass to the south after about 40 miles of flight between the huge snow-clad peaks. We had a nice summer afternoon for our crossing, and had a good look at the 'Cristo' — the statue of Christ with arms outstretched, as we flew past the precipitous ridge. Sombre markings commemorated aircraft that had not made a successful crossing.

We were soon able to turn south and continue towards Santiago's Los Cerillos airport. The westbound flight had taken four and a half hours, the hour extra being accounted for by winds and a slow descent to avoid discomfort to the passengers' ears.

The return to London was again routed via the Azores, with the help of a good tail-wind, and we arrived home in mid January, carrying gifts from many points en route. Such were the shortages of luxury goods in Britain during the post-war period that it became common practice for crews to be requested by friends and acquaintances to bring them specific items. Customs were very unsympathetic to crews, and their rules decreed few concessions. They thought we had access to a world of plenty and that this was in some way immoral and against the interest of His Majesty's government. Our real shortage was cash.

Another Tudor trip followed in short order, with some added excitement. Landing into Keflavik in heavy snow and crosswind conditions we were blown uncontrollably to the edge of the runway, and the left outboard propeller struck a snow bank, bending it beyond repair. This caused a three day-delay while a new prop was flown in and the engine inspected carefully for any related damage.

When crossing the Andes towards Santiago above a cloud layer, at 27,000 feet, with the Merlins pounding away close to maximum continuous power, there was a loud bang, and a crack appeared across the left-hand pilot's window.

At that time the captain was navigating, the headwind was about 130 knots, and we were in the vicinity of Aconcagua. I was in the left seat, with the first officer on the right. Luckily the crack was not in the pressure-bearing part of the laminate, and was caused by thermal shock. The idea of a rapid descent was unattractive for obvious reasons, and we delayed this until well clear of the cordillera. My heart rate rose to proof values for a short period.

The general character of BSAA operations during my period of service was of an airline poised to become a very professional force, hampered by financial stringency and the wrong aircraft types. Contagious enthusiasm existed at all levels. Experience was spread thinly, and had yet to be accumulated. The expansion of the air transport industry had provided many opportunities which could not be satisfied with the available resources. The war had provided a cheap source of trained airmen and ground maintenance personnel, but the transition to a peacetime philosophy proved more fraught with problems.

There was a rude interruption to this changeover when on 5 July 1948 the Soviet government started to blockade Berlin, cutting off supplies to the isolated city. The Airlift was successful in eventually lifting the blockade, and provided an opportunity for civil operators to augment the main lift mounted by military aircraft from the United States and Britain.

BSAA to Berlin

The Berlin airlift had been operating for some time when BSAA took delivery of Tudor 5s for the purpose of carrying light diesel fuel into Gatow. Based at Wunstorf, a pre-war Luftwaffe airfield situated near Hanover, the Tudor 5s were fitted with fuselage tanks containing 2,000 gallons of diesel, taking up most of the internal volume. The aircraft was a stretched version of the 4, with a much longer nose, and was originally intended for shorter-range, high-density routes, although fitted with the same wing and engines. I was drafted for several sessions in Germany but before this started was fortunate in being around for the birth of our son.

Looking back at this period I wonder how wives coped with the difficulties caused by the absence of husbands during such events. The resilience of the opposite sex is indeed remarkable. Today the health and other services are far better developed and more easily available than they were then. Shortages of qualified staff, beds, drugs, and other items would not be alleviated for years, despite the creation of a National Health Scheme. We were able to qualify for hospital confinement in view of it being a first birth, but after the experience my wife insisted on giving home birth to our two daughters. She had only been released from hospital for five days when I received instructions to report for an airlift assignment.

The arrangements at Wunstorf were a mixture of the luxurious and the primitive. We used the old officers' mess, were served by some of the staff who had been there for many years, and found the bar convivial after flying. For many of us it was a return to a wartime ambience. The airfield was in the midst of an evergreen forest which was quite uninteresting and monotonous. We were accommodated initially at the airfield, sharing one room to a crew, but moved out to a local village after a suitable small inn was discovered. This meant the loss of catering facilities, and use of the fascinating equipment in a large wash-room and toilet room adjacent to the mess dining room. This had the highest quality furnishings, and included polished long chromium bars installed at each urinal, no doubt to assist those officers unable to carry their beer or liquor. These we named 'Honkers'.

Flights to Gatow were arranged in 'streams' of aircraft. This was necessary because of the differing cruising speeds for each type. The British civil contingent at Wunstorf included Haltons (a civil conversion of the Halifax bomber), Yorks; a few converted Lancasters; some DC-3s; two Tudors belonging to an outfit called Fairflight run by AVM Bennett; and our Tudors. Anything in the way of food and fuel was cargo, with the Yorks carrying coal.

The other two airports, Tegel and Tempelhof, were the destinations for streams of American C-47s and C-54s, which were also routed into Gatow when carrying coal. Each stream flew with its aircraft required to keep a constant airspeed, separated by about two minutes flying time. Good speed control was essential. It was possible to mix aircraft types if this was achieved, but the C-47/Dakotas were slower than most of the other types, and it was tricky to fit them in, especially if they were joining a stream that had departed from another airfield. The corridors were very narrow, and carefully policed by the Soviet forces. Navigation methods varied with aircraft equipment. We used Gee, radio compass, and for landing, BABS.

An old squadron friend was flying in a Skyways York as the lead aircraft of a faster stream, and overtook the last aircraft of a Dakota stream on final approach. We never quite found out why the York flipped over and crashed a few miles short of Gatow, although there was suspicion that it had stalled at low airspeed. Diversion to left or right would have taken them into unprotected airspace. Our instruction in the event of inability to land was to return to Wunstorf with our load of diesel. The co-pilot on that aircraft was Bob Newman, big, cheerful, and seemingly indestructible.

We usually did two return trips each day. One of the trips into Gatow was more memorable than the others. I had arranged to deliver a parcel of food, including coffee and other items that were sorely missing in the beleaguered city. A distant relative had married a German in 1937, spending the war in Berlin. I was able to arrange a meeting during our short time on the ground.

We walked over to a Quonset hut for a hot cuppa and butty from the NAAFI, to experience once again shades of a service life which we felt had been resuscitated. Our usual BSAA uniform had been replaced with a battledress-type dark blue blouse of heavy serge, and we felt neo-military, although the subject of curiosity by USAF, and RAF types. The woman was waiting beside the hut, attended by a military policeman. Drably dressed, she appeared thin and careworn, but cheerful. I had only a few minutes to hand over the parcel and a few letters, before we were called out to take the empty Tudor back for another load of DERV. The damp and bleak airfield was enlivened by the noise of aircraft taking off on their return journeys, with the taxiways full of manoeuvring craft, brakes squealing as they turned into the parking area.

Fog was the only enemy that managed to halt the airlift, for three successive days, stranding us in Wunstorf on constant standby, waiting for the opportunity to get airborne. One evening while we were having a get-together with other crews in the old Luftwaffe bar we heard the noise of a light aircraft departing. Visibility was about one hundred yards, with sky obscured. This turned out to be AVM Bennett in his Percival Proctor (a single-engined, ex-RAF, communications aircraft), on his way to London. He must have had some very important business to reach, as there was no other aircraft movement in north Germany that night.

Don Bennett

Bennett, the son of an Australian farmer, had a remarkable career. He joined the RAF in the early 1930s, and then, as an Imperial Airways captain, he had pioneered long-distance navigation, and had piloted the seaplane Mercury, the upper component of the Mayo composite aircraft, to capture the world's long-distance record with a flight from England to South Africa. He helped to organise the delivery of American war-planes to Britain, and the Return Ferry Service to bring pilots back for further trips. Returning to the RAF as second-in-command of a navigators' training school, he was soon a wing commander in Bomber Command, leading a squadron engaged in action. The initial idea of a Pathfinder Force was his. He was allowed to select crews, and they were required to complete double the number of operational trips, sixty, compared to the main force. Many did not reach this limit.

He was an informed, creative, well qualified, and a driving thorn in the side of a sometimes resistant higher command. He admired those who had the 'press-on' spirit. In BSAA, as the Chief Executive, he initially employed many ex-Pathfinder pilots, creating a pseudo-squadron atmosphere, and did not discourage those who wanted to get the job done, even if this meant venturing into areas that perhaps might seem questionable today.

Examples of his extraordinary talent for survival include an escape from Norway via Sweden across a snow-covered mountain range after being shot down when attacking the battleship Tirpitz in a fjord; and in BSAA after taking off in a Tudor that still had the elevator control locks fitted, depriving him of pitch control. In the latter case he managed to land using the small trim tab surfaces on the elevators combined with power changes to keep a measure of control.

Some of us took advantage of the foggy period to borrow an old wartime Volkswagen, and visit Hamburg. One member of the party had been instrumental in creating a portion of the destruction that we saw. The city was still mainly rubble, interspersed with cleared roads, and an occasional habitation or shop. Poorly-dressed people gazed at us in curiosity. I was depressed by the evidence of mass destruction, far worse than the severe damage inflicted on London, and reflected on the death of so many crews in Bomber Command to achieve the result. Some sections of the city were obviously being rebuilt to a good standard, possibly with money provided by erstwhile enemies.

The wartime atmosphere of the airlift was in contrast to our South American operational area and not long afterwards I was scheduled out on a Lancastrian freighter trip to Jamaica. We used the same aircraft throughout, and flew some seventy hours flight time in nine days, during which we managed to spend only six nights in bed. We called at Dakar, Natal, Trinidad, Kingston, and Georgetown, British Guiana. The aircraft was so full of bags and boxes that we had to board through the top emergency escape hatch.

The Consul

On return from this trip I was summoned to the Chief Training Captain, Frank Walton, who later became Flight Operations Director of BOAC. They were setting up a small unit to give pilots experience of radio range, ADF, and ILS. The Instrument Rating was about to become a requirement. All BSAA aircraft were to have this equipment and the Tudors now being delivered would all be updated. Three First Officers were being given the job of safety pilots. Their task would be to convert to the Airspeed Consul, a civil version of the Oxford twin-engined trainer, and to fly locally with all pilots while they practised using these landing and navigational aids. When we thought that the individual had reached a satisfactory standard of handling and knowledge, we would put them up for a test flight with a training captain to issue their rating. I was among those qualified for this task as I had a licence endorsed for the Consul, and experience of the instrument aids. In fact we were in essence instrument flying instructors, and this was recognised later on by the issuing of instructor's endorsements on our licences by the Guild of Air Pilots and Air Navigators (GAPAN), whose panel of examiners was the authority in those days.

Between route trips I spent many hours flying with my colleagues at one time or other. Most wished to try their hand at landing the Consul, but we had been told to avoid this, as the type was well known for its tendency to ground loop on landing. I found it embarrassing to refuse captains, and suspect that this caused equivalent reaction from one or two strong characters when down the route with them.

Sperry Zero Reader

An interesting interlude was involvement with the Sperry Gyroscope Company in some trials of their Zero Reader. This was a flight director, displaying crossed needles on an instrument, to which signals from the ILS, mixed with aircraft attitude, were fed. Such was the rate of response and the design of the display that it was easier for the average pilot to fly an instrument approach, as flight commands were mixed in nicely with the alignment cues. After adjusting various inputs to the pilot display we managed to tweak the system to a very good performance. I was able to complete some approaches and landings in very low visibility.

Demonstration flights were arranged for many interesting and influential people. From BOAC we saw Captains Buddy Messenger, Sam Buxton, and Bernard Frost. From BSAA Captains Gordon Store, Walter Wellwood, Jimmy Fordham, and Johnny Wheatley. The Ministries sent Messrs Scott, Hall, and Fraser. GAPAN sent the clerk, Major Cordes, and from Vickers Weybridge came the test pilots Mutt Summers and Jock Bryce. Last but not least was George Edwards, Vickers' chief designer. The upshot of these visits was an order from B0AC for the Zero Reader to be installed in its fleet of Boeing 377 Stratocruisers.

We were also required to renew first officer's licences by giving them the required six landings and take-offs. The amount of route handling was insufficient, and this was an economical solution. This involved conversion to the Consul's errant ways, and proved to be entertaining for some, and a trial for others.

Demise of BSAA

The event that finally caused the demise of BSAA was the disappearance of the Tudor 4, *Star Ariel*, after departure from Bermuda for Nassau on a nice clear day. The cause has never been exactly determined, although many theories emerged. Certainly it was not shortage of fuel, nor because of weather, or navigational error. Such was the record of the airline, with so many accidents during its short life, coupled with uncertainty over the airworthiness of the Tudor, that there was pressure on the government to ground it. A decision was made that the routes would be taken over by BOAC and that we would be merged into their seniority list.

For many of our captains this was indeed a successful move, as they absorbed command vacancies that were expected because of expansion and delivery of 22 new Canadair 4 Argonauts, causing much unhappiness in the ranks of BOAC senior first officers. Many saw their command prospects put back by ten years or more. For the BSAA first officers the merger brought no joy either. They had been expecting rapid promotion with the advent of the large Tudor orders, and now faced a very long wait. The merger, like all such events, caused many problems and misunderstandings that were still around when I retired from British Airways. All the BSAA pilots possessed First Class navigation licences, whereas few BOAC pilots possessed this qualification, as that airline used specialist navigators, who were undoubtedly most competent. Ten years were to elapse, until the introduction of the Boeing 707, before BOAC would use pilots as navigators in a three-pilot crew, similar to the original BSAA policy.

So here I was, wearing a BOAC uniform, and at the end of the decade taking the conversion course on to the Argonaut. I was to fly mostly on the South American routes once again, and with many of the ex-BSAA crews.

BOAC Argonauts

British Overseas Airways Corporation was created on 1 April 1940, by the merger of Imperial Airways and the pre-war British Airways. The first Chairman and Managing Director was Sir John Reith, of British Broadcasting Corporation fame. When BSAA was merged with BOAC the Chairman was Sir Harold Hartley, already the sixth Chairman in eight years, to be followed in 1949 by Sir Miles Thomas.

The war had denied the British aircraft industry any opportunity to develop civil transport aircraft. This had been left to the USA, as all resources had to be devoted to the war effort, building fighters and bombers. As a result, in 1949, the fleet strength contained several American types. Lockheed Constellations 049 and 749 were used on the North American and Australian routes respectively. The Boeing 377 Stratocruiser was corning into service on the North Atlantic. Flying boats had just been retired, after many years of popular use. The Avro York was still used, but would soon be relegated to become a freighter.

The Canadair DC-4M Argonaut was a pressurised cross between a DC-6 and DC-4, carrying 40 passengers initially, and powered by four Rolls-Royce Merlin 626 engines of 1,760 horsepower each. Twenty-two of these machines were ordered from the constructors in Montreal, (thus avoiding a drain on US dollar reserves) and Canadair managed to deliver them early. They proved to be reliable but noisy, despite the fitting of a special crossover system designed to alleviate noise from inboard exhaust stacks.

Flights to South America were resumed by BOAC, using the Argonauts. The west coast route was abandoned, and Santiago

A BOAC Argonaut at Santiago.

was served from Buenos Aires. The east coast route ran to Madrid, Lisbon, Dakar, Natal, Rio de Janeiro, Montevideo, Buenos Aires, and Santiago. Recife was later substituted for Natal. The Argonaut was also used extensively on routes to Hong Kong, Japan, the Middle East, and Africa.

Argonaut training

I was sent on a conversion course to become qualified on the Argonaut, and was impressed with the standard of training, conducted in yet another wartime temporary building. The site was destined to become a large training centre within the next ten years. After ground schooling, and passing a comprehensive written paper set by the Air Registration Board, we took the train to Bournemouth for flight training.

Hum airport was used as an alternate destination during late autumn and winter, when dense fog often caused arriving flights to divert from London. The good local weather resulted in BOAC keeping equipment and personnel available. The rail service to London was excellent.

The Argonaut performed splendidly. With a tricycle undercarriage it was a delight to handle compared to a generation of tailwheel types. Propellers could be selected to produce braking thrust after landing, and the Merlins had two-speed superchargers to allow high altitude cruise. There were many similarities to the Avro Tudor, which had been certified with the same engines and maximum weight, but lineage from the Douglas company showed in many respects. The still air range of the Tudor 4 series was slightly better, as was climb performance. Perhaps this was because of the wing aerodynamics and overall drag co-efficient. However, the Argonaut's vastly improved handling in crosswinds more than compensated for any minor losses of performance.

My instructor was Captain Phil Brentnall, later head of flight training in British Airways. I was checked out by the late Captain Tom Stoney, destined to be manager of the Comet 4 fleet, and commander of the first west-east airline jet passenger service across the Atlantic on 4 October 1958.

After an uncomfortable period in our little rented bungalow close to the Thames, and the birth of a son, we had managed to find enough resources to purchase a derelict estate, containing a large house built in 1862. Twenty-two acres of grounds were included in the sale at a reasonable price. In 1950 the Labour government would not permit building new homes, but it was possible to obtain permits to convert older properties, or to rebuild bomb-damaged abodes. We started to convert the ten-bedroom Victorian structure into three separated living units. Employment of direct labour, and the many daily complexities of construction and administration, were perforce most often the responsibility of my wife. I was absent all too often, while she coped with the rudimentary conditions, living in a construction site.

BOAC routes

My first route trip with BOAC was to Cairo, with an ex-flying boat captain who was on his last trip before retirement. He had started flying in the RFC during the First World War, and had been with Imperial Airways since 1928. This introduction to the airline reminded me that there was a huge pool of experience that would contribute to my personal knowledge and safety. However, a few of the old-timers were finding life very different in 1950 from wartime and pre-war days. While most had adapted to new equipment and methods, a few would never be at ease with the new restrictions of air traffic control and management.

The next two and a half years did not allow me much exposure to the older BOAC commanders, as most of my trips were to South America, with only an occasional visit to the Middle East. There were two basic trip lengths, one lasting 14 days turning round at Rio, and the other a full 21 days, to Santiago. The idea of route specialisation for the captains was sensible, and promoted by the Ministry of Civil Aviation. Familiarity with the topography, weather, and airports contributed towards safety and regularity. Wisely there was no attempt to throw away the accumulated experience gained by the ex-BSAA crews.

Each part of the world has some special operational interest for the itinerant aviator. Depending on the type of aircraft, this will be determined by the en route altitudes flown, and the weather and environment. On the route to South America there were sections that could prove troublesome. The crossing from Dakar to Natal or Recife was normally flown at night, and involved flight through the inter-tropical convergence zone, where hurricanes are spawned, and where travelling storms are common.

The economic cruising height for the Argonaut above the South Atlantic was around 15,000 feet. We had no weather radar, and to avoid cloud we could only peer out into the night sky hoping to see the outlines. A good moon was a great bonus, but often there was only a starlit background as we sought guidance. Much of the heavy cloud was buried in stratified layers, and when flying in this there was little warning of trouble, though often foreshadowed by the presence of St Elmo's Fire,[1] accompanied by howling static noise on the radio receivers. Sometimes there was a preliminary series of minor turbulent bumps.

The drill was to warn the cabin crew, to strap the passengers in, and to adopt the rough-air speed by reducing power. All cockpit lighting would be turned on to maximum brilliance, to avoid being blinded by lightning The Pioneer autopilot was good, and well damped to avoid sudden control inputs, although unable to contain large up or down drafts. As the turbulence increased, so would the apparent speed changes shown by rapidly varying airspeed needle indications. One pilot would stay in control of the aircraft, ready to cut out the autopilot if the basic aircraft attitude was disturbed, while the other pilot concentrated on engine handling to keep the speed within safe limits while avoiding excessive corrections.

An Argonaut crew was composed of captain, co-pilot, navigator, and radio officer. The duties of flight engineer were assumed by the co-pilot, who had the responsibility of all refuelling operations, transit inspection, and in-flight systems handling.

On one occasion we had been riding out the bucking airwaves for a long time, and had begun to wonder if the airframe was up to the task of absorbing so much punishment. The commander was Captain Nigel Pelly, the pilot who flew Neville Chamberlain to the infamous Munich conference with Adolf Hitler. At that time he was a captain with the original British Airways. A perfect English gentleman, Nigel was much loved by all who flew with him. He was afflicted with a drooping right eyelid, which required stimulus to prop open. When viewed from the right seat he would appear quite soundly asleep, but this was misleading if rather unnerving. During our encounter with the malevolent forces of nature this eye remained wide open. When we were again in clearer weather it began to assume a more normal droop.

---

1   Corona discharge, a blueish glow occurring at propeller extremities, wing-tips, and windshield when flying in dry snow, ice crystals, or close to thunderstorms.

The aircraft had a circular lounge area at the rear of the cabin, with nicely padded seating around a table. This was most popular on long journeys, and provided a focal point for socialising. On the way back from Santiago, on the same trip, we had just taken off from Rio, and were flying past the Sugar Loaf mountain towards the harbour entrance when the aircraft became very tail heavy. I was alarmed that almost full forward trim was needed to compensate for the nose- up force. Calling the steward, we were amazed to hear that he needed our help in seating the passengers properly. We were carrying a group of girls in their mid-teens, together with two nuns as their minders, on a special charter that would take them through London to Rome for a Holy Year celebration. When we had switched off the seat belt sign after take-off there had been a rush by girls to obtain seats around the lounge table, and a fight to resolve priority. Nigel went back and managed to sort order from chaos, and our trim was restored. These girls all came from well-to-do families. Their next action was to establish a gambling table in the lounge area, despite complaints from the nuns. Only another rough ride from Recife to Dakar was enough to stop their antics.

Rio — the Cidade Maravelhosa

Rio de Janeiro was a fascinating city to visit. The local brand of spoken Portuguese was guttural and twangy, but we soon learned to order food and drink. Our long stopovers were caused by the low frequency of services in each direction. Arriving from Dakar through the night we would usually have been up for 28 hours before being able to fall into bed. About 16 of these hours would be on duty, and 14 actually airborne. The Hotel Serrador was situated at the end of the Avenida Rio Branco, the main tree-lined and busy artery of the downtown city. Our arrival was usually at around about ten in the morning, and, exhausted, I fell into bed as soon as possible. Once I woke in the darkness, looked at my watch, thought it was six in the evening, to discover that it was morning, and I had slept solidly for more than eighteen hours.

Those crews who were in Rio at carnival time were treated to the sight of many decorated floats proceeding up the Avenida

Rio Branco, around the hotel, and back down the avenue. This was more than half a mile in length, full of musical and visual extravaganza, so there was little sleep to be had, for there was no let-up until the early morning of each day. I had to take my bedding in to the bathroom to get sleep before departure, avoiding the blaring brass, and constant samba beat. Joining the mass humanity on the crowded streets was a jostling experience of inter-racial good humour, laced with unexplained explosions. Many windows were blown out of buildings by car loads of shouting and waving men, who tossed bundles of powerful firecrackers into any open window or door.

The swimming in Rio was dangerous, as Bracker's death had evidenced recently, and the currents regularly deposited drowned bodies on one little strip called the 'Red Beach'. Streets were populated by private entrepreneurial transport, jeepney type vehicles called lotacaos. These drove at flat-out speed weaving and twisting, braking suddenly to pick up or discharge. Mixed in with them, old buses discharged clouds of aromatic and choking smoky fumes. The strip at Copacabana was then a rather dirty beach, set off by the famous and typically Portuguese pavement designs, looking out on the departing air traffic from the harbour entrance. The city airport, Santos Dumont, could be viewed from the 860-feet-high Pao de Azucar (Sugar Loaf). From the top of the 2,310 feet Corcovado peak could be seen the city of Niteroi, and many ferry boats criss-crossing the magnificent harbour scene. At the western end lay Governardor Island, and Galeao airport. Still used by the Brazilian air force, it had a long runway suitable for our use. (Today, Galeao is a thriving international airport and Rio is connected across Guanabra Bay to Niteroi by a 17-kilometre bridge.)

The route south followed the coastline closely, and could usually be relied upon to produce some weather problems. About 360 miles north of Montevideo, the city of Porto Alegre marked the area where southern air masses collided with the warmer air from the north. This resulted in lines of thunderstorms and heavy cloud that often lay right across our path. Attempts to weave a way through the mass of heavy cloud could be unsuccessful, and often meant either turning back or taking a beating. The problem here was that these clouds were packed with hail and ice, unlike the inter-tropical region. One solution was to turn out over the ocean, and then descend to below the cloud base, to cross the disturbed region.

The attitude of many captains varied towards their co-pilots, and vice versa. This potentially dangerous interface has long been recognised as a prime subject for education and training. In the early 1950s there were some who had not learned to handle stressful situations without losing the cooperation of their crew members. One characteristic was the inability to accept warning of danger, and to stubbornly persist in a course of action. Many pilots had never flown as a co-pilot, and some did not accept the courtesy, or even the obligation, to allow colleagues a chance to develop handling and other skills. On one occasion, close to Porto Alegre, we flew into an area of severe hail despite my attempt to convince the captain that it would be best to divert. The result was substantial damage, with radiator matrices flattened, engine cowlings, wing leading edges dented, and rubber de-icing boots shredded from the wings.

Places and people

Buenos Aires in 1950 was a cosmopolitan and civilised place. We were accommodated in the City Hotel, a traditional first class establishment close to the main square. The atmosphere was European, and the main shopping area contained luxury goods that were hard to obtain in Britain. Anglophiles were abundant, and we could eat at various clubs, where the magnificent local beef could be sampled.

The Andes crossing to Santiago in an Argonaut was similar to that in the Tudor, with engines at high power to maintain a safe altitude, and a long period spent descending over the city. We now stayed in a company rest house, built close to the foothills, with towering snow-clad mountains above. Situated in an old orange grove, a stream ran through the site giving a soothing burble of running water, calculated to cure insomnia. A military riding school was just up the road, and the local quinta (bar) served both establishments. We liked being able to stay out of the noisy and dusty city, and were able to get transport to a fine golf course for a breath of the mountain air, and some much needed exercise.

Like most places that are close to high mountains in temperate regions, it could rain quite heavily at times. The bedrooms were on the top floor of the house, and the roof was red-clay-tiled in the Spanish style. One night I was awakened by the sounds of running water and thunder. The water was actually running from the ceiling and had soaked my bedclothes. Jumping out of bed I was startled to find that I stood in water. The tiled floor was surrounded by a lip, creating a well, from which water overflowed. Opening the door I could see the water cascading down the stairs into the hall below. Soon joined by the rest of the crew, we found solace in the dining room, lit a log fire, and dried out. Next morning all was steam, sunshine, and heat.

The Argonaut had a good suite of modem radio navigation and landing aids including ILS, twin Marconi ADFs, and at the navigator's position a Lamplough drift recorder. This device was a viewer of the surface with alignable lines allowing aircraft drift to be read off on a scale. The eye piece had a protective two-inch-deep soft rubber rim, which was ideal for comfortable viewing. Unsympathetic check navigators, when supervising new personnel, had developed the habit of applying a deep coat of powdered lead pencil dust to this rim. The consequential black eye was allowed to remain until arrival at customs and immigration. The unfortunate candidate would sometimes discover his disfigurement during a toilet visit, or wonder why the stewardess was so amused. This was a version of the golden rivet story that gulled some new girls to search the floor for this precious item.

Senegal

Dakar in Senegal was another place where the corporation had installed a rest house. This was placed close to the main fish market, with accompanying smells and noise. Yoff airport was close to the coast, and subject to fog and low stratus cloud during the night. When the inter-tropical front moved north, line squalls could move through the area, but for much of the year weather was much better than at the old flying boat base at Bathurst. Splendid beaches with wonderful waves allowed me to develop a liking for body surfing. The colonial French atmosphere, with architecture similar to that in the south of France, was reinforced by outdoor cafés, some good restaurants, and an abundance of coiffeurs.

These establishments were frequented by some crew members, not to have a makeover, but rather to view the range of scents. Everything, including Chanel, Joy, Mitsouko, Shalimar, and most other exotic perfumes could be found at ridiculously low prices. Such items were in very short supply in Rio and quite a few people succumbed to temptation, transporting a few bottles for resale. Distribution was no problem for them, as the hotel room staff were willing and able to comply. Overseas allowances on a per-diem basis were accumulated and could be withdrawn from a pay-book system. They were inadequate to cover any out-of-pocket expenditures during a three week trip. The only problem was that this trade involved non-declaration to the customs on arrival. The thought that a couple of bottles of scent would be for the personal use of our stewardess was reasonable, but for most of the male crew it involved risk of infraction, and possible disciplinary action that could lead to job loss. Despite this risk the practice was fairly widespread, and seems to have been with some collusion by customs, who were often seen to interview the chief steward for a few minutes, after which we would proceed with baggage un-searched.

The temptations were too much for one first officer who had decided that he would pack a holdall with bottles of the most expensive brands. He left this on the co-pilot's seat after disembarking, probably for someone local to collect. Unfortunately a police security guard was first on the scene. This crew member was dismissed from employment, after paying a very large fine. Many knew that he had been showing signs of large scale 'business' transactions by his spending habits and his loose talk. He managed to find a job flying for another major airline, and was promoted to command far more quickly than those whom he left in BOAC. The old habits prevailed however, and he became involved in drugs, ending up in prison with a fairly long sentence. A standing order in the airline banned any staff from having a second employer, or from trading, an instruction that many saw as unenforceable, even illegal. The temptations and opportunities provided by rapid travel across continents were used by some to their lasting advantage in developing business contacts. They reasoned that most board members and senior executives, even of BOAC, were only part-time, and had several allegiances.

Argonaut departures

The departure from Rio was usually on the direct route north to Recife, and not via the harbour entrance. This saved conflict with air traffic at the city airport, and also mileage, but involved flight up a valley over rising ground to the town of Petropolis. The ground rose to match the climb rate of a fully loaded Argonaut, and it seemed as if we were flying up the main street of this town to just clear a large church. Watching the buildings ahead of us, which seemed well above our projected flight path, I wondered if there would be some down-draft wind effect that would drag us into the market square, so visible below. I do not remember many dreams, but have a recurrent vision of this departure, with hills on both sides of the aircraft, and involving weaving to avoid roof tops.

The hot weather climb performance of the Argonaut was not exactly spirited. The liquid-cooled Merlins tended to overheat if prolonged high power was used in tropical temperatures. Opening the radiator flaps to increase airflow and cooling produced more aerodynamic drag, and was counterproductive. The coolant, a mixture of water and ethylene-glycol, would vent from the top of each engine cowling as a plume. This usually happened when the indicated temperatures were showing maximum permissible values yet power reduction was impossible. An engine failure at such a point would have been more than embarrassing. This problem mainly arose at a few very hot and high airfields. Kano, Nigeria, was the worst place, where quite some time could elapse after becoming airborne before the climb rate was enough to allow a careful power reduction, and a juggle with the radiator flaps. An Argonaut was destroyed after take-off at Kano, where a contributory cause was down-draft currents from a local storm. The aircraft descended into the ground with maximum engine power in use. This was recorded as an act of God, but today's aircraft would have escaped such wrath.

Crossing the Alps

The route pattern flown by the 22 aircraft was extensive, and I was occasionally rostered to fly a Middle Eastern service. These usually landed at Rome's Ciampino airport before going on to various destinations such as Amman, Cairo, Aden, Damascus, Baghdad, Basra, Bahrain, or Tehran. The flights would often be via Frankfurt, on the way to Rome. Crossing the Alps was always interesting. On a clear day the scenery is quite magnificent, and arguably even more visually inspiring than the Himalayas. When associated with dense cloud and high winds it was different. Apart from the usual problem of being unable to identify thunderstorms there was the standing-wave problem. When strong north westerly winds blow over the Alpine massif they create a series of wave disturbances in the southern or lee side. These can produce very powerful up and down currents and vicious rotor turbulence. It was not unusual to meet these waves flying towards London. After passing over Turin, and into the lee of high ground ahead, the first indication of trouble would be a drop in the airspeed, sometimes accompanied by turbulence. Application of more power to keep the speed would only give temporary relief. The heights that we normally flew on this route placed us in the worst zone for wave encounter, but the effect can go well up towards the stratosphere and today's jet levels. Continuing flight towards the mountains would mean loss of height initially, and then perhaps a compensatory updraft as we flew through the wave. The next wave would often prove more active, and threaten a safe crossing clearance. The remedy was to turn away from the mountains, and when out of the waves to climb above them if possible. There were occasions when a diversion to the west across France would be the best decision.

The Rome stopover

Rome was a central point for BOAC services throughout the 1950s and 1960s. A bilateral agreement between Italy and the UK gave a favourable incentive. We stayed in the Hotel Quirinale, on the Via Nazionale, an elegant and old-style establishment connected by a passageway to the main opera house. After many years we became familiar with the staff, always receiving excellent food and service. During the Second World War the hotel had been used by the Gestapo, and reputedly was the scene of some bloodthirsty events. Our rooms were in a wing at the rear of the buildings, they were large with lofty ceilings and shuttered windows which opened on to streets where the ever present Vespa noise vied with that of the Fiat 500. The floors were parquet strip, and squeaked ominously. The rumour had it that we were in the part used for interrogations, and that it was haunted.

Despite this, the delights of the Borghese Gardens close by, together with the food and general ambience of the lovely city, were more than enough to compensate. This was in the period before mass tourism, and when the Vias Veneto and Corso were uncrowded, and without fear of crime. The single runway at Ciampino would soon be supplemented by the new airport at Fiumicino (later named Leonardo da Vinci). The arrival from the south on a fine early morning, over Castel Gandolfo and the Alban hills, was a unique visual experience

The world's first jet airliner

Towards the end of 1951, introduction of the first airline passenger jet aircraft was imminent. Reaction among the BOAC pilots to this prospect brought forward many who wished to become involved in a new style of flight. Others, who in the past had seen their careers upset by association with an unsuccessful type, were more cautious.

Throughout my career the two groups continued to exist, like opposed political parties. The Comet 1 was essentially a medium-range aircraft (by today's standards), and would therefore not fly on the prestigious transatlantic routes, where the Stratocruiser and Constellation still predominated; but it was suitable for routes to the British Commonwealth in the eastern hemisphere.

I was hoping to be moved from the Argonauts, for the long trips were beginning to have an effect on my domestic life. With a young son, and still involved in the aftermath of the house conversion, my wife was very lonely, and had recently given birth to our daughter Susan. I reasoned that trips on the Comet would be shorter because of the greater distance travelled in a working day, and that they would not be to the Americas.

Captain Roly Alderson headed the Comet Development Unit, and became the Fleet Manager. He was an ex-Imperial Airways commander, who had been flying the long-range Empire flying boat *Cavalier* on 22 January 1939, en route between New York and Bermuda, when forced to land after two engines failed because of icing. Of thirteen people on board, ten survived, and were rescued after more than ten hours in the water.

Comet 1 training

Selection of the crews who would fly the jet was conditioned by the decision to use the co-pilot as navigator. The crew was two pilots, radio officer, and flight engineer. The use of the engineer was necessary as an equipment bay was accessible in flight, and specialized knowledge would prove helpful at overseas airports. The BOAC flight engineers at that time were recruited from those who had been qualified aircraft ground engineers with considerable background and experience. The radio officer was needed, as the era of telephonic radio — i.e. communication by voice rather than Morse code — had not yet been finally consolidated.

Each co-pilot was required to possess a navigator's licence. Inevitably this favoured selection of the ex-BSAA co-pilots. I was able to obtain a posting to the Comet 1 because of this advantage, although a contributory factor was that I completed a short course on gas turbine technology at the Power Jets School, at Farnborough, Hants. This was arranged through the good offices of a friend, Don Brown, who was Principal of the School. He had been a designer with Miles and had been associated with an abortive supersonic project, the M.52.

The Comet 1 first flew on 27 July 1949, and was delivered to BOAC in February 1952. The first jet service carrying revenue passengers left Heathrow on 2 May, for Johannesburg, via Rome, Cairo, Wadi Seidna, Entebbe, and Livingstone. Much worldwide publicity had resulted from the development of this aircraft. Carrying 36 passengers over ranges of 1,500 nautical miles at a cruise speed of 400 knots, nearly twice the speed of the propeller-driven aircraft of the day, it was a revolutionary step forward in the development of air transport.

My transfer to the Comet Flight was effective at the beginning of August, and I began a technical course at the de Havilland main plant and airfield, at Hatfield in Hertfordshire, north of London. We were a group of four captains and four co-pilots. The course lasted six weeks, and we visited the main assembly hall each day, where the production line was in full swing, and found daily hands-on contact with the hardware to be of substantial value. Our introduction to the course on the first morning was interesting enough. Sitting in the inevitable wartime hut, we had a view of a de Havilland Venom, which was about to depart on a test flight. The Venom was a larger version of the Vampire fighter, twin-boomed, and powered by a single de Havilland Ghost engine, similar to those used in the Comet 1. An asbestos blanket was thrown over the tailplane between the twin fins and rudders, and with good purpose, for the start was quite spectacular, involving flames from the jet pipe that billowed out behind the tail. After fire-extinguishers had been brought into play the aircraft was restarted with no apparent ill-effect. We knew that it was going to be a different world.

I had to live locally during the week as the commuting distance was too great, and although we now were the proud possessors of a 1934 Talbot, for which I paid £100, the condition of this car precluded excessive mileage. Others of the course joined me in securing rooms in a hotel near London Colney. The course was quite intensive, and fascinating. Hydraulically powered flying controls were installed which provided no progressive feed back of aerodynamic effect to the controls. We would be flying at high levels in the stratosphere, at twice the altitude of propeller-driven airliners. Speeds were nearly doubled. Many of the practical differences were only evident after an initial flight on the route.

On one of the hangar visits I was running my hand along aluminium alloy fuselage structure, behind the wing, and noticed how easy it was to flex the metal. We were impressed by the thinness of the alloy sheet which, as I recall, was 22 gauge. Power was supplied by four very reliable centrifugal compressor type Ghost engines, each producing only 5,000 pounds of static thrust for take-off. Weight-saving was a major requirement. In fact, with the Ghosts, the aircraft could have used more power.

Our sight of a newly painted Comet, ready for delivery, was inspiring. The aerodynamic cleanness of the aircraft, accentuated by a sleek nose profile, gave us the impression that this could be an exceptional performer, and good to handle. It looked right. The wing's leading edge was swept back 25 degrees and, with engines contained within the wing and installed close to the fuselage, was uncluttered save for a couple of wing fences. All our ground instructors were naturally most enthusiastic about their baby.

Tragedy at Farnborough

During late September, towards the end of the course, the annual Farnborough Airshow attracted me. Our son Christopher was nearly four. We lived close to the Royal Aircraft Establishment, and I thought that a visit would be interesting as various new aircraft were on display. I knew that the de Havilland 110, a twin-engined advanced fighter/ bomber, still undergoing development, would be flown by John Derry, the test pilot. I had met him the previous day when he had given us a short talk. The aircraft he was to use for his display became unserviceable, and he had to return to Hatfield to obtain the standby 110.

My son and I were seated on the hillside overlooking the runway as he joined the airfield circuit, making a very low and tight turn around the airfield perimeter. As the black aircraft pulled in towards the runway it exploded into fragments. The engines continued on their previous path, still rotating and screaming as they flashed low over our heads and buried themselves into the crowded hillside, killing and injuring many people. The centre-section, stub wings, and cockpit fluttered down onto the runway with a thump, killing Derry and his observer.

This accident was reputedly caused by the detachment of a mass balance weight on a control surface, leading to flutter and overloading, but I have never been able to confirm this information.

Monday morning at Hatfield was less than cheerful, as was to be expected, but we still had to finish the last part of our curriculum and take the Air Registration Board's written technical examination. This completed, we were ready to start our flying on the Comet.

Passenger jet flying — take-off

The aircraft were based at Heathrow, but Blackbushe, west of London, and close to where we lived, was used for the landing practice. My instructors, now BOAC training captains, were three ex-BSAA people, Ernie Radley, Frank Griffin, and James Linton. The comprehensive flying syllabus included a high-altitude demonstration of aerodynamic, nose-down 'tuck' after reaching high Mach Number; an emergency descent, stalls, recovery from unusual positions, a series of landings at light and heavy weights with one or two engines throttled back to simulate failure, a flapless landing and instrument approaches. Most of this is accomplished in simulators today. The amount of airspace used in the 'recovery from unusual positions' was interesting. At around 12,000 feet, with my vision of the outside sky obscured by a hood, the Comet was put into a series of manoeuvres causing the instruments to give false readings. This was because of their lag in following the rapid changes. The aircraft was then handed to me for recovery from a state where speed was increasing rapidly, climb or descent was uncertain, and G force was abnormal. Careful control inputs, using the wing-mounted speed brakes to kill the speed, and use of the altimeter to level off a climb or dive, were necessary. I have always wondered what these exercises did to the aircraft structure, which was only stressed to civil transport limits. It was certainly valuable training, but not repeated in subsequent jet conversions.

A flight navigation and planning session introduced us to the novel idea of working the basic fuel flight plan backward s. Captain A M A Majendie was nominated as Flight Captain, second in command to Captain Peter Cane, who was appointed as Flight Superintendent. 'Maj', as many called him, was a young, bright, and able person. Among other things he had devised that the best way to avoid having to juggle payload, weight, and fuel interminably, to discover range and reserve requirements, by calculating the flight plan in reverse order, from arrival to departure. As co-pilots and navigators we had the assistance of flight planning staff at home base, but elsewhere we had to prepare the flight plan.

The Comet 1 accelerated quite slowly on take-off. To ensure that performance was available, full engine power was applied before brake release, so that fuel flow, jet pipe temperature, and revolutions could be checked. When brakes were released the transition was made smoother by the use of a clutched release mechanism, allowing a progressive and smooth acceleration.

The noise generated by this pioneer aircraft was considerable. When we first heard a take-off at Blackbushe, about six miles from where we lived, it sounded like continuous loud thunder. As a result, night flying training after 10 pm was banned on the insistence of the local communities.

Climb rate at the maximum weight of 105,000 pounds (47,727 kilograms) was sluggish but once a good speed was achieved, improved rapidly, taking about 40 minutes, and 200 nautical miles to reach an initial cruise level of 35,000 feet. The cruise procedure then involved climbing steadily as fuel was consumed, maintaining a speed 30 percent above the minimum drag speed. This resulted in an average cruise true airspeed of 400 knots, and a final altitude of 39,000 - 40,000 feet. For an average 1,500 nautical mile journey the cruise would be maintained for about 2 hours 45 minutes, followed by 30 minutes of descent. A payload of about 4.5 tonnes, or 36 passengers plus mail, baggage and some freight, could be carried with fuel for a 200 nautical mile diversion to an alternate, plus reserve fuel for another hour's flight.

We were kitted out with flying helmets made of light material, and always had to use these, as the crew intercommunication and radio setup were integral. This was rather hot and irksome. The real need for these became apparent at high altitudes, where it was mandatory for one pilot to have an oxygen mask clipped to the helmet, ready for immediate use, and at very high levels to fix the mask into position with a demand oxygen system flow immediately available. Cabin altitude was kept at 8,000 feet when we were cruising at 40,000 feet. The structure was designed for a maximum differential pressure of 8.25 pounds per square inch, a far greater degree of pressurisation than had ever been necessary for piston-engined aircraft flying at half that altitude.

Comet 1 to India

My first trip was on 28 November 1952, only four days after completing flight training. Services had been extended to Ceylon (Sri Lanka) in June, and Singapore in July. The first day's work involved leaving London at 12.40 pm, flying via Rome, and Beirut, arriving at Bahrain at 10.55 am, which was 1.55 pm local time. I was in the right-hand seat on each segment until 20,000 feet was reached, then took up the navigator's position behind the captain, Jim Hengle, where a conventional navigation log was kept, with positions fixed by the use of radio bearings and sextant. I was being supervised by another first officer, and would be required to complete two trips before receiving my operations certificate. The Hughes periscopic sextant was similar to that fitted to the Argonaut. Duties as navigator ended at 20,000 feet on the descent, when I again took up the co-pilot's seat. Responsibility for preparation of the fuel flight plans at Rome and Beirut was mine, checked and counter-signed by the captain.

The flight proceeded very smoothly, and descents were made accurately by the use of Rebecca/Eureka radar transponder equipment. The Corporation had decided to equip each destination with ex-RAF sets, which allowed distance from the station to be recorded in the aircraft. This was also compatible with a number of installations at RAF stations overseas, and showed on a radar scope as a blip. Reception was limited to line-of-sight by the curvature of the earth, and was usually received in time for us to plan an efficient descent path. Coming down too early would deprive us of fuel and range for a possible diversion, and was very costly. Although the Comet 1 had no reverse thrust, the huge 'barn-door' landing flaps provided enough drag to slow us quickly after touchdown. The aircraft seemed to sing along smoothly with an audible whine in the cruise, and performed beautifully, although engine synchronisation required attention to avoid a constant cyclic beat. Our 36 passengers, carried in first class seating, included a sprinkling of service officers and their wives, businessmen of various nationalities, and a couple of positioning crew. Two stewards and a stewardess provided a light meal on each of the longer segments.

Adjustment of descent was helped by the allowable selection of wing spoilers, surfaces that projected from the wings to reduce lift and provide drag, which could be used at any speed up to Vne (not to be exceeded speed) 300 knots/ 0.77 Mach. The operational limit was Vno (normal operating speed) 275 knots/ 0.72 Mach. Descent was scheduled at 220 knots. When meeting turbulence in the cruise we reduced speed by about 20 knots by raising the nose to adopt a reduced margin of 15 % over the minimum drag speed. This was also the long-range cruise procedure, depending on wind component.

Bahrain airport was hot and humid. We stayed in the BOAC rest house, just across a causeway connecting the airport island, Muharraq, to the main island of Manamah. Enclosed by mud walls, the place was a haven of isolation from the dust and heat outside. The bar was a regular meeting place for parched locals and oil company employees. In 1952, the development of today's modem city had not begun. The only industry to be seen was boat building, involving construction of traditional dhows for trade across the Indian Ocean. The airport was mainly an RAF Base, with civil attachments.

Engine failure

The next Comet arrived in Bahrain three days later. I had already realised that my hopes of shorter trips were too ambitious because of the low frequency. Take-off was again late at night, and dawn broke when we landed at Karachi. After an hour's turnaround we departed for Bombay, and were thence destined for Colombo. This was not to be. As we were about to commence descent to Bombay, number 4 engine decided to quit. The twin needle revolution gauge wound down progressively. A bearing had failed in the accessory gearbox.

After a smooth three-engined landing by Jim Hengle, we parked on a hot asphalt hard-standing well away from the main terminal. Investigation revealed that we needed to change the engine. Luckily there was one in the company stock at Bombay, only recently released from bond by customs. An engine change was fairly simple, as accessibility was very good. A full team with the right equipment, experienced in the job, could do this in a few hours. Here, however, there were only the one fully qualified station ground engineer and a couple of locally employed helpers. Our flight engineer was invaluable in the circumstances, as was the supervisory first officer Bruce Arterton, who worked for many hours to help out. He was very knowledgeable about the procedure.

I was walking across to the company office to send a signal to London, when another figure joined me - my father, no less. He had just arrived as a passenger from Delhi on a Deccan Airways DC-3, and noting the Comet, had thought to enquire about my whereabouts. We had not met for three years since I saw him off on a BOAC York from Heathrow, when I was still employed by BSAA He now lived in Calcutta, and was general manager in India for Blackwood Hodge, the tractor outfit. For many years he was associated with large dam projects throughout India. During the Second World War, in India, one of the Argonaut training captains, Colin Butler, was Group Captain commanding the station where he was administration chief. They used to share weekend trips to Delhi in the squadron Harvard. After exchanging greetings, and expressing surprise to be meeting like this in Bombay, he asked me where we would be staying in town. This was established as the Ambassador Hotel where coincidentally he was also booked.

The engine change was completed by late afternoon, and a noisy old Bedford bus took us to the hotel through roads jammed by people and cows. On arrival, after a swift clean up, we arrived at my father's room, to indulge in mutual introductions and reminiscences.

Next afternoon we received instruction from London to retrace our steps to Karachi and Bahrain. The descent into Bahrain was remarkable as the spoiler air-brakes were selected out at 33,000 feet and only retracted at 3,000 feet on approach to the runway, as we were delayed in obtaining clearance to descend. The weather was clear with excellent visibility and runway lights were in sight from many miles away. I was very impressed with the operational flexibility. We had been issued with a booklet showing statistical summaries of the expected winds at our cruise levels for each month of the year and soon found that these were far more accurate than anything provided by the various meteorological offices en route. Westbound in the winter we were bucking high winds, which would often reach 100 knots. Care had to be exercised to keep out of the strongest wind core, and to make full allowances for the necessary extra fuel.

After a night in the rest house, we departed for Cairo, again at an ungodly hour, 2.20 am, landing at dawn for a brief transit, and then over the central Mediterranean to Rome, where we spent four days until the next Comet arrived. The flight home ended up as a diversion to Hurn, because of thick fog.

I was pleased with my new working environment. There was much to learn. We were very busy on each short flight. The flying was satisfying, and morale was excellent. For some reason it was three weeks before my second trip was scheduled. This suited me, as Christmas could be spent with the family, an event that could never be planned with any certainty. This trip was commanded by Captain Don Macintosh, and the supervising First Officer was Denis Whitham, who lived only a hundred yards away from us, and had been seconded to BOAC during the war after initial RAF training. He had been based in Durban, flying the Horseshoe route (the wartime route around the Indian Ocean, from South Africa to Australia) on flying boats before becoming one of the first co-pilots on the Comet.

Comet 1 to Africa

We flew to Johannesburg, via the routeing previously described. Our slip (stopover) stations were Rome, and Entebbe in Uganda. The small airport building was where, some years later, an Israeli commando force mounted a spectacular rescue of hijacked and imprisoned passengers. After landing into the prevailing wind, a turn off onto a taxiway would point you downhill towards the parking area, adjacent to this building. A few captains had devised a scheme to arrive outside the terminal in complete silence. They would shut down the engines about three hundred yards before reaching the building. Like many jet engines, the Ghosts emitted an ear-piercing dying wail as they ran down. Braking was assured by pressure in the hydraulic brake accumulators. Such arrivals were indeed quite dramatic, making a strong impression on the small audience waiting to take the onward flight. When management got to know of this, the practice was banned.

Entebbe airport is close to the shore line of Lake Victoria and we stayed in the suitably named Lake Victoria Hotel. One item on the menu was 'Lake fish to order'. The fish was very edible and well prepared, but like so much else after dark was accompanied by a cloud of lake flies. We called it 'Lake flies to order.' Uganda was still a British colony and smart black military policemen stood guard as we completed our pre-flight routines. Local swimming in the lake was inadvisable because of the presence of parasitical skin borers, but there was a small swimming club close to the shoreline, on high ground overlooking the lake and airport. On one occasion having been able to get there very soon after arrival, I was sitting by this pool, and witnessed a near-accident.

The departing Comet, taking off southwards towards the lake, came into sight, and as it became airborne, sank towards the lake and out of sight, being temporarily blanked off from my view by the ground contours. After a short while, during which I was sure that it must have hit the water, the aircraft reappeared in a climb, and set off towards the south The cause was a take-off made with the flaps fully down in the landing position. This was, in my opinion, bound to happen sooner or later, because of the way the before-take off check lists were written. One of the first things called for, after starting to taxi, was selection of full landing flap, followed by selection back up to the take-off setting. This practice, intended to ensure a full checkout of functioning, was a throwback to a DC-3 type of procedure. A more careful last minute check would have discovered this potentially disastrous configuration and basic airmanship should have intervened. However, it did not and Murphy's law was again demonstrated. Soon after this incident the check list procedure was revised.

Apart from the usual early morning thunderstorm, which left the red earth sticky and steaming, the days at Entebbe were very pleasant. The lake is 3,727 feet above mean sea level. There were two squash courts close to the airport, and we had formed a competition ladder (a kind of league table). Many carried their racquets personally, although equipment was available through the club. High altitude squash is quite demanding and rather different. Trajectories and speeds are changed.

After another four days waiting, our next aircraft arrived. The flight to Livingstone (Northern Rhodesia, now Zambia) took only three-and-a-half hours and, after a rapid transit, marred by continual power failures at the airport, we set off for Johannesburg (Palmietfontein), catching a good view of the Victoria Falls and the mighty Zambezi as we climbed past. Across Africa I was astounded to see that, at 40,000 feet, we were below the tops of the thunderstorms by thousands of feet, nullifying the information so diligently presented by meteorologists in the early 1940s.

We had no weather radar, and it was a worrisome business weaving around these heavy build ups. There were many problems, especially at night. The autopilot was designed to disconnect when limit switches sensed control inputs that might overtax the structure. These switches were very sensitive, and reacted to jolting air currents by causing autopilot cut-out with a little click and a disconnect warning light. It was usually possible to re-engage the autopilot, only to have it repeat the cut-out. The captain had his hands full as he attempted to steer through disturbed areas. Navigation was also made difficult by radio interference coming from the stormy electrical discharges. Radio compass indications were affected, attracted by heavy clouds.

With only one pilot at the controls, in a demanding weather situation, the workload could be excessive. I also wondered about what would happen if the captain became ill, and if this would be recognised in time for speedy action. I was never party to any discussions about the crew makeup on the Comet 1, but I believe that we would have been much safer with both pilots' seats occupied at all times. There was one case where a Comet 1 became quite lost for about an hour when approaching the Khartoum area in heavy cloud at night, flying round in circles. Luckily this was resolved in time, but fuel was very low when they landed. The captain assumed full responsibility, but the absence of weather radar and of better navigational guidance aids contributed to his problems.

Johannesburg was a mixture of civilization and nastiness. Poverty and squalor were in full view on the drive in from the airport, and violence clearly evident. We visited the Wanderers' Club after receiving an invitation from the secretary. Denis Whitham arranged a special membership, on behalf of our crews, so that we could play squash and also golf.

We were night-stopping with the same aircraft, and next morning ferried the Comet from Palmietfontein to the new Jan Smuts international airport. The new runway was much longer and allowed us to take off at a higher weight. Most of the African airports were at high altitude. Johannesburg is 5,500 feet above mean sea level, and our fuel and payload weights were restricted by this. The full customs and immigration services were not yet ready and our arrivals had to be at the old airport.

I was now becoming more familiar with the navigational demands. While climbing to cruise level there was time to pre-compute from the manuals calculations for two or three astronomical fixes. This allowed more opportunity to watch the real time situation as the cruise developed. This was quite necessary, as was demonstrated on the night flight from Cairo to Rome. The forecast issued by the Cairo met office showed a strong westerly wind of 110 knots. The statistical booklet agreed. We set off on the cruise segment at 36,000 feet under a starry sky, climbing at a slow rate as the fuel was consumed. I had allowed for a starboard wind drift, and the first three star shots confirmed a position fix showing that we were close to our intended track. The next set of sextant observations caused my eyebrows to raise, and to query my own accuracy. After taking each shot I plotted the result immediately, having precomputed the calculations. The first two shots produced position lines that crossed to show us about 40 miles south of our route. I advised the captain to turn starboard to a heading that applied a large correction for port drift as I took another star shot. This confirmed my position fix as accurate. However I was under supervision, and naturally such a large heading alteration produced unease.

We were probably now in range of the radar transponder at the RAF station at Malta (Luqa), and I switched to its frequency channel. With relief I saw the blip at the top of the screen, showing a range of about 190 nautical miles. There had been an unforecast wind change, blowing down the Adriatic from the north west. We completed our descent to the Rome area, passing over the Strait of Messina, 50 miles to the south of our intended route, and we arrived at Ciampino without losing any time. This event helped to reinforce the need for personal accuracy, vigilance, care, and confidence in one's ability, this being confirmed many times during the next fifteen months.

Productive flying

My operations certificate was issued, and life as a productive jet aviator began. The rest of my time on the Comet 1 was never dull and was always revealing new facets about this fascinating operation, many of which were encounters with problems that had not been foreseen. But I gradually accumulated an unease about the aircraft.

The first trip was a repeat of the route to Johannesburg, and we met the known engine fuel-filter icing problem. Kerosene contains a small percentage of water and absorbs moisture. Ice crystals forming at high altitude accumulated on the filter screens, gradually reducing fuel flow delivery to the Ghost engines. The symptom was slow and progressive reduction in power, indicated by the rpm winding down on the twin-needle gauges. The aircraft would begin to descend during the nominal 'cruise-climb,' as power was lost. There were no fuel heaters then (now fitted to all jets as standard equipment). Various ideas were adopted to alleviate this problem. One was to attempt a blow-out of the filter ice by increasing fuel pressure delivery. The fuel pumps on the Ghost were a swash-plate type, with two settings, partial and full delivery. A switch for each engine controlled this setting. Full pressure was used for take-off and landing. The blow-out procedure was to select full fuel pressure for a very short period, giving a pressure surge to move the ice, but prolonged use of the additional pressure would send a surge of fuel to the engine, and cause other problems. This was amply demonstrated by the captain as we flew from Rome to Cairo. Three engines began to run down slowly, so he switched to full pressure on two, quite successfully stabilising the rpm. The third was not so successful, for he held the selection on for too long. We heard a 'whoof', and the engine ran down to windmill speed. There had been a 'rich extinction,' dousing the flame. The flight deck was suddenly honoured by the presence of our distraught stewardess, who announced that a long flame had erupted as far back as the tail plane. We were quite close to the descent point so there was no operational problem. The engine was relit at 20,000 feet, the maximum height for this procedure, and all went well afterwards. Modifications were made to the filters in later months.

Accident in Rome

On 26 October 1952 the first of a series of accidents caused great concern among our ranks. Captain Harry Foote, with First Officer Syd Josling as co-pilot, were taking off from Ciampino on their way east. The Comet 1 did not become airborne and ran off the end of the runway into the 'prepared overrun.' This area was supposed to be cleared of obstacles, so that take-off weight calculations could allow higher weights to be used, and also to provide an emergency stopping strip. The aircraft had sat there making a hissing sound. It did not catch fire, demonstrating the superior crashworthy qualities of kerosene when compared to aviation gasoline, because of the reduction in vapour. This does not apply at high altitude, when the risk factor is reversed. In this accident some of the risk was removed as the 'prepared overrun' contained large boulders which ripped the bottom of the aircraft, allowing fuel to escape before it came to a halt.

Although this accident would probably not have occurred if the nose had been held lower during the take-off roll, it was really because of the leading edge wing profile design, which caused airflow separation, and loss of lift at high wing angles of attack. This problem was also the basic cause of an accident at Karachi on 3 March 1953. A Comet 1A belonging to Canadian Pacific Airlines crashed shortly after take-off, destroying the aircraft, and killing all on board. They were on a delivery flight via Sydney Australia, and Honolulu.

Harry Foote was blamed for the Rome accident, and transferred to fly the freighter Yorks. He redeemed himself splendidly soon afterwards. A propeller flew off one engine during the cruise, knocking the adjacent engine out of action. The free propeller cut a pattern of helical incisions along the fuselage, and hit the centre fin before falling away. Using the remaining two engines he flew the aircraft to a safe landing. Those who knew that the York did not fly very well even on three engines were most impressed with this feat. Viewed from one side the York appeared quite normal; from the other side it looked as if it had been hit by heavy gunfire.

To counter the dangers of pulling the nose too high on take-off we were instructed by a tersely worded signal to 'Keep the nose-wheels in light contact until V2.' This was not accompanied by any background information and involved giving the twin nose-wheel tyres a beating as they pounded along the runway. A revised leading edge profile was designed. This was fitted to new Comet variants, and would have been retro-fitted to our fleet. As a result of these accidents it is now part of the mandatory certification process for a test flight to be made to demonstrate that a safe take-off is always possible despite any excessive nose-up control input from the pilot.

The Tokyo route began on 4 April 1953. I was allocated a trip to Singapore, during which we flew the first Tokyo service from Karachi to Calcutta, Rangoon, and Bangkok, on its way to Japan.

The aircraft was maintaining published schedules with impressive regularity and we became quite confident that we had a winner despite the various problems. I remember meeting a pilot friend outside the circular terminal at Karachi airport. We were waiting for our respective aircraft to arrive. Dust devils swept across the barren landscape and kite hawks circled in the morning sun. We swapped information and I learned that his airline, KLM, had more command vacancies and was paid better than ours. However, we were flying at nearly twice the speed and height but he was not especially impressed with that, and voiced doubts about our safety.

The Comet had an equipment bay that could be reached in flight from a hatch in the floor at the rear of the flight deck. I noticed the amount of time our flight engineers had to spend down this hole. The hydraulic systems needed refilling during our short cruise periods. They leaked constantly and were designed to be quite independent of each other, supplying main, standby, and emergency power to flight controls, air brakes, flaps, and undercarriage. Unfortunately we found out that each of the three separate systems leaked at exactly the same rate, indicating interconnection. This was proved to occur via feed from common return lines, fed by leaky valves

John Cunningham demonstrates the Comet 1 prototype at the 1949 Farnborough Airshow.

in the flight control selector system. On one of my flights the engineer used fifteen cans of fluid for this purpose. The cabin crew had to guard against falling down this hole, and the casualty rate of stewardesses' stockings was similar to that in BSAA Lancastrian days. I think that they were able to negotiate an allowance for this.

Our passengers loved the rapid and vibration-free flight. We were able to top most European weather and sailed across the Alps in quick time. Load factors were very good, and publicity was positive. Those flying Comet 1s were a very small group, numbering about 140 crew members by the cessation of services. Most of the other BOAC flying personnel remained in ignorance of what we were doing, despite all the publicity. Rumours were abundant — a gulf existed between those involved on the western transatlantic route, and those flying BOAC routes elsewhere in the world. Those in the western division were paid a little more, ostensibly to compensate for the greater difficulties they had to overcome. Many of the most senior captains were flying the Boeing 377 Stratocruiser, and did face some tricky operational problems, as their aircraft could not make London-New York non-stop against the prevailing headwinds.

Misgivings about the Comet

A hard core of opinion existed among other BOAC crews who considered the Comet 1 operation to be dangerous. Conservatism and caution were the main reasons. Many felt no incentive to volunteer to leave their tried and tested current types for such a radical change. Further than this, there was no financial incentive.

BALPA was lobbied by the Comet 1 pilots' union council for support to claim a pay rise, to be called a 'jet differential.' The rationale was that individual productivity was higher and that the co-pilots needed additional qualifications. The council also dwelled on many details of the problems that had to be overcome (of which more later). A majority opinion within the union resisted support except to review the safety issues and criticise the crew complement. A bitter internal dispute ensued, only finally resolved by the withdrawal of piston-engined aircraft in the late Fifties.

We were accumulating some reasons for disquiet. At Calcutta a Comet had been damaged when moving along a curved section of taxiway at night. The Comet's taxi lights were very low-powered, and did not provide adequate illumination. They were always supplemented by the use of one of the two landing lights which heated rapidly because of their power and uncooled mounting. These lights could be kept on only briefly, and it was the practice to alternate between them by switching manually. The switches were positioned on the left cockpit wall, behind and below the left seat so that the captain had to look down and backwards to make the selection. This switch panel was poorly lit, and also contained the taxi light selectors.

The nose wheel steering was controlled by a wheel mounted on the left side of the cockpit and was self-centering. This was not duplicated for the co-pilot.

The accident was caused by the captain moving his left hand off the steering to select an alternate landing light. The nose wheel steering centred causing the aircraft to run off the edge of the asphalt and bury one main wheel assembly in soft ground. He then attempted to move the Comet quickly back onto the taxiway by applying high power. This was unsuccessful and caused substantial damage to the aircraft. He was held responsible, and had his seniority reduced, a penalty which would prove very expensive to him for the rest of his career. By common consent he was one of the best pilots in BOAC. A modification was introduced to reposition the landing/taxi light control panel to the forward upper cockpit panel, where both pilots could reach it. The disciplinary action by management was not viewed with favour by pilots, and did not contribute to morale or safety.

Bangkok

Bangkok was a fascinating place in 1953, before the Vietnam war, mass tourism, and prostitution combined to change things for the worse. The hotel that we used was second-rate, and we were stranded there for four days at a time, waiting for the next service. After dark the mosquitoes were vicious and could bite through two layers of socks. We were on a regular diet of paludrine or mepacrine, anti-malarial drugs. Many of the days were spent at the Royal Bangkok Sporting Club where there was a race course. A commonly-held rumour was that the horses were halted to rearrange their order when out of sight round a blind bend. The pace seemed to confirm this and was slow enough in the oppressive heat and humidity. Swimming and squash alternated with excessive sun exposure and reading.

The bureaucracy encountered at the airport when an aircraft was in transit was incredible. The captain had to sign dozens of incomprehensible and untranslated forms that were thrust at him by several levels of officialdom. They would not release the aircraft without this ritual.

Chicken at Calcutta

Late in April 1953 we were in transit at Calcutta (Dum Dum), having flown from Bangkok via Rangoon. Captain Alan Mervyn Smith was the commander, a good pilot, and so urbane that he was named Alan Smooth. The night was black and overcast. There were many thunderstorms in the area. The meteorological briefing officer had advised us of a nor'wester that would be arriving quite soon. These vicious storms are generated late in April and May by pressure and temperature changes on the Himalayan ranges and can race down on Calcutta at high speed, bearing excessive wind strength. Our next call was to be Delhi where we would hand over to another crew. The Met Office had just received a new weather radar set with a range of about 100 nautical miles, and was trying it out. They advised us that the best climb-out to avoid the local storms would be on a westerly heading. Our plan was to reach high altitude and then turn north-west towards Delhi once we could see around the storms, hoping that starlight would allow this.

After take-off and as height was gained we saw towering bubbling clouds close on each side. At about 20,000 feet, it was evident that a turn onto our route would soon be essential to conserve fuel for we were 50° to the south of our correct heading towards Delhi. But this was out of the question, as we would have to enter heavy cloud. Suddenly there was a searing forked lightning discharge which connected the clouds on each side and seemed to go right through the cockpit. I dare say that this was illusory, but the associated turbulence was not reassuring either. I looked at Alan, and found him looking at me. My eyes were reacting from the blinding flash and must have looked as alarmed as his. I would still swear that his eyes glowed as he closed the throttles. I selected full wing spoilers, and he turned the aircraft round 180°, pointing the nose at the airport lights, which we could see ahead and below. Landing a few minutes later, back in Calcutta, we decided to night stop until the storms were past. The aircraft was parked away from the main hangar, which proved to be fortunate. The nor'wester roared through only three hours later, detaching parts of the hangar roof. I have always wondered about our silent consensus, and must admit that I was scared stiff after the lightning flash. Our journey into Calcutta was a nightmare of flooded roads, cattle, people, and darkness and I thought that it was probably more dangerous than the flight. This opinion was soon modified by later events.

Red face at Juhu

Since the beginning of aviation pilots have made forced landings, for one reason or another. There have also been landings at the wrong airport, or on the wrong runway. Taxiways have been misidentified as runways, and approaches have been made towards bright street lighting instead of the dim lighting supplied by too many airports. The use of all possible guidance cues, including the use of instrument landing aids in good visibility, has become prudent practice. Misidentification occurs for a variety of reasons, including lack of familiarity with the area, poor lighting, bad visibility, or overconfidence.

We had such an instance when a Comet 1 landed at Juhu instead of Bombay's Santa Cruz airport. This small airfield had a short runway lined up on the same heading as the correct runway, and was a few miles closer to the coastline so that it lay between the coast and the main airport. They managed to stop satisfactorily and were, of course, supremely embarrassed to discover the location, which was a field fit for DC-3s but not for jets. Before the aircraft could be ferried to the correct destination, passengers were disembarked, a training captain was sent from England, and a very careful performance calculation completed to ensure that it was indeed safe to take off again, with minimum fuel and crew.

Another accident

On the 2 May 1953, on my next trip, we were on the ground at Rangoon, on the way to Bangkok. It was 11 am on a fine sunny day. Another Comet, G-ALYV, landed on its way home from Tokyo. We were flying G-ALYX. It was quite unusual to cross on the ground like this. We met the other crew for a lime juice and a chat to swap information. The captain was Maurice Haddon, and the first officer was Bill Strange, who had been on our course at Hatfield. They were full of tips about where to shop in Tokyo, showing us a few of their purchases. Bill had some special toys for his children. Their destination was Delhi, after calling at Calcutta. We departed for Bangkok as they were starting engines. After arrival we were transported by the usual noisy and smelly bus to our hotel. After a shower and change of clothing I was outside by a small pool close to the restaurant and arranging a table for dinner when the captain appeared with the news that he had just been rung to advise that YV had crashed close to Calcutta. Naturally this was very alarming to us. We knew that the weather around Calcutta was deteriorating when we departed, and that thunderstorms were expected. Speculation was intense, and theories abounded.

The cause of the aircraft break-up at high altitude has never been finally established, although at the time it was blamed on excessive gust loading in a heavy storm, and perhaps loss of control leading to excessive speed. One of the tailplanes was found on the ground as the first piece of wreckage in a path of destruction, leading to the view that it had failed under abnormal stress. Later views centred around the cause being structural failure of the pressurised cabin.

BOAC services continued, although many of us had doubts about this latest disaster. Many nagging problems were now surfacing. In hot and humid climates we were experiencing severe misting and condensation of the windshield panels on descent. This obscured the glass and we had to wipe a towel across the panels constantly to allow vision. Some help was provided by the selection of air flow controls to route all inbound pressurised air supply, from the engine tappings and heat exchangers, to the pilots' windshield ducting. This dried the eyeballs up rapidly and created a lot of noise. Night approaches were especially difficult as runway or approach lights were distorted and refracted by the moisture.

Stratocruiser interlude

The Tokyo route required the use of LORAN, a navigation aid with which I was already familiar. To obtain current experience, and to be checked out on its use, I was scheduled on a B-377 Stratocruiser service to New York. The outbound captain was Ken Buxton; inbound Sam Buxton, both very senior pilots. Outbound we had to land to refuel at Keflavik, the Icelandic airport near Reykjavik, but managed the transatlantic return flight non-stop, taking 11 hours 15 minutes. The difference between this type of aviation, and the Comet operation was, of course, substantial. The Stratocruiser was perhaps the epitome of airline luxury at the time but flights could be uncomfortable and bumpy, through ice-ridden skies at low-levels, listening to half-hourly weather reports and the constant static interfering with radio range reception. Two bunks were provided for crew rest but captains did not usually isolate themselves from the operation. Relaxation rather than actual sleep was the normal habit. One navigator, two flight engineers, and a radio officer completed the crew. The aircraft had a spacious flight deck, providing additional observer seats on each side of the pilots, allowing a four-abreast view of the flight path ahead through a large expanse of glass. Engine reliability was a problem at times, and there were also instances of uncontrollable propellers (runaways), with excessive revolutions in fine pitch causing penalising drag. The 28-cylinder Pratt and Whitney R-4360 four-row radial engines provided a total of 14,000 horsepower, twice that of the Argonaut, giving the aircraft a cruise speed some 50 knots higher.

It was educational to watch these captains eating their dinner in a small passenger cabin just behind the flight deck.

Crew, staff, and passenger relations required discretion and tact, and the personality of a commander could determine how successful the flight might be, on the ground and in the air. He had not yet been isolated by modern pressures and practice from a hands-on liaison with all phases of the operation,. Many of the senior pilots cultivated an aura of authoritative respect. This was certainly effective in improving coordination and safety. Their experience had ensured that a regular transatlantic connection between the new and old worlds could be sustained. The transition to jet aviation would be easily mastered by some, although many would retire before jets flew from London to New York.

There was little sympathy from our fellow pilots flying the North Atlantic route for those of us engaged in the Comet 1 operation. We were strangers, doing something which, in their opinion, was possibly unsafe and quite probably uneconomical.

Comet 1 to the Far East

My next trip was to Tokyo, lasting 22 days. We followed the usual route calls to Bangkok, then via Manila, to Okinawa. I was not impressed with one characteristic of our ADF installation. When tuned in to a powerful beacon on Okinawa the indication had reverse sensing, pointing the wrong way, needing one to subtract 180°. Apparently this only happened when using frequencies above 900 kcs (khz) and was because of the use of suppressed antennae mounted flush in a fuselage cut-out. Another surprise was the short period during which I was able to use the LORAN. The set's inverter power-supply cooling was inadequate, and overheating soon caused failure, leaving astro navigation as the only means to fix position until making landfall close to Kagoshima on the island of Kyushu.

In 1953 the Korean War had only just ended. Tokyo was full of forces personnel, and the departure of General MacArthur two years earlier had not reduced the impression of military government. Haneda airport seemed very busy, and quite disorganised, as we made our way through to where the

Comet stood, waiting for our attention as we prepared to return home. The weather forecast showed very strong headwinds of nearly 200 knots, as we flew westward towards Kagoshima before turning south to Okinawa. There would be a navigational dilemma, for as we flew south the wind strength would decrease rapidly when leaving the jet stream flow off the Chinese mainland. At some point there would be need for a large heading change to reduce the large offset drift correction. Assuming that the LORAN would not work, I arranged to use an astro position close to our descent point and told the captain of my plan to alter heading directly towards the Naha airfield on Okinawa.

We set off from Tokyo, bucking into the strong wind and very turbulent air. On reaching the turning point we took up a heading that allowed 30° of drift angle. The autopilot limit switches were causing disconnects, and I was trying to keep the sextant bubble under control, also trying to see if the LORAN would work, without success. The radio beacon was not transmitting. As I tried to use the sun, moon, and a planet for position lines the air became smoother and I guessed that the wind was calming. The fix, when plotted on the chart, showed us too far west. I stepped forward to the captain and advised him to alter course 50° to the east. This caused his eyebrows to lift gently, as I explained the situation. We were about 220 nautical miles from our destination. He accepted the alteration, and after a few minutes we were able to make contact with the American controllers, which at least indicated proximity, and then saw the island showing as a shadow under clouds on the horizon. This second excursion off a planned route reinforced the need to be very vigilant. Our fuel reserves seemed adequate on paper, but at low-levels did not confer much range. A premature descent could be threatening to flight endurance. Diversions to alternates required climb to higher levels and in some cases were scheduled as a climb, perhaps to 30,000 feet, immediately followed by a descent. The theoretical saving could often be lost by traffic control problems.

More teething troubles

There were other deficiencies and limitations which have now received the attention of the aviation industry but which we were meeting in their early stages. Only a single electrical main busbar fed essential services on the Comet 1. On one occasion there was complete electrical failure because of a shorted-out busbar, which had been delivered with the protective shellac coating still unremoved. At the top of the climb en route between Khartoum and Beirut, all the circuit breakers triggered to cut electrical power. The flight engineer was Alan Johnson, who had been associated with the Comet 1 since its inception, and who had been attached to the BOAC development unit. He managed to use a length of fuse wire to establish power to re-energise one main alternator, and Captains Phil Brentnall and Maurice Aries flew the aircraft back to Khartoum to a safe landing.

During descent in icing conditions, using low engine power, the centrifugal compressors and intakes accumulated ice. There was insufficient hot air unless the descent rate was slowed by increasing power, causing other problems. However, we were relatively free from airframe ice, except at lower levels, as the speed provided enough kinetic heating.

After a turn was made at high altitude the artificial horizon and the zero reader level flight indications would indicate a false horizon, and take some time before regaining accuracy. This caused difficulties. There was only one master remote-type compass system, with inadequate failure indication provision, and only a Pl2 basic compass as backup.

We could not test the integrity of the engine fire warning system. A fourth hydraulic system provided essential services, and was supplied by a standby pump which had a very short time rating. It would overheat too quickly, and was not adequate for prolonged use. The fuselage fire detection system could not differentiate between smoke or hydraulic mist.

A few incidents involved icing of the static air pressure sensing holes which fed information to the basic pressure instruments. The heating of these orifices was inadequate. Selection of an alternative source of pressure sensing inside the aircraft was available, involving loss of accuracy, but providing survivability.

Despite these various development problems, and with reasonable background information provided by our management through the medium of regular flight notice circulars and orders, most services operated on schedule and to the minute. Passenger loyalty was maintained, but crew concerns about the many problems began to spread, receiving the attention of BALPA.

Another problem was dealt with expeditiously. The outbound and inbound routes we used were identical. Above 30,000 feet it was assumed that we had the air to ourselves. Our cruise-climb technique involved constantly changing altitude, climbing at about 40 feet per minute as weight reduced with fuel consumption. The risk of meeting another aircraft was considered to be infinitesimal. Then, within a short period, there were three sightings during the cruise. We were approaching a cloud bank over the Burmese coastline one afternoon when another Comet suddenly appeared on our right side, on the opposite heading, at the same height, and only a few hundred feet away. We flashed by at the closing speed of 800 feet, and established radio contact. We had not been advised of their presence. Within two weeks all our routes were revised, to be separated enough for safer passage. There were no upper level airways as yet, nor any aids to enable accurate guidance along them.

Problems of inter-slipping

Sir Miles Thomas was BOAC's Chairman throughout the period of Comet 1 operation. He was approachable, well liked, and practical. The Johannesburg route had been achieved with the agreement of the South African government. This provided for South African Airways to supply flight and cabin crews for some of our services, which were operated under a pool arrangement. The original plans called for us to take over alternative Cornets that had been flown in by a SAA crew, so-called inter-slipping. There were many misgivings about this idea among BOAC pilots. These were mainly founded on the unknown background of SAA pilots using our equipment, although I believe that much of the resistance stemmed from a general unhappiness with employment conditions. Pay was low, much less than that of comparable European airlines, responsibility was high, and few of us could even afford to take a vacation. The idea that a foreign group of crews would in effect be absorbing employment opportunities caused some misgivings.

The unhappiness was reflected in many ways through contact with management, resulting in a special meeting. Sir Miles Thomas called all available Comet pilots to the BOAC headquarters building one afternoon. Situated on the Great West Road, half way between central London and Heathrow, this was the old Beecham administrative building. Remote from the daily hurly-burly of airport operation, and from the individual aircraft fleet administrations, which were still diversely situated, this place seemed remote from our daily problems. I was one of about twenty pilots asked to attend the meeting, which took place in the boardroom, with Sir Miles listening carefully to the views of our group. He was left in no doubt that the only way we would accept SAA use of our Comets would be for them to fly the complete route pattern, using their own crews throughout, separately from us. This was the arrangement finally implemented. Naturally this lengthened the duration of our trips to South Africa and increased the crew numbers needed, a significant cost to each airline. This first expression of collective unhappiness was not routed though BALPA. It was another instance of the isolation we were feeling from the main group of pilots.

Lull before the storm

By the end of 1953 we had become more experienced with our new environment and aircraft. Most flights were relatively routine, considering the teething problems, and the accidents to date. Familiarity bred dexterity. We knew that the Comet operation had been extraordinarily publicised, assuming major importance to a nation starved of encouragement in the bleak post-war aftermath. Passengers flocked to travel with us, loving the time-saving and smooth flight. To be associated with such a national project conferred a sense of importance that could cloud judgment.

Air traffic controllers were now quite knowledgeable about our flight performance capability and needs. I arrived home on Christmas Eve from a trip to Tokyo, on schedule to the minute. We had brought G-ALYP into Rome from Karachi, via Bahrain and Beirut, and had only ten hours off before picking up another aircraft for the flight home. Our usual northbound route crossed the island of Elba, where we would be approaching our initial cruise height of 36,000 feet.

After arrival at Heathrow in the early morning I promptly forgot all about aircraft and airline. I had been successful in the lottery for Christmas vacation, securing two weeks of my annual allocation. The difficulty of obtaining time off with the family during summer, school holidays, or at other festive times, is part of an airline crew member's life. We tried many methods of sharing out opportunity, but I spent many of these anniversaries away from home.

Our conversion of the big old house was complete and we had ended up with the servants' wing, selling off the other two sections, which were now self contained. Our four-year-old son was beginning nursery school, and Susan was a lovely eighteen-month-old with a mass of blonde curly hair. The days passed all too soon, with festive occasions involving relatives and friends.

I was rostered out for another long Far Eastern trip. We were still building strength and training new people. Some

153

of us had been appointed to act as supervisory navigators, so that we could help to check out the latest co-pilots. This was interesting, but a trifle onerous, but it did mean that an additional crew member was carried, so that in the event of trouble the captain could receive more help.

Cabin service aboard a BOAC Comet 1.

Comet disasters

On 10 January I was listening to the radio, and heard news of the Comet 1 crash close to Elba. G-ALYP had fallen into the Mediterranean. An announcement said that all Comets had been grounded, pending investigation. This meant that my trip, scheduled to begin the next day, was cancelled. When I heard the details of this event it seemed like a case of *déjà vu*. I was certainly not really surprised, for a recent visit to the Comet maintenance hangar at Heathrow had alerted me to some information. The visit was arranged to show my father-in-law over an aircraft, to give him some idea of modern aviation, and my job. He had retired as the commander of ground forces in East Africa, and was a survivor of the two World Wars.

A friend in the engineering hierarchy accompanied us on our tour, and responded to my questions truthfully. The large upswept tailplanes were sometimes being changed when major check routines were scheduled, as they were developing cracks. Cracks were also developing in the wing area where the undercarriage was mounted, and which needed watching. There was some concern about the effect of exhaust from the inboard engines on the fuselage skin, as they were very closely mounted in the wing roots. I knew about problems being experienced by modem British aircraft that had been constructed using a newer aluminium alloy with high zinc content. This new alloy was not in use by the American industry. Its advantage was that the tensile strength was improved and so less material was needed, but it was more brittle. Structures were more prone to fatigue and the new alloy seemed to have a poor record with several new types of aircraft.

'Yoke Peter' (the crashed aircraft) had a crew of six and twenty nine passengers on board. The captain was Alan Gibson, a most personable and competent pilot. One of our Argonauts was using the same radio channel and heard the last message 'Did you get my....', after which witnesses on Elba saw the aircraft plunging down as a globe of fire, rotating as it came down into the sea. The last full report had been made passing 26,500 feet, climbing to the planned cruise height of 36,000 feet.

I could immediately relate to the exact point in flight, having so recently flown the same procedure. The aircraft was our first Comet 1 to enter service, and had flown a total of 3,681 hours, covered more than a million miles, carrying thousands of passengers. Consulting my personal log book I saw that it showed sixteen flights on the aircraft within the last few months. I was motivated to discover information about the accident and the exact status of the Comet series.

The manufacturer, our airline corporation, and the Air Registration Board (the certifying authority) were advising the Air Safety Board and its chairman, Air Chief Marshal Sir Frederick Bowhill, as that body considered this latest accident and the probable cause.

Within BALPA we had formed a local Comet pilots' council. I became a member of this as I wished to follow the accident inquiry closely. The Royal Navy had been instructed by Admiral Earl Mountbatten, Commander-in Chief, Mediterranean, to 'recover the Comet'. Two special ships, HMS *Barhill*, and HMS *Salvor* were supplied with specialised equipment from the UK, and were based in Malta. Another vessel, HMS *Wakeful*, carrying television equipment, arrived at Elba on 25 January. The Navy located the crash wreckage very rapidly, and soon began to recover much of the aircraft for onward transportation to the Royal Aircraft Establishment at Farnborough. Meanwhile an exhaustive and detailed analysis of possible causes, however remote, was initiated. This resulted in a list of more than fifty desirable modifications to the aircraft, with the objective of clearing the way for a resumption of full commercial services, despite the lack of any positive identification of the accident cause.

Union concern

Within BALPA there was a degree of turmoil. After many months of unsuccessful negotiation for a long-awaited pay rise the Boards of BEA and BOAC had come forward with a very small offer. BALPA had made no claim for any jet pay, despite active representation by the Comet pilots. After the Elba accident it seemed that this claim was equated with danger, or 'development' compensation by the Central Board of BALPA, which took the view that the crew complement was a man short anyway. At the time the Comet pilots were convinced that they were being asked to perform additional duties in a very stressful situation. They also thought that their productivity was considerably greater. The technical section of the union did its best to track the moving situation, to little effect. Liaison between the Comet pilots and the rest of BALPA suffered, and the union's effectiveness was minimal.

BOAC let it be known that, provided the Central Board of BALPA formally filed a claim for extra pay, then the Comet pilots would indeed be offered something. This claim was never made, for a number of complex reasons. These mainly hinged around the constitution of the Central Board where representatives from the other fleets, BEA, and independent operators, sat in majority. They were unwilling to concede support for our claim. As can be imagined, this led to reaction amongst our ranks, especially as the main defence of the opponents was criticism of the safety standards maintained by our Comet operation.

While this was generating morale problems, additionally to the aftermath of the Elba crash, we were faced with the realisation that services were to be restarted as soon as possible. Most of the Yoke Peter wreckage had been pulled up from the bottom of the Mediterranean in a magnificent effort by thc Royal Navy. For many of us it seemed prudent to await a detailed inspection of the remnants before leaping into the air in blind faith that all would be well. Naturally there was concern in the press, and in Parliament. A statement by the Minister of

Transport and Civil Aviation justified resumption of services, with the government taking full responsibility on the advice of the Air Safety Board. My first encounter with a type simulator occurred on 9 February, when involved in a refresher session of three hours using the new Comet 1 simulator. Equipped with a mass of vacuum tubes, the main computer sat in a large room, supervised by a team of technicians. There was no visual or motion simulation. I spent three hours refreshing various procedures in an unhappy frame of mind.

On 25 February 1954 all flight deck crews were called to the hangar area at Heathrow airport for a briefing by the BOAC Engineering Director, designed to bring us up-to-date with regard to the modifications introduced since the suspension of services. About 140 pilots, engineer officers, and radio officers listened to a description of the work that was being done to make the aircraft safer. The list was comprehensive and contained action on some of our nagging problems, such as misting, hydraulic leaks, etc. The idea was to deal with most of our outstanding problems and to assume that the cause of the accident would be covered. After a question and answer session, during which concern was expressed at the early resumption before the Elba wreckage had been recovered and inspected, the assembly was asked to signify support for the resumption of services. A show of hands indicated an even split of views for and against, and a count was taken. There was a majority of one for resumption. Enough crew members were willing to restart services. In view of this, the meeting was asked to record a unanimous vote so as to avoid the harmful effect of publicizing the split opinions. This was approved, albeit with misgivings. I was one of those who felt that we should not risk the reputation of the aircraft, and hazard any more lives until the causes of the accidents had been thoroughly investigated. I considered that the momentum established by the promotion of the Comet I as a national achievement dominated the government's decision to proceed. I stood up and was counted as opposing the premature resumption of services.

Once more into the breach...

I renewed acquaintance with the Comet 1 on 15 March, for a short re-familiarisation flight, with three other pilots. We flew four circuits each, and were deemed ready for the restart. We were ignorant of what arrangements had been made by South African Airways to join the resumption, which was, for us, initially only on the Johannesburg route.

Notification of my allocation of a trip showed that the first pilots to fly the resumed services would be made up of one management pilot and one BALPA council member. I have never discovered how this arbitrary decision was made but have always assumed that it was in some way associated with our opposition to the resumption.

Captain Tom Stoney and I were rostered out of London as positioning crew to Rome, ready to collect the first Comet. It felt strange to be in an Argonaut, struggling along at low-level, and taking four hours to complete the journey.

On 23 March we flew Comet 1, Yoke X-Ray, via the usual stops, to Entebbe. The next aircraft through was Yoke Yoke, which we flew to Johannesburg (Jan Smuts) night-stopping, and then back to Entebbe. The SAA flights had also restarted. The aircraft was behaving well and we were able to keep on schedule, carrying good loads of passengers. Conversation was muted amongst the crew when on the ground: we had much on our minds. My wife had been very quiet when dropping me off at the airport and I knew that she was concerned. She was pregnant with our third child. It was difficult to conceal my resentment at being singled out so soon for the restarted services (bearing in mind my known apprehension) in view of the volunteers available. Tom Stoney was not entirely happy himself. I was allowed to make a couple of landings and take-offs. We made sure that the nose-wheels stayed in contact with the runway until the recommended speed. My last landing was at Entebbe, in the early afternoon, approaching from the south over Lake Victoria, and it was a good one. The aircraft was very nice to handle on the approach, but it was not advisable to come in low, or slow, as I had already discovered on one earlier approach to Rome (Ciampino). On that occasion I found that very high power was needed to overcome the drag created with the nose high, and have since thought that this was because of the wing leading edge profile.

Another close call

We flew Yoke X-Ray from Entebbe to Rome on 2 April, arriving on a sunny spring day, having a full three days off to enjoy the lovely city. My final flight on the Comet 1, from Rome to London, was on 6 April 1954. We took over Yoke Yoke again, after it had already completed another round trip to South Africa. This was the last BOAC service flown by the world's first jet passenger aircraft. We arrived at 7.30 am, and when I picked up my company mail there was notification that my next trip would start in ten days time.

The weather was so good that we arranged to travel down to visit Jeane's parents, who lived in Bembridge on the Isle of Wight. We managed to catch a ferry from Portsmouth to Ryde on the afternoon of 8 April. It was not until morning that I learned of the next accident. My father-in-law had been renovating a thorn hedge on one side of their property. Returning to the house he brought out the *Times* paper which he handed it to me without speaking.

Yoke Yoke had crashed off Naples, close to the island of Ponza. A South African Airways crew was flying one of their services. There were no survivors and it appeared that the circumstances were identical to those involving Yoke Peter. Seven crew and fourteen passengers had lost their lives. The aircraft had been on the way from Rome to Cairo, and had flown a total of 2,704 hours. The last message was transmitted at 7.05 pm, when the aircraft reported that they were climbing to 35,000 feet.

It would be an understatement to say that this news was sensational. So many aspects were involved. The Comets were grounded and a full Court of Inquiry would investigate the causes of both Elba and Ponza crashes. Personally, it was another lucky escape for me, and a very close call. At the time this aspect took second place to a lasting resolve. I became committed to ensuring that there would be a better process for the preservation and improvement of aviation safety, and I confess that I did harbour resentment towards a system that had, in my opinion, risked life needlessly.

From a de Havilland advertisement for the Comet 1.

Back to the pistons

U ntil grounded, the Comets, during 20 months of scheduled services, had carried 55,000 passengers, and flown many millions of miles. The gap created by the loss of this capacity on the BOAC routes produced severe practical and economic effects. For the crews there would obviously be the question of employment, and the maintenance of their flying qualifications and licences. Within two weeks we were informed of a temporary arrangement. This involved secondment back to our previous aircraft type, pending decisions about the possible use of the Comet 2. The simulator continued in operation for the time being. My Argonaut qualification had expired, and would require refresher flying to revalidate this. The airline, understandably, could not allocate aircraft time for this, so the only economical way for me to be used was as a full-time navigator.

My pilot's licence had to be kept valid, achieved by a brief visit to Croydon, where the Airways Aero Club was based. I completed two circuits and landings in an Auster Aiglet with Bill Brinsden, one of the instructors, and found that this little aircraft had a few quirks. The flap selection lever hung from the roof of the cabin and as one hand selected landing flaps the aircraft seemed to rotate vertically around the lever, causing laughter from the instructor's seat. Of course this expense was quite pointless, but was needed to keep a valid licence.

One month after the Elba crash I found myself on an Argonaut, under supervision as a navigator. The leisurely pace was relaxing. To be supervised was part of the game. Our Fleet Navigation section had to ensure that our group of pilot-navigators could maintain the standards set by the rest of the fleet's specialists. We flew to Cairo, and back via Frankfurt, taking three days. Then I was off on my own. It soon felt as if I had never been away from the Argonaut, but Comet problems and memories continued to haunt me. The Comet pilots' local council in BALPA continued to exist, as there was much experience to record, collate, and represent to union, airline, and the regulators.

BOAC decided to stop flying South American routes. This provided additional capacity for the more profitable eastern and African services, and went some way to replace the lost Comet capacity.

Belatedly, our claim for jet pay had been finally approved by BALPA Central Board. This was rather irrelevant in the circumstances, although important for the future. Then I received notification to attend a three-week Comet 2 familiarisation course. This was interesting as many improvements were to be built into the later aircraft, which was powered by Avon engines of 7,300 pound thrust. The hydraulic leak problems had been caused by a batch of faulty seals. Many of the outstanding deficiencies were being rectified. The wing leading edge profile was modified. The basic fuselage structure, however, was almost the same. This version of the aircraft did not enter commercial service, although the RAF flew a heavily modified version for some years, starting the first real transatlantic scheduled jet service to Gander, thus preceding BOAC's 1958 Comet 4 service to New York.

The Middle East

Kuwait was a regular port of call. The landing surface was hard sand, marked with oiled strips, and the terminal building was hut-like. Visibility was often reduced by dust. Damascus was notorious for a steady, strong crosswind, blowing down from the mountains separating Syria and Lebanon. In 1954 the city was crawling with ill-clad troops but was surprisingly green and pleasant to a crew travelling home from the Far East. We would often land there and take a taxi ride across the border to Beirut. This was very nerve-racking, sitting in an old Mercedes driven with excess speed around blind bends on mountain roads without guard rails. Despite misgivings, our crews managed to escape injury, although there were a few minor collisions. Occasionally we had a ride across in a chartered DC-3, a trip reminiscent of all that was rudimentary in the Middle Eastern area at that time. A tired and dirty aircraft, with soiled seats and a lack-lustre cabin attendant could be tolerated for the short journey, but we usually took off without any pre-flight engine run-up checks, which was not exactly reassuring, then weaving around mountains and clouds before arriving in sometimes questionable style. Beirut was pleasant. We stayed at the Bristol Hotel and frequented the St George's Club on the shore line, to sit and soak up the Mediterranean sunshine, relaxing in the knowledge that we were on the way home (trips averaged 16 days to the east). We also called at Nicosia, Amman, Basra, Baghdad, and Bahrain, as part of the web of BOAC routes leading to the Indian sub-continent and the Far East.

After four months of navigating I was rostered to a training session to renew my piloting qualification on the Argonaut, and from then on was crewed with another similarly qualified co-pilot, sharing navigation and piloting.

The Comet inquiry

The court of inquiry into the Comet disasters opened at Church House, Westminster, in London on 20 October 1954. I was able to follow the proceedings quite closely. The Royal Aircraft Establishment at Farnborough had secured a complete BOAC Comet 1, Yoke Uncle, and subjected it to a water tank test, accompanied by structural flexing and pressurisation similar to the usual flight cycle. This revealed that metal fatigue and structural failure of the fuselage would occur at a low total of flight hours. More than 100 hours were flown by RAF crews using a Comet 1 without revealing any contributory evidence. The Elba wreckage from Yoke Peter revealed an explosive destruction of the fuselage, starting at a cut-out frame for the suppressed ADF aerial. The frame had been manufactured by a process that had concentrated stress at the corners of the rectangular shape. Cracks had been detected during the manufacturing process, and had been drilled to stop them propagating. The test specimen failed in a different place, and although the salvaged pieces of Yoke Peter showed that the failure path included the drilled part, the inquiry concluded that this was not the primary cause of the failure. The inquiry also remarked upon insufficient consultation during design and testing between de Havilland and the RAE, whose Dr Walker, head of the structure department, stated that he thought that de Havilland ought to have been more cooperative. However he admitted that his department had not called for fatigue testing of the fuselage, only the wings.

My interest in the technical findings went beyond a consuming interest in the cause of explosive decompression of two, and possibly three, certificated civil jet aircraft. The future was clear. We had entered the jet age. There was no turning back. All our accumulated experience would have to be used. When Sir Arnold Hall, Director of the RAE, gave evidence to the court of inquiry he covered a wide range of issues, apart from the basic cause, which he considered to be metal fatigue. I was particularly concerned about the deficiencies in organisation and control between the Air Registration Board, the RAE, and the manufacturers. We had been flying an aircraft that had a very short structural life. The alloys used for some parts of the structure were new, and known to be more prone to fatigue. Apart from the fuselage, other areas indicated the need for extensive redesign. The wings had substantial cracking, which would have required modification. The fuselage skin behind the engines was subject to sonic batter, and had been weakened because of a change in the crystal structure of the metal alloy. The tailplanes were cracking. We had been on the peak of a dangerous learning curve. I thought that re-evaluation would show the industry that risks had been taken which should, and could have been avoided. I was more than ever sure that the decision to restart flying after the Elba crash — at least with such undue haste — was wrong. The presence of political control was unhealthy. Here we had a nationalised airline corporation, under Treasury control, administered by a board appointed by a political process. The ultimate authority to decide the resumption of Comet services was the Minister of Transport and Civil Aviation. His decision was made after reference to the ARB, and the Air Safety Board. I wondered if the RAE had been consulted.

After the benefit of hindsight, and nearly five decades later, the same problems may still exist in some degree when the airworthiness of a civil airliner type is questioned, although there is now a more cautionary approach. The design and testing of structures improves exponentially towards a level of absolute perfection that can never be achieved. The concept of 'fail-safe,' as opposed to 'safe-life' is now predominant in major structural design and certification, but is limited by the difficulty of inspection. Metal fatigue and corrosion have caused major repair and modification to be required for almost all jet airliners since 1954. Public safety is in the hands of safety boards, accident inspectors, certifying authorities, manufacturers, airlines, and, for better or worse, politicians.

West Africa

We served West Africa at Accra and Lagos via Tripoli, and Kano. Castel Benito airport had changed little since my RAF days. Tripoli was always very quiet, a mixture of eastern and western architecture, with a pleasant corniche. Many sites of great architectural antiquity are situated along the coastline within a few hours of the city and were worth investigating. Leptis Magna was scattered alongside the coast road, where Phoenicians, Carthaginians, and European armies had traded, travelled, and fought.

The flight to Kano from Tripoli was usually at night, taking just less than seven hours over the Sahara. Weather was normally clear for the first four hours, and we strained our eyes to make out the light at Ghat, a small place on the Libyan-Algerian border, which would confirm our position. The darkness below hid the shapes and undulations of the terrain and served to accentuate a starlit sky. We were conscious of the need to navigate accurately, for a BOAC Hermes had become lost because of a navigational error on the same route. This aircraft had deviated to the west of the correct route, eventually crash-landing on the desert in western Mauritania, more than 1,300 miles from Kano, as the fuel ran out. After several days they were rescued by the French Foreign Legion, who were helped by Bedouin tribesmen. All survived, with the exception of the co-pilot.

The last hour or two of the flight could experience increasing heavy cloud, and encounters with tropical thunderstorms. Kano is a large city, populated by more than half a million people, and teemed with activity. Situated 12° north of the Equator on a plateau some 2,000 feet above sea level, there is a wide range of ethnic diversity. At the time there was no hint of the violent civil war that would divide Nigeria in coming years. Crews usually bought locally-produced baskets, woven in many colours, filling them with fruit to supplement an inadequate home diet. We had one of these huge baskets as a laundry receptacle for many years.

On the way to Lagos or Accra we would inevitably expect weather problems and would have some exciting encounters with the active blue-black line squalls that grow to envelop hundreds of square miles. The coastal regions of Ghana and Nigeria, low-lying and humid, have many good beaches. Our aircraft were well patronised by a two-way flow of administrators, businessmen, and local nationals. The attractive variety of local dress, for both sexes, was evident in our passenger cabins, where flowing robes and decorative headgear leavened the western formality of European clothing.

North Atlantic

December 1955 marked the beginning of my renewed association with this route. Boeing B-377 Stratocruisers still provided the capacity to serve New York and Boston. The Britannia series of prop-jet aircraft was having engine problems, causing late delivery. The Britannia 312, a long-range version intended for use on the Atlantic, was to replace the Stratocruiser. Redesign of the Comet 3 to become the long range Comet 4 had begun. Development of the Boeing 707 and DC-8 jets was proceeding. Expansion of BOAC capacity on the lucrative American routes required a pool of pilots with experience of the route conditions. One group was allocated to obtain exposure to these special problems. This required me to alternate Argonaut trips with Stratocruisers. One would take me to New York, the next to Africa or the Far East. Services were scheduled to call at Manchester and Prestwick but the runway at Manchester's Ringway airport was not quite long enough for the Stratocruiser to use. The US Air Force base at Burtonwood, near Manchester, was used instead, by special arrangement, supplementing its normal role for Strategic Air Command, as with many UK airfields in the 1950s.

A Boeing 377 Stratocruiser at Prestwick Airport.

The 'Seven Seas'

During the next six months it became evident that our group would be transferred to the new Douglas DC-7C fleet, ten of which had been ordered as an insurance against the late delivery of the Britannias. Competition was increasing, and the range of the 'Seven Seas', as the aircraft was named, was good enough to guarantee non-stop flight between London and New York throughout the year, except in the most severe headwind conditions. Meanwhile I became reacquainted with the winter operation on the North Atlantic route.

New York's Idlewild (now JFK) airport was very busy. The peak arrival time was in the afternoon, when aircraft converged from all directions. The controllers spoke rapidly and unless you became familiar with local names and procedures there was the danger of misunderstanding leading to conflict. Air traffic control routeing clearances were read out at length, and had to be repeated verbatim. Within the airport circuit, in visual conditions, there could be many aircraft, separated and spaced by their pilots, using local landmarks to report position. When weather required the use of instrument approaches there were delays, and these meant holding in the stack.

We would remain in contact with our company office, which would advise the best alternate. The possibility of further landing delay would be assessed against remaining endurance. This, essentially, is still the system in use today.

We flew a daily shuttle service to Nassau, out and back. This averaged five hours flight time in each direction, and could involve a really lumpy and bumpy ride in the winter weather that often lies along the American coastline, and in the summer through vestiges of hurricane remnants. Visiting Oakes field again, after an absence of twelve years, was interesting and nostalgic. The hard standings where so many B-25 Mitchells had parked were silently empty, but the temperature was still as balmy.

'Seven Seas'

We started our ground school at the beginning of August 1956. At home we were feeling the economic pinch. My salary had increased by about 50 per cent since BSAA days, with incremental grade progress and long service.

Although inflation was low, the expense of three children, two of whom were now at school, had precluded any idea of a holiday. We decided that we would plan for one in 1957, come hell or high water. The country was gradually becoming more prosperous, and wartime restrictions and shortages were now past history, to be replaced by hope for a better life.

BALPA had just negotiated a new agreement which provided compensation for the additional duties that we would take on with the DC-7C. The radio officer had become a victim of technology and our crew would consist of two pilots plus an engineer, supplemented on the oceanic routes by a navigator, plus a third pilot for very long duty periods. After a course lasting four weeks at the BOAC Cranebank training centre and an ARB examination, the twelve members of our course found ourselves in Manhattan, New York. We made a daily journey to Jackson Heights, close to La Guardia airport, where the Pan American Airways DC-7C simulator was located. The instructors were all Pan Am staff, and very helpful.

The DC-7 had been in airline service for some time, and so there was much experience of a practical nature to impart. Our 7C variant had an extended wingspan, provided by an extra section of wing inserted inboard of the inner engines on each side. This allowed additional fuel-tankage, and more lift to carry the load. A disadvantage was the increased swing that happened when an outer engine failed. The fin and rudder were elongated to provide more control, although this was not a perfect solution as it also caused a rolling force. The engines were Wright turbo-compound R-3350s, giving a total power of 13,600 horsepower, nearly twice that of the Argonaut. Three power-recovery turbines on each engine were placed in the exhaust stream and provided additional power to the crankshaft through a fluid coupling. The inboard units were visible, and glowed white-hot in view of the passenger cabin. They were very noticeable at night, and could cause unease to the uninitiated.

After a week during which I flew the simulator for 16 hours, and a further 16 hours as co-pilot, we had developed a good knowledge of the operation, and returned to England for introduction to the aircraft.

Flying again

Shannon airport in Ireland was an ideal training airport. Although still in regular use by transatlantic airlines, the traffic was less than elsewhere, allowing good utilisation of the aircraft, and improved safety. Flight training safety has always been a concern, with an accident rate considerably higher than that for passenger flights. The prevalence of rain and high winds at this airport actually helped to build pilot confidence in understanding the handling performance of a new type.

My instructor was once again Phil Brentnall, aided by Ernie Rodley, and I found the DC-7C pleasant to fly and well equipped. At last we had a weather radar set, with scopes for each pilot. Some of the electronic equipment was supplied by British firms. A radar method of determining exact altitude could be used to resolve atmospheric pressure differences and interpret wind effects. The flight engineer sat on a folding seat between the pilots. An engine analyser monitored a number of vital systems. The engines were susceptible to carburettor icing, and care was needed to avoid sudden power loss. Choice of cruising levels could avoid most of this problem. An autofeathering system proved to be trouble-free.

Introduction of a new type in an airline is always interesting for those involved. New technology, revised certification, improved performance, and other benefits are usual. A period of acquaintance consolidates initial impressions. The DC-7C was well liked by most crews. Some missed the spaciousness of the Stratocruiser flight deck, and passengers certainly missed the availability of Pullman-style bunks, but these would be available once again when the Britannia 312 entered service.

In mid-November, I was despatched to Los Angeles, where a new DC-7C awaited a crew to take delivery. We were to start a new route across the United States from New York to San Francisco, and by arrangement with United Air Lines I spent time observing the operation of a DC-7 on the way to Los Angeles. The smooth flight took nearly ten hours from New York's Idlewild, giving me a chance to become accustomed to the traffic control, and other procedures. The crew was typically laconic and laid back but most helpful.

The Douglas plant at Santa Monica, close to Hollywood, was a hive of production, but we were informed that our particular aircraft was plagued by fuel leaks. The delay was cushioned by the supply of a company car from Douglas. A tour of the San Gabriel and San Bernadino areas was delightful. Visits to the film studios and a moment's pause at the intersection of Hollywood and Vine introduced us to the ambience of 'Tinsel Town.'

After two weeks we were ready to embark on an aviation tour of North America. Our first session involved completing approaches at Fresno, Bakersfield, Oakland, and Sacramento before landing at San Francisco for a brief night-stop. Next day we visited Reno on our way to Idlewild. After another quick hotel stop we left the next morning to complete approaches at Philadelphia, Baltimore, Washington National, Syracuse, and Moncton, before landing at Gander. After an hour on the ground we were on the way home to London, very impressed with our new aircraft.

'Seven Seas' routes

My first passenger-carrying flight was with Gordon Store as Captain. I do not think he remembered that initial BSAA selection board. He had been appointed Fleet Manager, and had Bernard Frost as his deputy. Bernard had been a first officer in Imperial Airways, and had been associated with the Mayo composite aircraft during 1938, when Don Bennett flew his record-breaking flights to America and South Africa. They made a fine management team. Most of the captains were drawn from those who had been flying Stratocruisers, although a few came from other sources. I was on the North Atlantic run once again, and was coincidentally situated among many of those who had expressed so many misgivings about the Comet 1 operation.

The flight, which was the first DC-7C commercial service for BOAC, on 6 January 1957, was supposed to be non-stop to Idlewild, but Gordon Store decided that we should refuel at Goose Bay because of the very bad weather forecast for the New York area. As it turned out we took over ten hours to reach Labrador, and after an hour's transit, a further five hours to arrive at Idlewild. This was not much of an improvement on the Stratocruiser, and the passengers were in less comfort. Our initial configuration was for 60 passengers in first class seating. Four Pullman-style berths could be installed in the rear cabin, but were not fitted. No fewer than four lavatories were supplied, a ratio that makes today's jets seem somewhat deficient. Two crew bunks were provided in the flight deck. Cruising speed was similar to that of the Stratocruiser, but the range was much better because of more efficient engines, and additional fuel capacity. Nevertheless it was apparent that some captains thought that the change was retrograde. They were to modify their views.

We had started services in mid-winter, and had to contend with some strong headwinds when westbound. Flights were scheduled to serve Manchester, Prestwick, Montreal, Boston, Chicago, Detroit, and New York. By the middle of the year we extended to fly from Idlewild to San Francisco, the first BOAC service approved to cross the continental US, albeit with no cabotage rights to carry traffic within the US. We started off by using Ringway airport at Manchester but soon reverted to Burtonwood while a runway extension was being constructed.

The non-stop flight from London to New York was usually made at about 8,000 to 10,000 feet, This kept us out of the stronger upper winds but reduced the true airspeed, causing some very long crossing times. Thirteen hours was average but fourteen hours or more could be experienced. The crew bunks were useful. The navigator would go off duty once we reached the Canadian coastline, and navigation was then pilot -controlled by use of the radio ranges, VORs, and beacons. We found the weather radar to be a wonderful asset. A teleprinter was installed close to the crew bunks. This proved to be most useful in providing weather reports, reducing our radio workload substantially. The radio officer had become redundant, and had been replaced by reliable High Frequency Radio Telephony (HF/RT).

This system is still the primary method of communication for all civil aircraft when they are out of range of the land -based VHF stations. For many years pilots have asked air line s, governments, and ICAO to introduce a satellite-based system. This, at last, seems to be accepted as a needed expense. Direct pilot-to-controller communication will replace the existing oceanic set-up where radio operators relay messages from a congested and sometimes unreliable network of conflicting radio frequencies.

Although the idea of resting on a long flight might have seemed strange to many passengers who may have wished that the captain should always be at the helm, it was essential to ensure that all crew members would be fresh enough to deal with the demands of a diversion to an alternate. This could involve a very high workload in a stressful situation when fuel reserves and weather conditions had to be carefully watched, and when complicated air traffic clearances and routeings could develop.

Feathering

The 'Seven Seas' was not free from engine problems. The cylinders had cast iron scraper rings that wore, causing high oil consumption. This required the carriage of a central auxiliary oil tank from which individual engine oil supplies could be replenished. The shut-down rate per 1,000 hours flown was very high. My personal experience during my time on the type included twelve three-engine landings, for a variety of causes. One particular case was interesting, when we were over Gander on the way to London, at 21,000 ft, using high blower supercharging. The night was very black, although a few Aurora Borealis shafts were visible to the north. I was in the left seat, and the captain was in the passenger compartment visiting the customers. There was a sudden thump. The manifold pressure on Number 1 engine had fallen substantially, to a level reflecting loss of supercharging. We had been warned that this would be a sign of blower failure, and that it could probably mean contamination of the oil system by metal fragments. These would block the oil system that controlled the operation of the propeller feathering circuit. Unless there was an immediate selection of feathering, to streamline the propeller blades, we could expect loss of control, and an over-speeding propeller. There had been enough incidents involving over-speeds to warrant extreme care. A runaway propeller could reach very high rpm, and create enough aerodynamic drag to reduce range and threaten loss of control. The best way to alleviate the condition was to descend to a low-level, if possible, which would reduce the speed and loads. Despite this there was a distinct risk that the propeller assembly could detach, and whirl away, or towards, the aircraft, depending on the side of the failure. A suggested procedure existed that recommended imparting energy to throw the assembly clear deliberately. This involved pushing the aircraft nose down or nose up to use gyroscopic effect just before the assembly broke off. This naturally required talent to spot the appropriate moment. At night this was easier, as the heat generated by the high rpm would show up as red-or white-hot around the reduction gear assembly behind the propeller.

With all this in mind I placed my thumb on the feathering button, and as I began to press it, found the flight engineer's finger helping me. Later, the strip-down of the engine revealed failure of the supercharger gear train, and a contaminated oil system. We had been lucky to avoid a runaway, and certain damage to the engine, if not to the airframe, or other engines.

Spacial phenomena

One dawn landing at Prestwick in 1957 will always be remembered. After parking the aircraft outside the Orangefield hotel, and as the passengers disembarked down the steps, I was suddenly conscious that one or two were looking skywards. The Soviets had launched Sputnik on 4 October and the world was suddenly a smaller place. Tracking across the sky right above our heads was a bright pinpoint of light, moving slowly and deliberately. The space race had begun.

It is now also possible to understand a strange happening to us when crossing the Newfoundland coastline at 21,000 feet on the way to London. Shortly after passing over Gander the dark night rapidly changed colour to display a rapidly shifting ray pattern typical of the usual aurora seen in northern or southern latitudes. The unusual aspect of this display was that it became blood red, and so widespread that much of the sky seemed to be that colour. We called Gander on the radio, but had no contact. All radio frequencies were inoperative. We were isolated in the midst of an unknown phenomenon, and remained that way for more than two hours.

At this stage of the cold war, with squadrons of B-47 jet bombers stationed in the UK. and relations deteriorating between east and west, we quite often considered where to fly should 'the bomb' be dropped. Uncertainty is the enemy of equanimity. Much later we learned that this event was caused by the deliberate discharge of metallic debris by a US rocket, which found its way into the radiation belt since called the

Van Allen, generating excessive electromagnetic radiation in the visible spectrum. All I can say is that it scared me.

The Windy City

Our service to Chicago was via Montreal and Detroit to the busy O'Hare airport. We left Detroit one morning in July, after a short transit. The weather was appalling over the whole area of mid and eastern North America, with heavy rain, thunder storms, and flooding. Arriving overhead at O'Hare we found that they were using only one runway, with one radio beacon serviceable, and using one radio frequency. Starting a holding pattern at 21,000 feet we worked our way down by 1,000 foot steps through torrential rain and turbulence, eventually starting an approach with a reported crosswind of 30 knots for landing. Breaking out of cloud at 300 feet we were amazed to see the flooding, which extended for many miles. The excellent handling qualities of the aircraft helped to ease the situation. Returning next afternoon we overflew Detroit and Montreal directly to Prestwick, avoiding the severe weather.

American journeys

Flights across the US were interesting. The air traffic control clearances issued by ground control at Idlewild were long, detailed, and spoken at inexcusable speed. Today this is replaced mostly by 'cleared as filed,' with a short supplementary departure routeing. We needed a sharp pencil, and sharper ears to avoid asking for repeated instructions. After weaving around the lower level airways we would reach our cruise level, and relative peace. Ground radar was in use to monitor progress along the airways, and to provide assistance when we needed to skirt around heavy weather. Two pilots and a flight engineer comprised the crew on thcsc internal flights, the first time that BOAC had adopted this configuration. It worked very well.

Some long detours were occasionally needed when crossing the mid-western and western sections of the country. One day we flew 200 miles due south, with the help of several controllers, to find a gap in an active frontal line of very heavy cloud, before breaking through to cross the Rockies. Low cloud and fog can cover San Francisco and travelling depressions from the Pacific can bring heavy rain and high winds.

San Francisco was a good source of passenger traffic, and loads were heavy. We stayed at the Clift Hotel, a pleasant and dignified establishment close to the market square, but stopovers were brief, as we took the same aircraft eastbound next morning. Average flight time from New York was nine and a quarter hours, with the return flight taking about eight hours. The sight of the Golden Gate Bridge standing out above the rolling fog and low cloud banks during an early morning departure was spectacular to our unfamiliar eyes.

We also ran a daily flight from New York to Bermuda, again using the three-man crew. This was a three-hour journey. Initially we flew the round trip, but were soon scheduled to slip for 24 hours. Kindley Field was still controlled by the US forces. Returning to the island colony after an interval of nine years recalled memories of Tudors and another era. But the crosswinds were still there, and we still used the island-holding reserve-fuel flight planning technique.

I think that the decision to adopt a 24-hour slip pattern was reasoned on the basis of crew duty times, and their meshing with the pattern of services ex-Idlewild, but I have a shrewd idea that a factor was the pressure by some Captains to partake of the golf available at the renowned Mid Ocean Club. We were accommodated in the clubhouse, and had free access to the course. The head professional was Archie Compston, in his semi-retirement, and it was sometimes possible to arrange a round with him. On one occasion I was crewed with a much-decorated ex-Coastal Command captain who, in the later stages of the Second World War, had the unique privilege of being allowed to choose his own operational patrol areas, and had sunk two submarines. He was an exceptional pilot, and had a wonderful sense of humour, treating his crews with civility and understanding. He could also be very irascible, especially with the airline traffic staff. Woe betide anyone who presented a load-and-balance trim sheet containing an error. Strong words would be issued in apparent anger. After the culprit left the flight deck he would turn and grin disarmingly at me without comment.

Bermuda was also the place where my airline career almost ended. We had eventually revised the schedule to cut out the night stop, which was replaced by a two-hour transit. After landing in the usual twenty-five-knot wind I left the aircraft by the front steps, crossing under the nose to reach the airport buildings. As I passed under the fuselage behind the nose-wheel a drop of hydraulic fluid blew into my left eye from a small drain spout protruding below the metal skin. There was an immediate sharp pain and reaction. The DC-7C hydraulic system used the first generation of non-flammable Skydrol fluid known to be very dangerous to the eyes. We carried a small kit to wash out the eyes in the event of contamination. I ran into the aircraft, the stewardess found the kit, and I spent the next hour alternately flushing the eye and using the antidote. I declared myself fit for the return flight but perhaps I should have consulted a doctor. My eye (and a 100 per cent fit pilot) was more important than an on time departure.

Career moves

The Britannia 102 was now in full operation on African routes, having overcome the unusual engine icing problem that had delayed entry into service. The Britannia 312 was now available to take over on the premier New York and San Francisco routes. There were also plans to start a trans-Pacific route via Honolulu to Japan, Australia, and New Zealand. The industry had introduced tourist fares in 1952, but the real boost in traffic occurred in 1958, after economy class and even cheaper fares were introduced. This led to the introduction of two-class seating in our aircraft.

The new Comet 4 was also about to enter service. Development of this redesigned successor to the ill-fated Comet 1 had involved a complete re-examination of the aircraft and its operation. BOAC had ordered 19 of these aircraft in 1955 and to hasten crew training and obtain operational experience with the Rolls-Royce Avon engines, the airline acquired two Comet 2Es. These were specially modified Comet 2s, fitted with a pair of Avon 118s of 7,300 pounds thrust in the inner positions and the Avon RA 29 Mk 524 engines destined for the Comet 4 in the outboard positions. 3,500 engine hours were flown during 1957 and 1958 by these aircraft on a series of flights between London and Beirut, followed by flights across the Atlantic to Gander. Twenty-one ex-Comet 1 captains crewed this development programme, as the airline raced to introduce the first civil jet airline service across the Atlantic.

Pan American Airways was planning to start Boeing 707 services on 19 October 1958, but the first BOAC Comet 4 services left London and New York on 4 October. We were back in the jet era again, this time permanently. Our DC-7Cs continued to serve Montreal and New York, and began services from New York to Nassau, Montego Bay, and Kingston. I was hoping to be transferred to the Comets to fly jets once more, but knew that if this took place I would probably lose any chance of promotion in the near future. The airline had also ordered Boeing 707s, which would soon begin to enter service. Command vacancies on the Seven Seas would be created for those of us with the appropriate seniority, as may of our captains would opt for the big jet.

The promotion blockage that had been caused by the absorption of so many BSAA captains was the cause of much unrest in the ranks of co-pilots. Traffic had grown but this had been achieved without an increase in total aircraft strength, as the newer types were larger and faster. Many of these co-pilots were in fact contemporary with the ex-services captains employed immediately after the war, and had begun to worry about total earnings and pensions as their ages advanced. Their main concern, as with pilots in today's airlines, was progress to the left seat and command. An extended salary scale was introduced, together with a new intermediate Senior First Officer rank, and a system was created that categorised individual command suitability, based on personal records and recommendations by management. Provided the criteria for promotion were met, seniority could be notionally acquired, to become effective after obtaining a command. This went some way to assuage the concerns, and had the advantage for the airline that there was no immediate cost, yet introduced an incentive to keep standards at a high level. Unfortunately the administration of the assessment for command suitability proved to be fallible. Different methods and opportunities existed on the various fleets of aircraft, and this led to some long-standing grievances causing BALPA many problems.

During this period there was a need to recruit and train replacement co-pilots. The RAF was once again the source of these pilots, mostly of ex-National Service short-term pilots with jet experience, albeit limited to a few hundred hours flying Meteors. They found themselves engaged on a long flight-navigator's course, as they were destined to serve initially as third pilot/navigators on the Boeing 707 or VC10. The days of the specialist navigator were drawing to a close, but did not finally end until the mid-1960s with the withdrawal of the older aircraft types.

Before one could be promoted there were still some hurdles to jump. I was scheduled on several complete trips, 'in command under supervision'. This involved acting as captain, taking all decisions, and doing all the flying, at the same time being assessed by a supervisory captain. This was a test of ability and personality, and could be quite stressful. Especially if, as some times happened, there was personal incompatibility. Some supervisory captains were very helpful and constructive, but others could be totally uncommunicative. Feedback of progress and assessment was imperfect. No news was usually good news.

Passing out

I was faced with a dilemma one afternoon in Bermuda. The trip was my last one before impending promotion. So far things had gone well, but wherever we had been, in a fairly long and busy itinerary, there had been an intense searching of my personal values and background. The supervisory captain was a former chief pilot, 6 feet 6 inches tall, very positive and directly competitive, with piercing light blue eyes. He tried me at squash, swimming, bridge, chess, and conversation. On this particular afternoon he suggested that we take the club's 14 foot dinghy out for a sail in the harbour, having discovered that I had used it before. Boats were swinging on their moorings as we whisked away from the jetty with me at the helm. Constant activity was needed to avoid hitting other boats. It was exhilarating, and called for many swift manoeuvres in a very gusty 20 knot wind. After about ten minutes of near misses I decided to call it quits. On reaching the jetty, without damage, my companion said that he would now take the helm. We set off, in whirligig fashion, skirting by a few tossing sail boats in a wild ride across the disturbed waters. Facing aft and dealing with the end of a sheet that seemed to have lost its way I was amazed to see an expression of utter horror on the helmsman's face. We were within a few feet of a gleaming white hull, and hit the central part with such force that the impact left a neat imprinted shape of our bow profile some two feet above the waterline. Most of the remaining afternoon was spent on reporting and negotiation. I left the matter of compensation in his safe hands after my offer was refused. The rest of the trip back to London was conducted with considerable restraint.

Promotion

After a final handling check at base with Captain Peter Mains-Smith, I received a letter advising of my promotion to captain, and with the accrued seniority, I would be half-way up the incremental salary scale. The Corporation had decided to introduce a scheme which involved promoting two pilots for each current command vacancy, which would require each new captain, now called a 'Captain X,' to fly half of the time as co-pilot, until the time that vacancies appeared to make this unnecessary. This enlightened move helped the bulge situation, and also created a pool of trained commanders for the expected expansion and the retirement of many old-timers.

Oil over troubled water

My first trip as a BOAC commander was on 8 September 1959, flying a DC-7C scheduled service from London to Prestwick and Idlewild. I had served a long apprenticeship, and felt qualified to take on the responsibility. The period spent by co-pilots before obtaining their captaincy can vary substantially. In most major airlines this is limited by a rigid seniority and bidding system. The vacancies depend on age structure of the pilots, retirement age, and the state of the international or national economy. Many airlines use a system that can bump a pilot down from command and up again, depending on vacancies. This is usually implemented only if there is complete acceptance of the principle that a pilot may exercise his company seniority to achieve a vacancy. BOAC did not use the bumping system, nor was there any bidding system that allowed the knock-on effect of double-training. The move to captaincy was for a probationary period in the first instance but was then permanent.

After leaving Prestwick we climbed to 8,000 feet for a long crossing to New York, a cruise procedure calculated to defeat the strong headwinds. I concentrated on obtaining some late weather updates, as there was an active depression moving through the US eastern seaboard. The flight engineer had advised that the technical log showed two engines were consuming oil at high rates. We were used to the Wright engine problem, but it did require watching carefully. Many times we had arrived after a long flight with one engine close to the minimum permissible oil quantity, even after using the transfer tank, which held 26 US gallons of oil and gasoline mix (to protect the viscosity). Our route on this occasion took us quite close to the southern tip of Greenland which I watched carefully on the weather radar, as we were well below the huge ice-capped plateau.

The oil consumption was being monitored by our flight engineer, and he advised me that the two engines were consuming oil at an increasing rate. Despite the use of our transfer tank, we would need to stop both engines at least two hours before the estimated time of arrival in New York. Each engine was using more than three gallons of oil per hour. We decided that the best option was to stop one engine, while it still had enough oil to be restarted in the event of need, and to concentrate the transfer on the remaining rogue. I also decided to land at Boston to fill up with oil. We still had plenty of fuel, but the long range of our Seven Seas was impaired by the rapidly wearing piston rings.

After a swift transit at Boston's Logan airport, we departed on the short flight to Idlewild. As we were turning onto the final approach close to the Scotland lightship, and lining up to land on runway 4R, the flight engineer apologetically advised me that the engine analyser showed two inoperative plugs in one cylinder of number two engine. This called for a precautionary shutdown to avoid engine damage.

This was my first command trip, and was about to set a record of two three-engined landings on the first day. Each would require an incident report, and be subject to investigation by both the airline and the regulators. We were less than five minutes from landing. I throttled the affected engine to idle setting without feathering the propeller and carried out my second three-engined landing of the morning without the need to initiate yet another report, as we had not actually stopped the engine. No damage was risked despite the inoperative plugs, as we avoided using any power.

When we had parked the aircraft and walked across to the BOAC flight planning and operations office, it was possible to meet the crew who would be taking the aircraft back to London. I was a bit dismayed when I saw that the captain was Peter Mains-Smith (the check captain who had signed me off on my pre-command flight test), feeling vulnerable to his reaction that we had perhaps made too much of the problems, especially as it was my first trip in command. The plugs were changed, and they set off on a direct flight to London. On my return to Heathrow I went into the fleet office to discuss these events. When mildly complaining that there should be a better procedure to limit high oil consuming engines to one per aircraft, I discovered that Peter Mains-Smith had been forced to land at Shannon to top up the oil, and that my concerns were accepted.

With the freedom conferred by promotion, which was quite delightful, came a degree of responsibility that required continuation of what I had learnt from my peers, adding the application of my own personal experience. As I was contemporary with most of the other crew members I found it easier to understand and relate to their problems and needs than some of the older-time captains. This helped to produce a pleasant working relationship. There were no illusions that this honeymoon period would last, however, for we were recruiting many new pilots who would perhaps regard us as dinosaurs until they discovered that we had something to offer. Rapid promotion to command of a large public transport aircraft, without any experience as a co-pilot, denied many post-war pilots the opportunity to acquire an understanding of the need to train and bring on new personnel in a positive atmosphere.

Soon after promotion, during a social function, when asked to declare my occupation, I was told that I did not look old enough for such a job. My response was that in few occupations did the apprenticeship take sixteen years.

The 1960s

In 1961, we were able to take our first real family holiday, a camping tour of France as far as Provence, before returning to plan the construction of a new house. Conditions in England were at last easing to allow such things, and a growing prosperity was also filling airline seats with a hint of the mass market yet to come. The Comet 4 was now in service on all our routes except the Atlantic, replaced by the Boeing 707-436, a Rolls-Royce Conway-powered version of this successful new type. The Comet 4 did not have enough range or payload to compete with other airlines using the larger Boeing or the Douglas DC-8, but remained in BOAC service until 1966, serving the eastern routes very successfully — mostly over routes where its smaller size was an advantage on the more thinly-travelled segments.

Monkey business

My position on the seniority list was low enough to deny me any bidding rights for captaincy on the jets. Our DC-7Cs were still intensively used. A couple had been converted to freighters, with thirteen pallets that were pre-loaded and shunted manually down the fuselage tube, running on rails. The aircraft shuddered and flexed as these were rattled along into place. We could load cargo within the hour and ran a scheduled transatlantic freight service with success. Much argument ensued about who would provide food for the crew during our long duty periods. The airline did not wish to add a steward to the crew, but succumbed to the request after he also took on the job of purser. There was little space for him as the cargo hold extended almost to the original front door.

We soon began to carry animals of every shape and size, including many monkeys that were destined for laboratories in the US. The freight conversion had a small rest compartment in the rear of the aircraft, close to the tail cone. A three inch high metal channel had been installed across the floor between the cargo and rest areas, probably designed to protect the rest area and rear equipment from contamination. On one occasion I was inspecting the cargo, dodging the malevolent and deliberate spraying by some monkeys, when I saw that the floor was awash with slopping urine, small waves of it running across the smooth surface as it ran against the metal channel. I made a mental note to start any climb carefully, and to attempt gentle deceleration after landing. The smell could last for long periods and permeate clothing.

We were always very concerned about weight and balance, as

many loads involved heavy machinery. Such things as ships' propeller shafts, aircraft engines and other large items needed to be secured very carefully. We were supposed to be protected from these things suddenly arriving without invitation on the flight deck, in the event of an abrupt stop, by the fitting of what was known as a 9g net. This I viewed with some caution. These aircraft could be reconverted to passenger use with relatively little work, but were then handicapped by the heavier floor structure, not to mention monkey fragrance, and a big freight door.

Paris again

Our capacity was used to supplement the BEA service from London Heathrow, to Paris Le Bourget, for a few months in the summers of 1960 and 1961. BEA was introducing a fleet of Comet 4Bs, a clipped-wing but longer-fuselaged version of the 4, but the airline was still short of aircraft to cope with increasing demand in peak periods. This use of the DC-7C, the longest range piston-engined airliner, on one of the shortest international routes was an example of ultimate expediency. We found it to be an interesting diversion from the usual routine across the Atlantic. Occasionally we would use the new airport at Orly. I found it nostalgic, remembering my encounter with the Languedoc in 1947. The DC-7C was fast at low-level, and we were able to beat the existing schedule by a good margin, despite it being devised for the Vickers Vanguard, a four-engined turboprop that was, astonishingly, built to compete with the Britannia.

Charters

We continued to run the scheduled service to Montreal, and freighter services to New York, but started flying charters to new destinations. These were mainly to bring immigrants from Barbados and Jamaica. Complete families came on board holding a few personal possessions, clad in their best suits or dresses, which were unsuitable for the rigours of a British winter. They broke out into communal song, mostly of religious content, as we flew them via New York to an uncertain future. There are many tales of how they were fleeced by unscrupulous taxi drivers, who dumped them in London suburbs described as Manchester or Birmingham. We must have carried many thousands of these innocent and aspiring people, on a swift return across the ocean over which so many of their ancestors had travelled arduously for many weeks in chains.

Havana

In September 1960 we were sent on a trip from New York to Havana, where Fidel Castro was consolidating his power. This was very different from the days under Batista's rule, and our BSAA services. This time there was no stopover, only an hour's transit while we boarded a full load of Cubans who were leaving the country permanently, either voluntarily or compulsorily. They had no baggage, only the clothes they wore. Most of their personal possessions had been confiscated, including watches and jewellery.

Armed guards in olive drab fatigues carried sub-machine guns at the ready, and watched with suspicion as I filed the necessary flight plan for Kingston, where we would exchange this load of emigrants for another load of Jamaicans bound for London. We were not allowed to start engines until a special sign was given by the guard commander. The hostility could have been sliced into visible portions. At the last minute armed guards appeared and escorted two distraught people off the aircraft, waving us to close the door. I was relieved to lift off and head south.

Turning circles

Many runways are 150 feet wide. Some are not paralleled by taxiways for their full length. This requires aircraft to enter and backtrack before lining up to depart. The danger involved, when this is coupled with low visibility and imperfect communication between aircraft and controllers, was demonstrated by a terrible accident in Tenerife, a collision of two 747s, which killed hundreds of people. Another aspect of this problem was demonstrated when we were scheduled to fly a charter from Bermuda to Buffalo. There were two sections to this large charter, one flown by a company Britannia 312, and one by our Seven Seas. The captain of the Britannia issued a challenge that they would be first on the ground in Buffalo. A fair degree of competitiveness existed between the two fleets. The Britannia was indeed faster than the Seven Seas at most levels, but we were able to outpace it during climb and descent. We departed in rapid succession after receiving identical clearances, with our altitude higher. The weather was poor on arrival, although reasonable enough for landing.

On transferring to the initial approach control we were instructed to join a holding pattern because of 'company traffic being unable to clear the active runway.' Apparently the Britannia had missed the last available turn-off, and had gone on to the runway extension, where there was no taxiway. A 180° turn was needed, but the Britannia apparently was unable to manoeuvre within the paved surface available, and had to be towed in to the ramp. When we finally arrived, and went to the American Airlines crew room, we found the other crew there, looking quite embarrassed. We cancelled the wager, calling it quits.

BALPA

Since the Comet 1 downfall I had been involved in following up how de Havilland, BOAC, and the government agencies were taking account of the lessons we had all learned. This was possible through the technical liaison channels that BALPA had established with the Air Registration Board, the airline, and the Ministry. As a member of the pilots' local council I was gradually drawn into a wide range of activity. The pilots' association was at last engaged in talks with both BEA and

BOAC to secure the principle of jet pay, but was unable to obtain any progress through the National Joint Council for Civil Air Transport, a forum that had a permanent bureaucracy which seemed inflexible, and unable to break the deadlock of governmental control or interference. The result of this was a reference of our claim to the Industrial Court for a ruling. Preparation of our brief for this hearing was made more complex by the fact that BEA was now flying the Comet 4B. Their pilots could see no reason why they should receive a lower salary than those in BOAC, despite the existence of our North Atlantic pay, or the need for co-pilots to obtain navigation licences.

I was part of a team that helped to advise our solicitors in their preparation of the brief for our barrister and his junior, to present at the court hearing. Although normal legal etiquette precludes any direct contact between barrister and client, on this occasion we were served differently. The junior barrister was the younger brother of a captain in our group. We had some hope that the background and complexities of our case would be put forward to the hearing without the essentials being lost by an unbriefed and busy principal barrister. We had retained an ex-Solicitor-General in the Labour government for this task. The BEA pilot group had retained the services of Roy Jenkins, a consultant who was well-known later for his subsequent career in government and two political parties, the European Union, and latterly as an eminent political historian.

The Industrial Court was close to the Houses of Parliament, and the old building seemed to possess an aura of conflict, a blend between a prison and a hospital. The hearing was expected to take a full day, involving submission of our case, questions from the appointed chairman, and responses from the airline corporations.

The morning session soon demonstrated that our expensive leading QC was misinformed about some vital aspects of our case, and that he had not put enough time into reading it. Our faith in the full understanding of the case by the junior being passed on to his leader was unjustified. During the lunch break our team went downstairs to a small dark room that was reserved for 'employees.' The leader produced his briefcase from which he extracted, not the expected copy of our brief, but a large packet of sandwiches. We spent the next fifty minutes setting him straight with a copy of the brief, and also consumed most of his sandwiches while he listened. The afternoon went more successfully.

The result of this claim was a partial victory, leaving a debris of anomaly and ill will littered across our contractual relations for many years.

The author gained his first command on the DC-7C. 'With the freedom conferred by promotion, which was quite delightful, came a degree of responsibility that required continuation of what I had learnt from my peers.'

The Comet 4

The Boeing 707 was in full service by the time our DC-7C operations began to wind down. My seniority as captain was still not enough to bid for a 707 vacancy, so I made a successful bid for the Comet. This meant that our home life would change yet again, and I would return to the African and eastern routes. The last trip on the Seven Seas involved an empty freighter from Montreal's Dorval airport to Idlewild. I was regretful at having to leave the Atlantic and North American routes, and also the DC-7C, all by now very familiar.

The new training course contained twelve pilots, and was conducted in the expanded training centre at Cranebank, a couple of miles from Heathrow Airport. As I had been in constant touch with the Comet development, and completed various follow-up courses, it was agreed that a self-study regime would be approved before taking the ARB examination. This freed up a course vacancy for one of the airline's medicos, who was an ex-RAF flying doctor. He went on to fly as a line co-pilot, gaining valuable insight and experience. After a few weeks buried in the books, plus various visits and help from the flight-engineering training section, I was able to pass the examination, and a special check-set of questions set by the company.

The aircraft was very different from a Comet 1 or unmodified 2. Problem areas had been carefully addressed. Structurally there was thicker fuselage skin, with circular window cut-outs, while more conventional copper based metal alloy was now used for construction. This, together with other steps, increased the fatigue life of the wing-root joints by a factor of about 50. The inboard engines were turned out away from the fuselage to reduce exhaust efflux batter. A revised electrical system provided much more protection. Fuel heaters ensured that engine supply would be maintained. Wind screens were heated by gold-film electrical wire circuits. There was a revised and more flexible autopilot. A two-speed elevator control gearing was selectable to minimise structural risks at higher airspeed. The Rolls-Royce Avon RA 29 Mk.524 engines had axial flow compressors, with more than twice the thrust (10,500 pounds). The airframe and engine intake de-icing systems were now very efficient. An ice detection system worked extremely well, and even had a small dummy airfoil vane that could be seen by the pilot to indicate ice contamination. A distance-measuring system was fitted although many overseas airports did not have matching equipment. The biggest bonus was the weather radar, which was often also used for identifying such things as desert pipelines, and cities, so that descent points could be judged precisely. Reverse thrust was available on the outboard engines, and Dunlop Maxaret anti-skid brakes were fitted, together with brake cooling fans. Stall warning was provided by a stick shaker. Seating was 60 first class, or 76 tourist class. Altogether, this was a far, far different aircraft from the innovative and trailblazing Comet 1.

One development was not entirely welcomed by many pilots. The Smiths Flight System replaced the old Sperry Zero Reader as the basic flight director. This was also installed in the Britannia, and involved some display orientation novelties that caused head-scratching at times. The indications and inputs were, however, well devised, and had nice rates of response. They could be coupled to the autopilot, which would produce an ILS approach to 300 feet above the runway. The demonstrated maximum crosswind for a manual landing was 28 knots. Remarkably, the power/weight relationship was such that an engine failure at cruise level would not require any descent, and, in fact, shutting down one engine could increase the range.

The Comet 4 simulator had limited motion capability, but was otherwise similar to the aircraft in many respects. There was no visual simulation. After fifteen hours of handling, and another fifteen hours acting as co-pilot, we were sufficiently advanced to begin flying. The aircraft was delightful to handle, precise, smooth, and overpowered. A comprehensive syllabus included many non-standard landing configurations. I was most impressed with both the training and the aircraft, compared to the Comet 1 conversion course I had undertaken more than nine years previously. After the usual flight check, and a visit to the Ministry for licence endorsement, it was time for my first trip under supervision. This retraced many familiar ports of call, all the way to Tokyo. Although there were many changes of procedure, I remained familiar with the weather and general environment, feeling comfortable with the new aircraft and operation.

The concept of noise abatement was becoming widespread, and new procedures were being devised by sensitive cities. Hong Kong was always interesting, still needing a precise ADF instrument approach when landing to the southeast in bad weather. We ended up at low-level in heavy rain, passing Green Island, looking for Stonecutters Island and then the 'chequerboard' before a last minute turn towards the runway. This unique landing aid was exactly that: a vivid warning in the form of a chequerboard-rectangle, coloured red and white, set against the last hill before turning right, southeast, into Kai Tak, after flying over the rooftops (and almost between them) of the Kowloon apartment buildings.

The reassuring aspect with this aircraft was its performance should one wish to go around again. Clearing the local mountains would be no problem. Visibility was now good through the improved windscreens, and the Comet 4 felt very solid and stable in the turbulence created by strong surface winds. Because of the 25° leading edge wing sweep-back; and the early onset of compressibility effect, the cruise speed was limited to Mach 0.75 which, when compared to the Boeing 707's Mach 0.82, was slower than desirable for a competitive airline. This meant that we would need a replacement at some time in the near future, if we were to stay competitive with the so-called big jets as the traffic built up. A further order for Boeings, and/or the Vickers VC10, was pending. We were still suffering from the delays brought about by the Comet 1 era. However, the aircraft could be flown into and out of some small airports, and was very flexible, proving popular with passengers. The longer fuselage and many differences had made the series 4 Comet a greatly improved aircraft from the series 1, although it was interesting for me to sit in the pilot's seat, and see the identical nose profile, as if the clock had been turned back. Improvements in the galley installation now produced a better standard of catering, but the ratio of toilets to persons on board had started its downward progress, a trend which is continuing today in the latest and shiniest types.

The additional range was a blessing, although the carriage of fuel in outboard pod tanks was a compromise that the de Havilland designers had adopted reluctantly. The engine pods of the DC-8 and the 707 provided relief by wing-attachment loading, which empty pod tanks could not match. The original decision to place engines inside the wing and close to the fuselage resulted in a clean wing, and good handling when an outboard engine failed, but has not been repeated in subsequent airliner designs, although the Soviets used the idea in their Tupolev Tu-104.

After another trip, this time to Singapore, I gained my operations certificate. We were flying into every Middle Eastern airport, or so it seemed. The African routes were extended and the The Far Eastern route pattern was also very comprehensive. Services to South America had also started again. By February 1960, route mileage was more than 70,000, and the weekly seat mileage total exceeded 23,000,000. Load factors were significantly higher than those of the competition. The aircraft was reliable, with the Avon 524 engines' unscheduled overhaul rate proving to be extremely low.

We ran some fast flights with few stops, and others which puddle-jumped into every possible place. As may be imagined, this range of destinations brought crews into contact with some very different conditions of air traffic control, weather, en route terrain, and local culture. There were many considerations, one of which was the constantly changing political situation and the safety of various destinations. The airline monitored the changing scene in each trouble spot but was usually unable to forecast trouble in time to withdraw any crew that happened to be slipping there. Many stories were told of individuals being close to, or involved in, disturbances. In 1962 Syria had only recently broken away from the United Arab Republic: an expanded Egypt headed by Colonel Nasser; and Damascus was subject to fluctuating incidents of violent demonstrations. One of our crews was having a snack lunch in a restaurant close to the city centre when a hail of gunfire was heard. Stepping outside, they found several bodies lying in the street, which was otherwise deserted.

Tehran trouble

The crew of our Comet 4s initially included a navigator, although the installation of a Doppler guidance system eventually eliminated him except for the longer oceanic segments. Tehran is surrounded by high ground, and the weather can be very poor at times, requiring a long instrument approach.

We were on our way east one night in March 1964 when there was heavy cloud over the area. Following the required tracks shown on the letdown procedure required very careful cross-checking of timing, and bearings from the non-directional radio beacons that were used for alignment. Another airline had crashed during the previous month while attempting the procedure and so we were alerted to the possibility of false and misleading radio bearings. We adopted the recommended method, using our two ADF sets, retuning them to obtain confirming cross bearings as we approached each turning point, descending in the black, gusty, and wet cloud.

The navigator began to query our procedure, causing a distraction, and introducing uncertainty. After more careful double-checking with the co-pilot, we were confident that we had not strayed from the approved procedure, and used the weather radar to give a rough check of our proximity to the higher ground. I was relieved when we broke cloud nicely lined up with the runway.

Touch and go

After landing, I had a quiet chat with the navigator who revealed that he had been a crew member on one of our Comet 4s that had almost been destroyed when landing at Nairobi. A mistake in setting the landing pilot's altimeter millibar datum to 938, instead of 839, had caused it to over-read by nearly 3,000 feet. The sight of runway lighting ahead warned them that they were very low, and full power was applied - but too late. As the descent rate was stopped they actually touched down and ran along the ground briefly. The wheel marks were later found in the game park.

Bird strikes

Birds are a hazard to aircraft. A high-flying Viscount was brought down by a migrating goose in Canada and there have been many cases of multiple strikes causing engine or structural damage. I have been hit on five occasions. One of these was during a Comet 4 take-off at Tripoli, when a pair of kite hawks rose into our path as we were on the runway approaching decision speed, after which we would be committed to become airborne. One bird whirled across my vision and over the nose, and the other walloped into number four engine, causing a huge cough and bang. We went straight into the abandoned take-off procedure, stopping well within the available runway. The bird had caused a compressor failure, damaging many of the Avon's blades.

The phenomenon is common in southern Asia, where birds of the kite hawk and vulture families have also been seen at great heights. The problem has not yet been solved, despite resident falcons, gunfire, patrols, and amplified recordings. A British Airways 767 hit a group of mallards during take-off at

Vancouver in 1997, and this caused power failure of one of the two engines. More research will perhaps bring information on how to protect aircraft, particularly at seaside airports close to main migration flight paths. Meanwhile, many large engines now have fan blades that can withstand impact from large birds without losing power.

Problems

The Comet 4 was such a good aircraft that it was easy to extract performance that was not exactly intended by the manufacturer nor by the certification authority. Having joined the fleet more than three years after its introduction, in 1958, I was very conscious that there was a degree of élan and confidence amongst the crews. This worthwhile characteristic may have contributed to a series of events that was nearly disastrous. The first personal experience I had of this was when being route-checked. An annual check was required which directed a route-check captain to witness a full day's flying. The check would involve all aspects of the operation, and served to maintain standardisation and feed back problems to management. Many route-check captains were senior and well respected, positive, and helpful. They were supernumerary, and not allowed to interfere with the captain or crew unless safety was threatened.

We were en route to Khartoum on a lovely clear night, with unlimited visibility, close to the distance from the airport when descent would be started. I was tapped on the shoulder by the check captain, who was observing from the jump seat. He suggested that we should delay the descent, and he would tell me how to fly a 40° flap profile. He thought that we could cut the time by as much as five minutes if we waited until we had 60 miles to go. I was a little doubtful about adopting this non-standard and unauthorised procedure, although it was within the permitted performance envelope; but curiosity prevailed, supported by a desire to avoid upsetting him by a refusal. We slowed up to the limiting 170 knots for lowering 40° flap, cancelling the associated undercarriage warning horn. The descent proceeded, accompanied by some slight buffeting, and we lowered the undercarriage at 3,000 feet, establishing a normal approach slope soon afterwards. This all seemed fairly innocuous, and we did save time, but I was worried about having to repeatedly cancel the insistent warning horn. The air loads on the flap mechanism were sustained over a longish period, and we might be causing wear and tear. The co-pilot told me that many pilots were in fact developing ways to stay up late and come down fast. Use of the air brakes all the way down from cruise level was quite common.

The 1960s witnessed an inevitable change in the make-up and experience levels of the pilot group within BOAC. The pre-Second World War generation had retired, and most of the wartime generation had moved into the left-hand seat as captains. The right-hand seat was now filled with pilots who were mainly from the RAF with limited total hours, albeit on jets such as the Gloster Meteor, having served their two-years of National Service in that capacity. They were good and they were keen, taking to the Comet 4 with enthusiasm.

The procedure of rapid descent from high altitude was fostered at this time by a series of published instrument letdown procedures titled 'Jet Penetration'. These were similar to the common military recovery procedure for jet fighters. Requirements of traffic separation and local conditions today have made these impractical.

Close encounters of a Comet kind

Our normal approach to Rome from the north was via a radio beacon, before transition to another beacon and the ILS beam, to line up with a runway at Fiumicino. The descent was usually rapid as the controllers knew that we could descend swiftly. The Comet 4 was called to show its strength one night when arriving from London. The first approach beacon was on the same frequency as a more powerful transmission elsewhere in Europe, and this caused the ADF indications to be deflected, with the effect that the approach was diverted inland over rising ground. Destruction of the aircraft was averted by the sight of trees ahead, lit up by the aircraft's lights. Maximum power was applied, but the Comet struck the upper parts of several trees before regaining height and landing safely. The Avons were credited with burning some chopped-up branches quite successfully, without any problems of indigestion.

Another event was further evidence of this strength. A visual approach was being made towards Madrid airport at night when the aircraft hit an unlit ridge of high ground about six miles from the runway. This severely damaged the undercarriage and hit one of the under-wing crash-switch levers that automatically shut off fuel to both engines on that side. A successful belly landing was then made at the airport. After repairs, the aircraft was flown back to London and re-entered service.

Rome was the scene of another event, involving a rapid descent and a landing with the gear still up. The touchdown was so smooth that the cabin crew were initially unaware of the situation. When the main cabin door was opened from outside the stewardess was amazed to be confronted with a face to-face encounter with a fireman. This incident led to investigations into operational standards and procedures.

Another instance of belly contact with a runway occurred at Stansted airport, north of London, where much local flying training was accomplished. During a touch-and-go landing, the gear was raised prematurely, and the aircraft settled back on to the runway. This seemed to be a classic case of confused command interpretation.

Unintentionally it opened up the underside of the Comet 4 and revealed corrosion problems where Redux adhesive had been applied. This led to extensive maintenance work on the fleet. Details of these potential disasters were published in the airline's internal safety-digest publication, with a follow-up of the probable causes. The Comet fleet had begun to acquire an unenviable reputation, and management action was taken to tighten things. Although these were isolated incidents amid a considerable volume of flying by the nineteen aircraft in the fleet, they were taken very seriously, and caused a re-evaluation of operational standards.

Training captaincy

Transfer of pilots to Boeing 707s continued, and a VC10 fleet was being formed. There were vacancies in the Comet Training Unit, as some of the senior training captains were selected for transfer. One or two people had suggested that it might be possible for me to join the Comet unit, which was confirmed after a meeting with the fleet training manager. My background with instrument training in BSAA, and other instructional duties, was perhaps a contributing factor to my selection. Anyway I was pleased with the idea as I enjoyed flying instruction, and knew that the best way to achieve a good knowledge and proficiency was to instruct. There was also a bonus. There would be less time away from the family, although still a considerable amount of route flying.

Ministry indoctrination

The duties of a BOAC training captain included the conversion of pilots on a new type, refresher flying for those who needed this, plus the revalidation of a pilot's type rating and instrument rating. These involved the simulator, now approved for some renewal tests, and the aircraft. The type rating was revalidated every six months, and the instrument rating every year. At these times there was also an opportunity to introduce revisions and new procedures. The training captain was also accompanied by a training flight engineer, and they operated essentially as a team. The training flight engineer was responsible for re-validation of a flight engineer's rating.

On the wings of a dove

Supervision and control of the system began with the Ministry. Approval for the individual training captain to conduct tests and to revalidate licences was delegated after an initial course of instruction had been passed. The Civil Aviation Flying Unit (CAFU), based at Stansted, was staffed by Ministry pilot examiners, and used de Havilland Dove 6 twin-engined aircraft to conduct the instrument rating initial test. The de Havilland Chipmunk was also used to conduct the general flying tests that were required before commercial licences could be issued.

Standards for the initial instrument rating test were stringent. The Dove had to be flown without any assistance, in instrument flight rules conditions, on an airways route, including a holding pattern, instrument let-down procedure, go-around (then called an overshoot), and a non-precision instrument approach. Various other requirements had to be satisfied, including dealing with a simulated engine failure, and instrument malfunction. There was an extensive oral test. This was a far cry from my original visit to the Olley hangar at Croydon in 1946.

I spent four days observing a series of tests, most of which resulted in candidate failure for a variety of causes. Then it was my turn to complete a full initial test, handling the Dove, which was strange to me, despite watching these daily events. The weather was not good, as we flew from Stansted to Birmingham's Elmdon Airport. This was fortunate in one way, as the lurching little aircraft masked my inaccuracies in holding speed and height, and after one and a half hours we were on the ground and I had managed to pass the test.

After a few more educational trips observing a mixture of inexperienced and experienced pilots grappling with these stressful tests, it was my turn to practise conducting a full test on a guinea-pig examiner captain. This brought out many points that would need to be watched if standards were to be maintained. These would have to be applied to the renewal tests that would be conducted on the Comet 4 aircraft and simulator. A final flight involved a comprehensive test as examiner.

Duality of responsibility to the airline and government required that a report of a failure be filed with both. The position of a delegated examiner is delicately poised between a rather slavish adherence to the legal standards set out by the Ministry's regulations, and the more practical needs of the airline.

The Comet 4 simulator was not adequate to replace the aircraft, either for initial conversion training, or landings, but had approval for the renewal of the instrument rating. The simulator sessions lasted four hours, with two pilots, each alternately acting as pilot-in-command and co-pilot. The flight sessions usually required three landings per pilot, customarily flown at Stansted or Bedford, and a short flight from and to Heathrow.

Communication

Air-to-ground communications were still a cause of problems, once outside the range of local VHF, and gave the non-flying pilot a few headaches. The H/F R/T worldwide network, still used today by international carriers, is organised into separate 'families' of frequencies, chosen so that they minimise interference between adjacent geographical areas, but at night radio waves skip vast distances as they bounce off the upper layers of the atmosphere. The amount of traffic can fill the ear with constant cacophony. Attempting to decipher a clearance from ATC can be difficult. The effect of electrical storms and other noise can distort reception. This system is still the primary long-distance communication, although a satellite relay system has long been available. Airlines have been reluctant to introduce that because of expense.

One night, when flying from Bahrain to Calcutta, the co-pilot was taking his turn at flying the segment, and I was using the radio telephone to pass a position report to the control centre in Karachi. Many stations could be heard using the same frequency, including Rangoon, Calcutta, Bombay, and others. Various aircraft were making their calls. In a network, if contact is made with one station, a report can be relayed by ground line to the correct destination, or by another transmission. Mutual help is the policy.

The noise and static on the frequency made it difficult to establish contact, but we eventually received the reply from Karachi to go ahead with the position report, 'words thrice,' a procedure used when reception is very marginal. This rather laborious transmission was completed, but was answered by the Calcutta operator, who read it back for confirmation three times. The skip distance of radio waves between Karachi and Calcutta may have had something to do with the ensuing transmission from the Karachi operator. 'Calcutta Calcutta Calcutta, this is Karachi this is Karachi this is Karachi.'

'Shut up, Shut up, Shut up,' said rather petulantly in the familiarly accented English. Pakistani-Indian relations were strained at the time. This had the desired effect, and Karachi then read back our position report accurately. All was well until we jousted with the airwaves again thirty minutes later.

Water leak over Paris

A night take-off from Heathrow to Rome involved the usual route close to Paris, which could be seen glittering below at our cruising height of 33,000 feet. Over Europe there were constant changes of radio frequency using VHF. In France the sectors were split by altitude levels and geographically. Over Holland, Belgium, and West Germany the proximity of national boundaries required constant changes of control and frequency. The jet age had not brought any improvement in the need to make so many reports, which seemed geared to another era, absorbing time better spent in other duties, such as keeping a good lookout.

We had just made yet another report when the co-pilot's flight instrument display froze and we were left with standby emergency lighting. Luckily the left side VHF continued to work, and I was able to ask for return clearance to Heathrow, as an initial move.

On arrival at Heathrow our passengers were now calmer after a soothing announcement. The problem had been caused by water flowing from a ruptured tank in the forward galley, which had shorted out electrical equipment in an underfloor bay. The batteries were replaced and after three hours we set off again for Rome without further troubles.

We were still staying at the Hotel Quirinale. By now, more than ten years had passed since the Comet 1 days, but the concierge still remembered me as he accepted our passports for the routine police check.

A pyrrhic victory

The reminder of Roman police brought back memories of 1953, and a crew visit to their central headquarters. This was to report the loss of a watch. We had been enjoying a beer in a bar close to the Via Sistina one evening during our three-day slip, and when the bill arrived could not collect enough lire to meet the inflated total. An arrangement was agreed allowing our captain to leave his wrist watch as security, on the basis that we would return next morning with the necessary cash. On arrival the next day we were met by the same waiter who professed complete ignorance of the transaction. The watch was a Rolex Oyster, and worth many times the lire we owed. We were annoyed by this chicanery and decided to report the event. The local police station was off an alleyway behind the Quirinale Palace, close to the hotel, and was a four-storey building in the typical shuttered and flat brick style, well worn, with woodwork needing a coat of paint. As we entered through large double doors the view was dominated by a large dais and desk, behind which sat a policeman, soundly asleep. It was the nodding hour of 1 pm, and the outside temperature was in the mid-eighties. Tactful shuffling and clearing of throats wakened him from his dreams, without embarrassment. Our first difficulty was immediately obvious, as he did not speak a word of English. We were finally able to convince him that a statement was needed, to protect other unwary clients of that bar, if not to recover the watch. This resulted in the appearance of a plain-clothes operative who beckoned us to follow him up three sets of stairs to the top floor. On the way he stopped to enter several rooms, looking for something. This turned out to be an antique typewriter, which was carried in triumph to an airless inquisition chamber.

Here we sat, choking back hysterical mirth as the interrogation proceeded. We did not know the address of the bar, the number of the watch, the name of the waiter, and could not recall with any accuracy the time of the event. Our detective began to show signs of restive impatience at these revelations as he typed away, his expression slowly changing to repressed and then outright laughter. We signed the paperwork, and left, confident that there would be small hope of recovering the watch.

That evening. as we met in the hotel lobby, the concierge beckoned us, handing a package to the captain containing his watch, with a brief note from the police wishing us compliments and apologies. This surprise was capped by a further development. When walking past the bar later, on we saw that a notice of closure had been attached to the door. This effectively denied us the only source of cheap beer within reasonable reach of the hotel. Other crew members attempted to use the watering hole, soon telling us of the closure. We kept a low profile.

BALPA again

Willie Watson, a former RAF Coastal Command pilot, Stratocruiser and Seven Seas Captain, had transferred to the Boeing 707-436. He was the chairman of the pilots' local council, and also of the combined BOAC pilots' councils committee. I succeeded him on the local council, which was responsible for concluding agreements affecting our fleet operations, such as scheduling and hotels.

Our local relations had been very good, at a time when both Bernard Frost and Gordon Store were in charge. Rumblings of discontent were beginning to surface as the early Sixties revealed the management aim to improve productivity. As a nationalised corporation, accountable to Parliament, and charged to provide the government with an annual return, BOAC had found it very difficult to overcome the setbacks caused by aircraft failure and the lack of suitably profitable aircraft from the UK industry. Government policy, expressed to the airline through the Treasury, invoked pay restraint and imposed strict guidelines that denied negotiators flexibility.

As air traffic began to increase, the frequency of flights on our route network increased. This allowed better utilisation of crews, who were not left at overseas slip stations for long periods. Another method the airline introduced was to reduce our time spent at home base, on stand-off. Some of this time was utilised as stand-by against delays and sickness, and was not free time. The days spent overseas during the post-war years had been excessive, because of infrequent services, and crew shortages. Now a similar situation was being created by a deliberate move to economise. No attempt was made to compensate for additional flying or days away. The airline used the government's policies as an excuse. We suspected that they were indivisible in their intransigence.

Willie Watson was killed when he crashed his light aircraft in bad weather, and this caused the appointment of Laurie Arthur as his replacement in the BALPA/BOAC chair. During 1964, for a variety of reasons, I suddenly became the chairman, involved in direct negotiations towards a new contract for the BOAC pilots. For many years now, the Association has employed specialist personnel to act on its behalf, but in those days the pilots elected someone from the ranks of their contemporaries to take on this responsibility. The background to my four years in this onerous position would provide material for a separate book. I cannot claim to have been wildly successful in attempting to protect the pilots from gradual erosion of their service conditions, or pay, and, indeed, made the fundamental mistake, in a vain attempt to ensure stability, of agreeing to a three-year contract which was overtaken by unpredictable inflation. Although there was a protection clause against this effect, the government vetoed any adjustment, allowing the airline to procrastinate. The effect was much unrest, my replacement as chairman, and a pilots' strike in 1968. We were going through intensive growing pains, as the big jets became our standard equipment, and airlines at last began to be profitable.

During this period I naturally achieved a certain notoriety, both with management, who saw me as a problem, and with the pilots, who were not seeing enough improvement. Once again the divisive effect of differing interests allowed the pilot group to lose effectiveness. Those flying the Boeing 707 understandably viewed their claims as more valid than others. The seed of a seniority bidding system, and a differential pay system, was sown, eventually resulting in large differences in pay and pension for many pilots of equivalent career service. These problems remain the cause of industrial disputes to this day, and as I write, pilot groups are on strike worldwide over the slice of the cake that they feel they are worth.

Throughout this time, although engaged in sometimes confrontational and difficult disputes, some of which involved contact with the Conservative government and its Labour successor, it was possible to sustain a good personal relationship with all but a few on the management side. The amount of help and cooperation received from many quarters helped to ease discharge of my flying duties, both on the route, and as training captain. My time was absorbed unfortunately to the detriment of my family obligations. My wife was most helpful and understanding. She was now teaching art and about to develop her successful career as a painter.

Learning curve

Many clichés exist about pilot experience. Operations manuals contain information distilled from many years of collective analysis. Pilots are continually bombarded with reminders and warnings. Aircraft are improved regularly to ensure that equipment specifications will include systems such as ground proximity warning, terminal collision avoidance, altitude alert, central warning indication, flight management, and automatic system back-up. None of these improvements can replace the basic need to gain experience and confidence. Pilots accrue valuable information to become safer as their career develops. Each mistake, if recognised as such, should result in an improved understanding and safer performance. That is why the flight recorder is such a valuable tool for providing information about problem areas, so that all can benefit and thus avoid repetition.

A smooth landing has always been a yardstick of pilot and passenger satisfaction. The Comet 4 could be placed on the ground with precision, and stopped quickly with anti-skid brakes and reverse thrust adding to the flap drag. One nagging problem that we faced was an above-average attrition of tyres. Some of this was caused by smooth landings in wet conditions. Burst tyres were too common, and showed evidence of the rubber compound being overheated by superheated steam, melting on initial contact with a wet runway. To obtain best braking efficiency it was necessary to have the full weight of the aircraft on the wheels.

When landing on short wet runways, extra care was needed, and it was recommended to fly into contact with the surface firmly and without delay so that brakes could be used. This was all very well. No special training or practice was provided to demonstrate the necessary technique. Perhaps it should have been part of the conversion syllabus.

Bader

One one occasion we were flying in to land at the old single-runway airport at Kuala Lumpur, on our way from Colombo to Singapore. A distinguished passenger was Douglas Bader, the fighter pilot who lost both his legs during RAF service, then associated with the Shell Petroleum company. The weather was very rainy, the runway was short, and the approach crossed a high railway embankment, on which a train could intrude into the cleared legal approach slope. We had to confirm that trains were absent before starting approach. With rain bucketing down I aligned onto the runway, crossing the embankment at the recommended threshold airspeed, and then adjusted the descent downwards slightly to aim at the markings for the displaced touch down point. As we passed over the line of arrows I eased the nose forward to touch down. This occurred suddenly and heavily enough for me to inwardly curse my luck. The wind was also swirling around erratically. The roll-out took most of the runway, despite brakes and reverse thrust.

During the short transit we walked across to a small area where soft drinks were available. Douglas Bader sat there looking at me with an expression that did not indicate sympathy.

'What happened?' he asked, in a sort of superior way.

I was nonplussed, and was grateful to the co-pilot, who answered 'We were getting it on the ground and stopping it.'

The conversation ended at that point as we left to prepare for the short flight to Singapore, where the co-pilot made a smooth landing. There is usually a reason for most things. Excuses are out of order, and explanations often unbelievable but the occasional hard landing does occur despite the use of normal techniques. Wind reporting can be inaccurate. There has always been a reluctance by controllers at some major airports to change the landing direction when the wind direction swings. Another factor is the use of short runways for landing, and long ones for take-off. Too often the pilot has all the elements stacked against him: a short, wet, runway and a strong crosswind with a tailwind component.

Shannon again

Returning, this time as instructor, in February 1963, we were converting the first group of Malaysian Airways crews to the Comet. A mix of expatriate captains, and young Chinese co-pilots formed the nucleus of what was later to become Singapore Airlines, after a lengthy metamorphosis. At that time BOAC and Qantas had a financial stake in the embryo airline. Singapore had for long been a well-served destination for many of our schedules. The presence of UK forces in the area during the long war against communist rebels, and the transition from former colonial days, had provided a strong traffic pool. The formation of the Malaysian Federation in December 1963 was yet to happen, with Singapore as a founding member, only to leave and become an independent republic in December 1965.

We were staying in the Old Grounds Hotel at Ennis, County Clare, a few miles north of the airport. Clive Houlder had taken over as officer in command of training, and had brought his wife over for an Irish break. He was approaching retirement, and had held the same position on the Argonauts. Tactful and pleasant, he possessed the judgment necessary to deal with any tensions in our current group of trainees. The main problem that I faced was related to my junior status in the training unit. After breakfast, on the first morning after arrival with the aircraft from London, I was outside the hotel for a spot of fresh air when Clive's wife collared me. She had their Jack Russell terrier on a leash and handed it to me with a flourish. I was informed that it would be my duty to walk the dog each morning. Clive came on the scene soon afterwards grinning hugely.

Too real

The Comet 4 simulator was kept in operation for eighteen hours every day. The motion system was unsophisticated, and did not give trouble, until the day when I was involved in a refresher session with a couple of pilots from East African Airways. That airline had an arrangement with us that we would complete their regular refresher training and rating renewal test during their London turnaround before going back to Nairobi. We were to practice an emergency descent from 35,000 ft, after a simulated pressurisation problem.

The Comet 4 procedure was to select the wing air-brakes out, and then reduce engine power, descending rapidly to a safer level where oxygen would not be required. Unfortunately on this occasion the handling pilot closed the throttles fully without selecting the air brakes. This caused a strong nose down trim force and we were soon pointed down at a steep angle with speed increasing rapidly. At that point he remembered to select the air brakes, but this did nothing to retrim the aircraft, merely accelerated the rate of descent. I remained a silent witness, expecting them to recover, but a further problem arose. The altimeters were rotating very swiftly, the analogue needles spinning round. This type of three-needle altimeter had been misread on a number of occasions, and had led to the crash of a BOAC Britannia during a test flight.

The descent was continued to ground level, at a steep angle, and at high speed. At the simulated impact the simulator rocked violently, all the lights went out, dust flew everywhere, with books and manuals tumbling. We all sat immobile for some seconds, stunned by the event. The simulator remained seized in the nose down attitude, so that we could not use the exit steps. A ladder had to be found, and we gingerly made our way down this to the floor. The pitch motion jack was broken, lolling uselessly below the unit.

We had a procedure that required the crew to state the passing altitudes, and for another member to confirm the call. This valuable experience was worth the cost of the repairs to the simulator, which proved to be relatively minimal. However, for an instant I did think I had perished, as did the training engineer, and his engineer trainee.

Deportee dilemma

The position of an aircraft commander can be very difficult when dealing with an unruly or disruptive passenger. A drunken and aggressive person can be restrained until no longer a threat, although this process can oblige the crew to take physical action, and this might lead to accusations and perhaps litigation. The laws of other countries can become a problem, and international conventions may not be observed.

We were about to start the engines on our Comet 4 to depart

for Rome and Cairo, when a uniformed policeman handed me a sheet of paper, without comment. I had to accept the responsibility of the deportation order, charging me to transport a named person out of the UK. The flight was terminating in Aden, and the man was an Aden national. I asked if he was violent or a danger, but received no information or background to the order. There was civil unrest in the Yemen and in Aden (which eventually led to the UK. relinquishing the colony). The steward confirmed that the unescorted deportee was seated, and quiet.

Trouble began after about an hour's flight en route from Rome to Cairo. Our man was standing in the rear of the cabin and shouting obscenities laced with condemnation of the British authorities. Adjacent passengers were becoming alarmed. The deportee was flailing his arms and raving constantly. I asked him to sit down and remain silent, but was met with shoving and further shouting in English and Arabic. The stewards manoeuvred him out of sight. I do not know what ensued, but have a shrewd idea. A short time later he came forward, chastened, and sat down. He was supplied with a drink, looked up at me and apologised.

He left the aircraft at Cairo and claimed to have been assaulted by the crew, and that he wished to be medically examined. He was handed into Egyptian custody and I was required to make a full report to the local police.

Luckily I knew that two witnesses would be needed to back up my statement of an in-flight disturbance, and had obtained these from passengers. But there was considerable local bias and hostility from people who had only heard the shouted accusations. I managed to warn the captain taking over our aircraft, and he refused to carry the man onward to Aden. The deportee was accommodated in a good hotel, from which he vanished. The episode was probably a successful attempt to disembark in Egypt.

Making several reports to the company and the UK governmental authorities, I was able to obtain an under standing of the legal situation. Once away from UK airspace, my duty was to treat the man as a normal passenger but this did not extend to a duty to deliver him to Aden. I was entitled to protect the aircraft and passengers by any reasonable means if any passenger became a threat. The position under Egyptian law was not clear. After this event it was agreed that commanders would be provided with more information. The Tokyo Convention governs procedures and legal responsibilities on board aircraft that are flying internationally, but there are too many non-signatories.

Farewell to the Comet

As 1965 drew to a close our Comet 4s were soon to be withdrawn from service. The Super VC10 fleet was being introduced into the North American pattern. The Boeing 707 fleet was in full operation, and achieving impressive utilisation. Productivity and profitability from these big jets were improved compared to the Comet 4. Vacancies on the VC10s were available in order of seniority, and many captains wished for a posting to the new British aircraft. This was stimulated by the excellent handling qualities of the Vickers product, which made it very popular. The aircraft was also popular with our passengers, helping to offset the slightly higher unit operating costs when compared to the Boeing. Structurally there was a lower maintenance cost, as the corrosion-proofing set a new industry standard. Another factor was the difficulty some older pilots had experienced when converting to the Boeing 707. There had been an abnormally high failure rate, with some pilots reverting to their previous types.

Because of my low number on the seniority list I had no option but to file a bid for the 707. This did not really worry me as many friends who were flying the type advised me that any problems that may have existed had been magnified. My last flight on the Comet series was on 29 October 1965, to Bedford for a series of landings, and a check by Clive Houlder to revalidate my rating for another six months, just in case of a return to the fleet. I was sorry to leave such a fine aircraft.

A BOAC Comet 4 over Hatfield House.

The Boeing 707

The ground school on the 707 was comprehensive and conducted at the extended and improved Cranebank centre. Instruction was excellent, and soon revealed many differences when compared to the Comet 4. The higher sweepback gave a speed increase over the Comet 4 of about 50 knots. Rolls-Royce Conway high bypass engines each produced 16,000 pounds of thrust. Passenger capacity was increased by more than 70 per cent, depending on configuration. Range was substantially extended to achieve regular non-stop westbound transatlantic schedules throughout the year.

Some early versions of the 707 series were delivered to airlines without any hydraulically-boosted rudder assistance. The rudder force needed to counteract an outboard engine failure during take-off was substantial and the initial group of BOAC pilots being converted on the aircraft by Boeing pilots in the US had revealed a problem. During one take-off, when practising an engine failure at decision speed, a wingtip had scraped the ground. Our aircraft had boosted rudder systems, and were fitted with a ventral fin to aid directional control.

This was history, of course, when I was being trained, but the aircraft was still vulnerable to the effects of outboard engine failure, and needed careful appreciation of the factors involved. Additionally, the inboard engine pods sat close to the ground, and a relatively small bank angle could bring them into contact with the runway surface, especially if this was accompanied by a hardish landing which could flex the wing. Over-controlling had to be avoided, as the 707-436 lateral control forces were light, and the roll rate was rapid, allowing large inputs to be made. Inevitably, many of the engine pod scrapes that airlines experienced with this aircraft were caused by control wheel input in gusty crosswind landings. BOAC recognised that there would be a number of such incidents, despite intensive efforts to train and warn pilots. They were treated as casualties, usually not apportioned to the individual pilot, but rather to extreme conditions. Nevertheless many pilots preferred the 707-436 to the later 707-336 series, which was quite a different aircraft to handle, having been modified extensively in association with leading edge flaps on the wings, and which had a reduced roll rate.

Australasia

After the ground part of my conversion course my wife and I managed to combine annual leave with official business to attend the 1966 International Federation of Airline Pilots' Associations (IFALPA) conference in Auckland. We had decided to visit one of my wife's old school friends, who now lived in Suva, the capital of Fiji. She was married to the secretary of Fiji Airways which was flying de Havilland Doves and Herons on a large inter-island network. Some flights were long enough to involve the captain in some quite difficult navigation. He would leave the flying to the co-pilot while viewing the southern stars through a sextant. We then flew from Nadi, the international airport, in an ancient DC-3, to Suva, to be met with another round of excellent hospitality, staying in a bungalow that had a wonderful hilltop location with extensive views of the lovely rolling and mountainous countryside.

Boeing crash

The date was 5 March 1966. We were still in Suva. One of BOAC's 707-436s, G-APFE, had crashed after taking off from Tokyo's Haneda airport, disintegrating in mid-air with total loss of life. The captain was Bernard Dobson, an ex-DC-7C pilot with whom I had flown on several occasions, and who had transferred to the 707 when it entered service. As can be imagined, this event revived many misgivings and memories. The investigation later determined that the most likely cause was very severe clear-air turbulence. They had flown downwind of 12,388 foot Mount Fuji, to enter an area of disturbed air. The wind speed that afternoon was more than 70 knots from the north-west. Ground observers had supposedly seen several tornadoes, and one had actually witnessed the aircraft breaking up. Unfortunately the flight recorder was destroyed, as it was not crash proof. I wondered what the future held, as past events had conspired to equip me with a very healthy doubt about ever receiving full information concerning aircraft on which my life and occupation depended.

After our three days in Suva, we retraced our steps to Nadi, this time in a Dove. I was able to sit in one of the pilots' seats as we followed the coastline to the international airport, where we boarded the Auckland-bound Boeing, a sister ship to Foxtrot Echo, the crashed 707.

Big jet flying

On 27 March 1966, I began what was to be a long association with the Boeing 707 — a magnificent aircraft. We were ferrying Foxtrot Papa to Shannon for our training session. This was *déjà vu* for me, having so recently been there as a training captain, now as a green pupil once more. The weather was appalling. Jim Hengle from Comet 1 days, our training captain in command of the trip, put me into the right-hand seat for the 90 minute flight on a very black night. Although familiar with the internal scenery from the 707 simulator, the sounds, smells, feel, and view were all new. We had to use weather radar to avoid heavy buildups as soon as we took off in pelting rain. The Boeing shook and shuddered throughout the trip as Jim handled it with great confidence to a landing at Shannon in a strong crosswind.

We were staying at the Shannon Shamrock hotel once again, having forsaken the delights of Ennis, and I re-acquainted myself with the manager's Irish wolfhound, a noble beast that tolerated our intrusion. The conversational 'hangar doors' were perpetually open with technical and aviation scuttlebut, interspersed with some very wet walks through the local countryside, mainly to Durty Nelly's for a snack and a Guinness stout.

The flying syllabus included some interesting exercises. The 707 did not have a vicious Dutch roll like the VC10 series, but once a yaw had induced a roll, the ensuing rapid gyration of bank angle and heading could be quite severe.

The need to compensate for large changes in pitch trim of the aircraft was accentuated by the sweepback, fuel distribution, and the changes of lift centre caused by the large speed range. There had been cases of the stabiliser operating motor 'running away' and causing severe out-of-trim control problems. Another and potentially hazardous failure was the jamming of the stabiliser in a fixed position. The solution was to compensate for the loss of trim by using the spoilers, which were mounted in pairs on each wing. Isolating one set provided for additional trim in the desired direction, nose-up or down. Isolating the outboard wing flaps provided additional trim effect. Initially I thought that the handling qualities were no match for the crispness of the Comet 4, but the systems design of the 707 was a model of logical simplicity. After 10 hours of flight training in appalling weather I was given a final check and instrument rating renewal by Ken Loveless and caught the next Aer Lingus flight to London.

Boeing 707 route flying

BOAC now used the Boeing 707 all around the world, both west and eastbound through many ports of call. Pilots were based in Sydney and Hong Kong. Further routes would be added as the airline introduced a fleet of eleven 707-336 aircraft.

My absence as a parent on so many occasions put a great load and responsibility on my wife, as our children had reached the teenage years, with all the vicissitudes that the 1960s brought forth. I was also still involved with BALPA, which absorbed much of my spare time when at home. It says a great deal for the tolerance of my wife, who gave the greatest support, that we navigated through this turbulent period. Although the job as training captain on the Comet 4 had kept me at home base for much of the year, this was about to change, as life as a regular 707 route captain meant more time away.

I was allocated to the eastern route initially, through very familiar territory, albeit with a longer range and larger aircraft. After a trip to Delhi, and then one to Hong Kong with route supervisory captains, it was time to earn my keep. The first take-off from Heathrow with a supervisory captain had proved quite exciting. The flight engineer discovered that the pressurisation control operated in the reverse sense to his inputs, and we experienced wild pressure surges. We returned to Heathrow, landing in torrential rain on the only runway not equipped with an instrument landing system.

Navigation over desert and water was still by conventional methods, using LORAN, and sextant. Many erstwhile co-pilots became adept at excellent navigation, but failed to obtain much aircraft handling. I was always careful to share the flying with them, but with a limited number of landings, shared by three, it was difficult for them to build their experience. I also needed to find out more about the aircraft's foibles. One instance of this occurred on a trip through Bangkok's Don Muang airport during my second trip after checkout. It was a sunny hot afternoon as we lined up to land. Crossing the runway threshold at the right speed and height, I eased the power back steadily and confidently but we hit the runway with a clatter and bang, and with enough force for the flight engineer to insist on a heavy landing check on the ramp. A careful inspection produced no evidence of any problems. The main effect was on my ego, which was probably ready for a fall anyway. Our touchdown had probably coincided with a hump in the runway, and the slight tailwind may also have had an effect. But after this I began to take even more notice of the wind and runway conditions.

Hong Kong

For the next eighteen months all my trips were routed to Hong Kong. Much has been written about the problems associated with bad weather arrivals at Kai Tak (now usurped by the new Chep Lap Kok airport built on reclaimed land off Lantau Island). Local knowledge of the likely wind conditions that could be met in the last part of an approach to runway 13, on a curve, and with high-rise apartments right, left and centre, was essential to prepare the pilot to place an aircraft correctly to anticipate sudden last-minute displacement from the runway centreline.

On one occasion we were sitting in the aircraft, completing preflight checks for departure, and watching arrivals. Our own aircraft, stationary, was buffeted by the strong wind, and its flexible structure transmitted the message that this was 'one of those days'. We witnessed successive approaching aircraft lining up from their turn past the visual chequerboard (mounted on a hillside to indicate where to aim before starting the final turn) and making approaches that required heading corrections to stay on line. One 707 from a well-known international airline crossed the runway threshold at about 100 feet, and well to the right side of the landing surface. The engine pods nearly touched the ground as the aircraft was banked into wind, skidding across and finally aligning to touchdown more than half way down the runway, and stopped just before the sea wall.

On another occasion, when the wind was blowing strongly from the north west, the approach to runway 31 through the harbour entrance in heavy rain and turbulence produced jolting air currents which threw the large Boeing around with airspeed needle indications flicking over a twenty-knot band as we passed the entrance, with sudden up and down drafts caused by local air currents off the hills. The airport could be closed for as long as two days by low cloud and fog. We sometimes had to spend time in Manila, waiting for things to improve. The new international airport should remove many of these difficulties, although some pilots may miss the excitement and challenge of Kai Tak. The safety record has been generally good, although a few large aircraft have plunged into the sea.

Zürich

The 707 was noisy and therefore unpopular with many a local city council and local resident. Many airports are now situated too close to densely populated areas, although the proximity may have been tolerable when they were first built. The luxury and economy of a straight climbout, using full power to obtain best speed and economic performance, is now generally denied by special noise-abatement procedures and routings. The use of reverse thrust on landing is prohibited at some airports. After becoming airborne, power reductions are required, and changes of heading to avoid sensitive areas.

Zürich was a regular port of call on our way to the east, and had set stringent limits for departing jets. We had an arrangement that provided the resulting perceived noise level for our departure via company radio soon after take-off. The route out of mountainous Switzerland involved some accurate flying and changes of tracking before joining the airways south. Our reputation for making a racket was under attack by local and airport authorities so our local company representative met each incoming captain to brief him on the need for care.

One day, during this transit routine, he suggested that I could reach the aircraft quicker if I used a bicycle. This idea was immediately appealing, as the walk took a good ten minutes. The airport would not allow use of our company transport on the movement ramp, despite the use of passenger buses. Clutching documents in one hand, I cycled off. As I increased speed downhill towards our Boeing I discovered the brakes to be totally ineffective. The speed was now too much to dismount, and the only option was to steer round the front end of my 707 in a large circle, hoping to slow up as I pointed uphill. The resulting manoeuvre threw me into a broadside slide, ending up, accurately but undignified, at the foot of the steps to the front door. A surprised stewardess suppressed her mirth as I dusted off my uniform and raced up the steps, leaving the failed steed to be retrieved by the ground engineer. I have often wondered if I was 'fixed-up' by that station officer.

We started the engines, and departed on schedule, managing to achieve noise results that did not 'ring the bell'. My loss of dignity had been observed by the co-pilot, and became the source of many amused replays during the next twelve days.

Tokyo aftermath

The Tokyo accident had triggered a worldwide examination of the Boeing 707, by now in use by many airlines. Boeing identified structural areas that would need inspection, although steadfastly maintaining that the accident could not have been caused by any of them. BOAC indicated that much work was needed to improve areas of the wing, tailplane, and fin. The wing skin attachment bolts were of stainless steel, and had been installed through holes machined into skin aluminium. Without protection treatment, cadmium oxide corrosion had spread into the adjacent skin, reducing strength. Thousands of these bolts had to be removed on each aircraft, and replaced to extend the structural life, and the company engineering department performed magnificently. Eventually the wings were treated using an excellent anti corrosion coating that had been developed for the VC10. The fin terminal fittings were inspected using eddy current technique, which revealed that half the airline's aircraft had significant cracks requiring attention or replacement of the fitting. The tailplane terminal fitting lugs had corrosion and cracking damage. BOAC and the ARB decided that it would be prudent to remove each aircraft's complete tailplane, revealing the need for a modified design, which was completed on a phased program. Meanwhile ultrasonic testing was conducted regularly, despite the Boeing recommendation that a visual check would suffice.

The repairs and modifications to our 707-436 and 707-336 aircraft were spread out over two winter maintenance programmes. The great care exercised by our company and the excellent information provided to crews were not unrelated to the Comet 1 experience.

North America again

In May 1967 I was back on the Atlantic after an absence of six years. The routes had proliferated to include many Caribbean destinations, as well as Canadian and American airports. Traffic growth was causing congestion in New York, with much holding before landing and many long line-ups for take-off clearance. It was pleasant to renew acquaintance with Bermuda and Nassau, and to visit Trinidad, Barbados, and Antigua, where landing could be quite interesting.

The short runway at Antigua ended close to the sea, and approach into the usual trade wind required the aircraft to pass between high ground to make a visual approach. This was usually at night, and when circling the airport it was not possible to see the runway, as hills were in the way. Although visual approach slope indicator (VASI) lighting installations had been fitted to some airports, some years passed before Antigua was provided with these, despite many complaints. This British approach guidance invention has improved aviation safety and aided pilot judgment for many years.

Antipodean detachment

Later in 1967 I applied successfully for a 3-month posting to Sydney, Australia. We rented accommodation in Manly, across the harbour, and took our children with us, to augment their education.

Our family left London for New York in a Super VC10, while I was in the 707 that was to take us all through to Honolulu. After reuniting in New York we arrived at Honolulu to find that our bags had been sent elsewhere. Fortunately I had arranged to take a week's annual vacation to allow adjustment to the time change and a nice break.

We were provided with funds to equip us with beach gear until the bags turned up three days later, and hardly missed our other clothing. After suffering intensive bombardment by the Fourth of July fireworks we were somewhat relieved to depart for Nadi and Sydney.

Australian air rules at this time were quite different from ours. An airport could be closed for operations when the civil aviation authority determined that this was necessary. On one such occasion, departing from Sydney for Nadi, we had reached the holding point before the take-off runway and were then advised to return to the ramp, as the airport was closed. I left the passengers on board and went to the air traffic control tower, to be told that a line squall was forecast to reach the area within the next 90 minutes. I asked him to accompany me to the weather office, where the radar screen showed that the advancing line of heavy cloud was not on our intended route, and it would be easy to avoid the area completely by a small diversion. After some diplomatic conversation, we were allowed to leave. We encountered heavy rain but the flight was uneventful

Many airports have rules prohibiting arrival before dawn and Sydney was no exception. The airport is surrounded by housing, and the nuisance effects of jet noise had become politically contentious. Landings were banned before 6 am, and an inbound schedule from Nadi was timed to arrive just after. Because of tailwinds we arrived ten minutes early one morning, having been bounced around in some nasty clear air turbulence — quite a regular occurrence in the Fiji-New Zealand-Sydney triangle. We were cleared to descend to 1,500 feet, and to take up a holding pattern over the outer marker NDB, which positioned us neatly over the most populated area of Sydney at a very low level until the airport opened. Rules are rules.

There was much to do between trips. We used the famous beach at Manly, where flags indicated shark warning, and life guards were on constant duty. We had bought an old Austin 110, large and quite dilapidated, which consumed oil voraciously and smelled of chickens, with a few feathers as evidence. This took us to the Bobbin Head boat marina, where a 27-foot cabin cruiser could be rented to explore the nearby Hawkesbury river for fishing, and swimming. Our son had developed a talent as a fisherman, catching trevally (similar to small tuna) off the local rocks, and he even sold a small shark to the local aquarium.

Singapore was not yet reconstructed and modernized. We stayed at Raffles, where the rooms were large, fragrant with hardwood panelling and older furniture. The service was impeccable, and Singapore Slings were still served at the long bar. Fans and wicker chairs complemented the evening breezes.

The three months went quickly. Return from the Sydney winter of clear skies and sixty degrees to similar weather in Britain's autumn eased our homecoming as we resumed the routine of schools and other tasks.

707 trainees

By the late 1960s the airline was about to experience some big changes, with the arrival of the widebodied Boeing 747, which was twice as big as the 707. A progressive transfer of crews to the new fleet would require their replacement. The traffic growth and retirements created a large demand for new co-pilots. The College for Air Training at Hamble had been formed to train a new generation of pilots for the airline corporations. The supply of ex-service pilots was no longer available in sufficient quantity. Recruitment of pilots from other airlines was also drying up. Hundreds were needed to crew the expanding aircraft fleet.

BALPA and BOAC had been negotiating about which way pilots could be utilised on the worldwide route pattern. The airline's aim was to improve productivity by increasing the annual number of flying hours per pilot. BALPA's aim was to ensure that this did not compromise safety, produce excessive fatigue, or recall the era when days of leisure at home between long trips overseas were rare.

The lead time necessary before a pilot could be a productive crew member on a 707 or VClO was conditioned by the need to possess a flight navigator's licence, and training to navigate, in addition to flying training, and conversion to one of these jets. This could total nearly three years for an ab initio candidate joining one of the schools. The airline faced many difficulties in deciding a recruitment plan, for the aircraft order book was fluid, and did not firm up during the period when decisions were necessary. Because of the demand for new pilots, we were also accepting graduates from the Perth and Oxford schools, which were run by non-corporation commercial ventures.

Joining the 707 training unit coincided with the beginning of an intensive conversion programme of inexperienced pilots on to the 707 and the VC1O fleets. This was to become a fascinating period in my flying life. Although primarily engaged in training, and checking, I continued to fly the 707 on worldwide routes.

Dual qualification

Our two variants of the Boeing 707 allowed a system of dual qualification so that qualified crews could fly either type. The differences between the 707-436 and 707-336 went far deeper than different engines. The 300 series had full span leading edge slats to replace the 400 series short section of leading edge flaps between the engines, and it also had reconfigured slotted flaps on the trailing edges of the wings. This allowed the maximum take-off weight to be increased by more than 10,000 kilograms. It was really a different aircraft. Four of our eleven 336s were configured as cargo aircraft, six as passenger aircraft, and one as a convertible. Two of the passenger aircraft were 336Bs, without the large freight door. Many differences of weight, limitations, and equipment existed between these eleven aircraft.

For the pilot the two basic types were different to fly, especially the way the take-off was handled. With the additional lift provided by the modified wing-flaps came a new procedure on take-off. The 707-336 used a single wing-flap setting of 14°, and no flap selection at 400 feet. Furthermore when the wing flaps were finally retracted to clean the aircraft up for climbout, the resulting trim changes were opposite in effect. The 436 nose rose, and the 336 nose fell.

An accident to a South African Airways 707-300 series aircraft when taking off at Windhoek, South West Africa (now Namibia), involved a crew which had also been flying the 707-400 series. This raised the question of whether there should be dual qualification. Airlines like to have their pilots qualified on more than one type as this is more economic for many reasons, but only completely safe if there is a regular and frequent exposure to each type. The mental load on pilots is considerably increased when they have to master significant differences in aircraft response and procedure, and they could revert to the wrong technique in time of stress.

The Guild

The Guild of Air Pilots and Air Navigators is a City of London livery company, and primarily exists to provide a professional focus for pilots and navigators. Past and present membership includes many of the most distinguished names in the development of British service and civil aviation. The Guild provides input to assist government and industry, being represented on many aviation-related organisations. As a strictly non-union body, striving to ensure the best standards within the civil aviation industry, its views are often sought. I had been a member since 1950 and joined the Aviation Training Committee in 1969. This brought me into contact with the Ministry of Aviation's Asymmetric Flight Training Committee. The main subject was to develop policy for the future that could improve safety during this type of training. There had been too many accidents, and the conditions in which pilots were trained to overcome engine failures needed regulation. This also led to involvement in making policy on the use of simulators. I continued as an active Guild member for the next five years, until becoming fully absorbed with Concorde.

Boeing 707-436, G-APFE, at JFK Airport. This aircraft was tragically lost in an accident close to Mount Fuji in March 1966.

Busy busy

The next seven years were packed with interesting flying. About a third of the time was spent flying commercial services across our world-wide route structure, which now approached Tokyo from several directions. A polar flight landed at Anchorage, Alaska, before routeing to Japan. There was a flight across the Soviet Union, landing in Moscow before a long stretch across the Siberian wastes, and another from Honolulu joined up with the old route from Hong Kong. Our 707s went everywhere except Africa, which was the VClO's preserve, with their superior hot-and-high take-off performance.

Over wartime Vietnam

Our route from Bangkok to Hong Kong usually crossed the Vietnamese coast close to Da Nang, before flying across the

South China Sea and well clear of Hainan. Often flown after sunset it was cluttered with tropical cloud and turbulence. The war continued below as we sped by above with our passengers consuming their dinners unaware of the proximity of hostilities. As we kept checking the weather radar, and prepared for the approach procedures at Kai Tak, we could see activity in the form of flares, and flashes close to the ground. Use of a discrete radio frequency that we had discovered allowed us to monitor some of the US army transmissions, usually involving control of gunship or helicopter procedures. I wondered about our vulnerability to missiles. We were not provided with much information. Some airlines had altered their routes to avoid overflying the war zones, but this meant a long detour to the south. Once, I managed to make contact with a major who was controlling the operation below us, and we swapped civilities. He had been out there for 17 months. Our brief talk revealed an unhappy man, due for 'R & R' in Bangkok.

The Thai capital was full of such people. Our captains stayed at the Oriental Hotel, then the best place in the city, on the banks of the Chao Phraya River, where the noise of motor craft vied with the traffic din on the roads. Although the city was full of racing traffic, crowded with servicemen and the inevitable hangers-on and bar-girls, it was still possible to watch a performance of elegant Thai dancing while taking tea in the lovely hotel gardens, sitting next to colonels from the US forces. The Wat Arun or Temple of Dawn was quite close to the hotel and its gilt outline gleamed in the afternoon lighting.

Salutary strike

Negotiations between BALPA and BOAC had reached an impasse by the spring of 1968. My successor as the pilots' chairman, Denis Whitham, was under great pressure from the majority of member s to achieve some sort of parity with the salaries being paid by European airlines. A climate of unrest had grown as a result of increased inflation and inflexible government policy. The airline corporation was controlled largely by the UK Treasury, which thought the pilots' demands to be excessive. Unable to resolve the many outstanding problems within the procedures of the National Joint Council For Civil Air Transport, a secret ballot was called to see if there was support for a strike. The vote was 90 per cent in favour.

Organisation of a worldwide stoppage of services involved the possibility of stranding many crews overseas. It was decided to fly all aircraft back to the UK, and to collect as many of these people as possible if space permitted. When the strike day arrived I was in Fiji, having just flown an aircraft in from Honolulu. After two days our crew managed to catch the last 707 back through Honolulu, to New York, and then the last VClO as far as Manchester on 21 June.

Resolution of the dispute involved the government', and a detailed investigation into the airline's administration and management. The strike was over within three weeks. During this time many pilots had found part-time jobs, as their salaries were cut off, and strike pay was minimal. The aftermath of this trauma continued for many years, warning all concerned that a better way was needed to resolve disputes and avoid mutual losses.

I was back in the air by 3 July, with a backlog of refresher flights to complete with those pilots whose recent experience had lapsed beyond legal limits.

Middle East diversion (politics don't mix)

A February evening in Delhi, fine and warm. We were to take a 707-436 as far as Tehran, where another crew would take over and fly to London via Tel Aviv. Aircraft landing in Israel were not permitted to fly over, or land, in any of the adjacent Arab countries. The possession of a passport with an Israeli visa could cause untold problems for a passenger, and the airline. Alternate diversionary airports had to be carefully selected to meet this requirement, and they were limited in number.

We checked the weather forecast for the short 3-hour flight to Tehran, and found it good, with scattered cloud for our night landing. The alternate airport was Abadan, some 360 nautical miles south-south-west of Tehran, where the forecast was for clear skies. As we approached the Iranian capital we were informed that the airport was closed because of a heavy snowstorm. This was the first information that such an event was remotely possible. After checking its latest weather, which was clear, we renominated Abadan as destination, saving fuel by staying high. A Qantas 707 was a few minutes ahead, also diverting from Tehran. This proved fortunate. The only approach aid was a single radio beacon, and this was not exactly lined up with the landing runway. We were on the same radio frequency as the other aircraft, and heard a deep Australian voice saying that fog was forming and that they had only just managed to see the runway in time to land. He said that we should do the letdown and 'look right to pick up the lights,' which consisted only of runway edge lighting. The advice was invaluable, and we were able to align with the runway at about 500 feet, just in time to make a landing. Otherwise we would have had to land at Basra, which was close, but in Iraq, with inevitable repercussions.

Our troubles then began. There were no ground handling arrangements for passengers from the two 707s. Refuelling took ages. The fog closed in. There was no accommodation for passengers or crews and Tehran was snowed under. I decided to make for Tel Aviv, but this meant backtracking over Iran again to avoid Iraq. After troubles in obtaining flight plan approval from the local traffic control office, staffed by two very sleepy gentlemen, we managed to depart after a total delay of four hours.

Arriving at Lod airport, Tel Aviv, as the sun rose, we were marshalled by a follow-me jeep to a remote spot in the parking area. When the main door was opened, armed Israeli soldiers guarded the steps, and our local traffic officer came into the flight deck and announced that a security alert was in progress. Our crew had been on duty thirteen hours, through the night, having left the Delhi hotel just after midday there. We were advised that, should we decide to delay to obtain crew rest, there was no accommodation for our passengers and they would have to stay on the aircraft. We were governed by UK law, which set maximum duty times. To stay within them would require us to stop before reaching London and delay for at least ten hours. Rome was the obvious choice, as it was en route. But we could not arrive in London before 6 am because of the night-time noise curfew. The law allowed commanders to extend duty periods in exceptional circumstances, but these had to be justified by special report to the Ministry.

I canvassed our crew individually and suggested that we could proceed with fuel for London, and I would use my discretionary power to extend the duty period, but land at Rome if we felt too tired. They agreed. The weather forecasts were good, but there was a strong headwind, making our day even longer. Shaking off the dust of Israeli problems we set off with some relief. I organised the engineer to sleep when we reached cruise level, and rotated the pilots so that we could each shut our eyes, for a short while. The cabin crew, who had been marvellous throughout, insisted on serving us tea every half hour. The take-off and landing were flown by a senior first officer, as it was his turn, and we completed the flight to London, all very tired.

The aftermath of this nineteen and a half hour duty period was the need to justify my decision to the government regulators. BOAC was, of course, delighted to have its passengers and aircraft arrive only a few hours late, without additional expense. The Ministry must have accepted my reasons for I never heard from them, but in hind sight I think that I would not have repeated it in similar circumstance. The need to stay fresh enough to deal with another diversion cannot be forgotten.

BEA Airtours

During 1971 the inclusive tour operator BEA Airtours had arranged to obtain some of our original 707-436s. They were flying the clipped-wing, shorter-haul Comet 4B, handed down, from the main-line BEA operation and now with high density seating. Their routes extended throughout the Mediterranean and they now wished to expand horizons with a longer range aircraft, as the Comets approached the end of their life.

We were charged with converting an initial group of their pilots to the 707, to be completed at Palma, Mallorca, where BEA had ground engineering staff, and the landing fees were attractive. Flight deck procedures were different from those in BOAC's, and I spent some time as an observer on various Comet flights from Gatwick. The 4B flew a little faster, and had a deeper windscreen panel, giving improved vision forward, but noises and smells were nostalgic reminders of years past. They used a third pilot, instead of our specialist flight engineer.

The inclusive-tour operation involved 'seat-back ' catering. Trays were wrapped in plastic film, and contained equally plastic-looking cold food, stowed in the rear of each seat back. The cabin crew served only soft drinks, but sold alcoholic drinks and duty-free goods, from which most of any profit was earned. Seat pitch was knee-bumping and cramping. The cost of these flights was low enough to attract tourists, coinciding with the proliferation of holiday/vacation development in Spain and elsewhere. The cabin was usually crammed with carry-on items on the return flight, taxing the open overhead bins and possibly creating a hazard.

We started the flight conversion in February 1972 with our BEA colleagues enjoying their introduction to the 707. Palma had not yet been swollen by the summer hordes, and it was pleasant to explore the attractive countryside. The local sparkling wines, which at that time were very affordable, some excellent restaurants, and the prevalent good weather: all these compensated for the chaotic situation when we were airborne. I found it difficult to find airspace to practise our high-speed runs, or an emergency descent, finally settling for a track that aimed towards Algeria, and terminated before crossing into their jurisdiction. We fitted in to the commercial traffic, with the cooperation of the local air traffic control, but the lack of positive radar monitoring precluded the use of Palma as a regular training base, as there were delays and disruptions that proved expensive and distracting.

BEA Airtours went on to use the 707-436 on long-distance charter work. Occasionally we saw our old aircraft in their original stamping grounds on the eastern routes, albeit under new colours. Perhaps they knew the way well enough to help their new crews.

Moscow

Our route from London to Tokyo via the former Soviet Union landed at Moscow's international airport, Sheremetievo. BEA and Aeroflot had been operating services between the two cities for many years, but for us it was a novel experience. Initial contact began when we were transferred to the control centre at Riga, Latvia. Speaking good English, a woman relayed our position to the Soviet controllers, and was our only contact with the land below. We were using a dedicated radio channel, and could not hear any other transmissions. Occasionally she would issue instructions; otherwise the frequency was silent. The arrival at Moscow was progressed by a series of short transmissions instructing us to descend, and change heading. Eventually we were directed on an intercept heading to the final landing approach, when we could use the western-type ILS. In the winter, the landing lights illuminated snowflakes moving up the beams with disturbing velocity. As soon as the runway came into sight it was possible to see the shapes of many parked and inactive 4-engined Ilyushin-62 jets surrounding the airport perimeter.

Navigation across Soviet territory to Siberia and Tokyo was by non directional radio beacons. We had been told that our progress would be monitored by their radar, and would be notified if we strayed from the approved routeing. We had to convert all metric height instructions into feet using a conversion card. Specific alternate airports were nominated to calculate fuel requirements, with Leningrad (now St. Petersburg) and Helsinki available from Moscow. We were told by the Soviet authorities that if an en route landing became essential there would always be an airport within reasonable distance. We would be directed there and advised of the radio beacon frequencies. Their standard airport had a 3,000 metre runway and was equipped with two radio beacons. The approach patterns were also standardized, involving a square letdown procedure similar to the one that we had used in BSAA to perplex the Brazilian controllers at Rio de Janeiro. We could use the airport at Khabarovsk, 780 miles north of Tokyo, if short of fuel on the long haul return flight between Japan and Moscow. Situated on the Amur river, close to the Chinese border, this large industrial city was the regional centre for the Far East division of Aeroflot.

The journey into the city of Moscow was by bus, with blacked out windows that hid the drab outside scene. We initially stayed at the Intercontinental Hotel, close to Red Square and the Kremlin. The downstairs bar, always seemed to be packed with heavy drinkers in the last stages of inebriation. Food was a real problem, as the battle to be served in any of the local restaurants could absorb several hours, and the result was usually disappointing. We decided to bring as much food with us as practicable, and pooled our supplies to create a combined snackery. The only local bargain was a fur hat, especially if bought in one of the shops that traded only in foreign currency.

Another hotel was the vast Ukrainia, an older edifice built in the grand Stalinist-wedding-cake style, perched close to the banks of the Moskva River. Each floor was guarded by a dragon lady and her assistant, booking us in and out. The number of uniformed personnel on the streets seemed to equal those dressed as civilians. We discussed security, bugging, and whether or not we were being followed. We had to obtain a special visa, after providing many personal details. Our aircraft were always guarded, with a Kalashnikov-toting trooper standing at the top of the steps with his long greatcoat flapping in the wind. Our passports were collected on arrival and returned on departure.

The very large rooms in the old hotel were furnished with solid and traditional furniture, and archaic telephones. After discussing the probability that their conversation was bugged, one crew decided to search for the offending item. After taking the telephone apart unsuccessfully they looked behind the wall art, again without result. Lifting a carpet in the central part of the room they discovered a shiny small metal object, and curiously unscrewing it to further investigate the metal box beneath, were astounded to hear the crash of a released chandelier down below.

Irish antics

A charter flight to Toronto, using the 707-436, was an occasion to remember. We were flight planned via Manchester and Shannon to pick up the rest of our passenger group who all belonged to an Irish-Canadian society. After a two hour delay at Manchester, we arrived in Shannon at 5 pm on a sunny July afternoon. Our passengers disembarked to sample the delights of duty-free shopping while we took on fuel.

We were unable to start number 2 engine for departure. A jet engine is really a can into which compressed air is fed, with fuel sprayed in and ignited. The Rolls-Royce Conway engine had two igniter plugs for this purpose. Both igniters had failed. We disembarked the passengers. There were no spare plugs at the airport, as our airline had relinquished its inventory after the worsening security problems.

They took a plug from the adjacent number 1 engine and fitted it into position. Testing its operation required selection from the flight deck. Someone had to listen, very close to the engine, and one of the ground engineers acted as a messenger to tell us the results.

'Try it again' said the messenger, and as I selected the start ignition switch there was a loud bang.

'Holy Mother of God, you've killed the poor devil.'

I really thought that we had done something unimaginable, but in reality what had occurred was the collapse of a box upon which the listener had been standing. When we had recovered our composure, we discovered that each of the other engines had only one serviceable igniter. London already knew. The policy was to allow this situation to develop, as there were spares at each station but only on our normal routes. As a result of this misplaced economy, we ran out of flight-duty-time, and had to night-stop to await the spares.

Polar wanderings

Our polar service to Japan went north-westwards via Anchorage in Alaska and although the route did not actually go north of 80° latitude, it did skirt the magnetic pole, causing magnetic compasses to be useless. We did not have inertial navigation equipment, and carried an extra navigating first officer whose main task was to correct our gyroscopes for heading accuracy by using a polar path compass to take astronomical sightings. Crossing the northern part of Greenland and Ellesmere Island we flew close to Tuktoyaktuk, in the Canadian North West Territories, before crossing Alaska. The 80-mile-long massif crowned with Mount McKinley (20,320 feet above mean sea level) was off to our right as we descended towards Anchorage. This, the highest mountain in North America, was impressive and both a foreboding sight to the aviator and a magnificent panorama for the passengers.

The frequency of this service was only twice a week, giving us a few days to explore and to become accustomed to the time-zone difference. Surrounded by glaciers and permanently snowy peaks, Anchorage is best seen in the long days of the northern summer. In the early Seventies urban development had not yet modified the older parts of the city, and we found many old hands willing to discuss local history. Most of the expansion of the area had been made possible by the float and ski planes. It seemed that almost everyone flew, and probably owned, or had access, to a small aircraft.

One of our flight engineers was invited on a fishing trip with the pilot of a Cessna 185 floatplane, which is a good load carrier, having a large cabin and excellent performance. They had a good day, catching many king salmon. The pilot was about to stock his storage refrigerator for the season. This was a series of holes cut in the permafrost below his back yard. When the time came for return, the aircraft was well laden with large salmon. They had landed on a straight stretch of river a few hundred feet in length, and where the take-off path ended when the river turned sharply left. The river was bounded with tall trees. As they sped across the water, and the floats came up on their steps, the aircraft at first refused to become airborne, but at last the pilot managed to break the drag of the water by rocking the wings to unstick one float, then two, and climb just in time to clear the trees.

Our next day's work took us to Tokyo and Osaka. We were still using Tokyo's Haneda, and it seemed strange to be in transit after so many years. Several days of flying to reach the Japanese capital had now been shortened by the reach of long-range aircraft. The route from Tokyo to Osaka is the second busiest in the world, exceeded only by Tokyo-Sapporo, although only taking just over an hour to fly. We were using the old airport, twenty years before the new Kansai airport was to be opened in 1994, and which would be built on an artificially-created island in Osaka Bay. Osaka is a major industrial city and port with a metropolitan population of more than eight million, and is the home of Japanese drama and puppet theatre. The overall impression is of intense activity.

A trip to Kyoto provided relief from the busy rush of Osaka. Although only about thirty miles north-east, it seemed another world. Full of wonderful gardens and buildings, Kyoto was the imperial capital until 1868, containing two palaces, and many museums, shrines,and temples. I found a street that had ceramic workshops on each side, where craftsmen were working. It was possible to watch the throwing, building, decoration, and glazing of ceramic objects. Many examples of individual creativity were on display. The foot operated throwing wheels, ancient in concept, were still being use d with consummate dexterity.

Distress

All civil aircraft keep a listening watch on the international civil aviation distress frequency of 121.5 megahertz VHF. Military aircraft also use a UHF frequency. Ships do not listen on these frequencies. I have often wondered, when over the lonely oceans, why it should be so difficult to make contact with shipping. With the use of global positioning satellite (GPS) navigation by even the smallest vessels, and most civil aircraft fitted with either GPS or inertial navigational equipment, the location of a ship should be easy.

Once we were flying from Bermuda to Nassau and heard a faint 'Mayday' transmission on the distress frequency. There was no acknowledgment of the call from other aircraft so I responded. We became the relay station between a US Coast Guard ship and the distressed aircraft. This was a small Britten-Norman Islander, which was bound for one of the little Bahamian out-islands. The pilot radioed that he had been unable to find the island, and was very low on fuel. He did not know his position. After twenty minutes, and some guesswork using headings supplied by the lost pilot, we decided that he had overflown his destination, and was well east of his intended track. I advised the Coast Guard of the possible position. As he said that he had only ten minutes of fuel remaining we were able to tell him that the Coast Guard vessel had a radio bearing, and then a radar fix on his aircraft. The little twin-engined airplane ditched as I listened to his last transmission.

We heard later that the rescue had been successful, with no loss of life, but wondered how many other ships were close enough to provide help. The maritime and aviation worlds seemed to need more cooperation.

707 Training Captain

The rapid expansion of our routes in the late Sixties, the adoption of three-pilot crewing, together with many retirements, caused a demand for a large flight training programme. This was concentrated on the VClO and 707 fleets. Sources of recruitment were varied. The College of Air Training at Hamble, in the south of England, was established to provide pilots for both BEA and BOAC. Many ex-services pilots, and those from other airlines, supplemented the Hamble intake. Hundreds of new pilots needed training to fly the big jets. There would probably never again be such a volume of flight training involving large civil aircraft. I was fascinated to be involved in this effort.

The first group of ex-Hamble cadets, who were soon to be nicknamed 'Hamsters', arrived in Shannon for their conversion to the big Boeing. Some of them had been intended for BEA, but had been transferred to us because of our urgent requirements. This did not please them, for they would have been able to gain more aircraft handling experience in the short haul airline. Hamble used the small Beech Baron, a light twin-engined executive-type aircraft, for the advanced flying portion of their course to obtain a commercial pilot's licence. The leap from this to a 707 or VClO was quite a challenge.

One morning, arriving for breakfast in the Shannon Shamrock Hotel with two of our training captains, we encountered a group of young men gathered in the lounge area. They were extremely informally attired. Some had long and unkempt hair, and the general impression was that we faced some problems in motivation, judging by their attitude. This was the first course from the school, ready for their baptism into airline life.

Our senior training captain, himself a fastidious dresser, lambasted them, warning that they should get their hair cut, clean up, and be properly attired when seen in public as examples for the airline and occupation. This had the required effect, although there was some resentment. When it came to flying, however, we were impressed by their ability to progress on the 707. We were building with excellent material, receptive, keen, and intelligent. The first session of landings with a new trainee cadet was usually great fun, and once they located the ground, they progressed rapidly. Introduction to an outboard engine failure during take-off was made with slow power loss, but they were soon able to cope with a sudden failure, although we avoided crosswinds over 10 knots. After completing an average of about 15 hours handling to obtain their Group 2 ratings as co-pilots, we would sign off their Ministry forms. Then they were off on a route trip as supernumeraries, to obtain experience of the normal airline environment and duties. Possession of a navigator's licence then meant further training and supervision to obtain an operations certificate as third pilot/navigator. During the next few years they were given further flying to upgrade their handling proficiency, and remove any crosswind or weather limitations.

Line captains were faced with a wide variety of proficiency when allowing a co-pilot to fly a route segment. There were two co-pilots, and an increasing amount of long-haul flights, reducing the number of opportunities. The smaller number of landings to be shared between three crew members inevitably meant that some would not receive enough exposure to build their experience.

The situation was further exacerbated when BALPA and BOAC introduced a bidding system for trips. This caused the establishment of a depressed class. Those of low seniority found it hard to accrue enough route utilisation, as a reserve category to cover sickness and unforeseen events was needed. Each month, bids were submitted by pilots to fly work-lines. Most of these contained trips with work content up to permitted maximum hours. About 15 per cent contained much less work, and were combined with standby, and other non-line activity. We had a continual task of giving captains and co-pilots a session of refresher flying to obtain sufficient handling. This was called 'recency' to comply with legal minima for regular handling, set by the Ministry,and was very expensive.

The Boeing 777, 747-400, 767/757 series, 737, and Airbus 320/330/340 are all two-pilot crew operations where the problem no longer exists in such proportion, although the very long flights now possible do reduce the number of landings available in each hundred hours of airborne time for the longer-range types. Simulators have now fortunately reached a degree of development that allows much of the need for recency to be more economically satisfied.

Air misses

We used many different airfields for our busy training programme, including Prestwick, Manchester, Bedford, St Mawgan, and Birmingham, but Shannon was always my favourite. Several other airlines also used the airport for training, and we followed a rigorous separation procedure to ensure enough space within the so-called visual circuit pattern, under the guidance of a tower controller.

One afternoon we were in the midst of a four-hour session, and were on final instrument approach with the cloud base at about 1,500 feet. Another 707 from a European airline was in the visual circuit below cloud, doing touch and-go landings. As we broke out of the wispy cloud base I was astounded to find that we were wing tip to wing tip, level with the other Boeing, with no more than a wingspan between us. I could see the pilot's face clearly. My immediate reaction was to select full power and climb away into the missed approach procedure. Luckily my trainee had established his track with enough inaccuracy to be slightly off the centerline, otherwise we would have descended into the other aircraft.

This event was reported over the radio as an 'air miss,' and was followed up by the required written report The tower controller had left his post just when the approach controller had attempted to report our impending arrival. This coordination problem was rectified, but the event led to a rather difficult decision for me. The controller asked me not to file the report. Our head of flight training also asked me not to file the report, saying that it would destroy the good relations between our company and the airport authorities. I could not agree to this. We had been close to certain death. Unless the facts were recorded there would be no guarantee that the information would be available for future procedure evaluation. I was also legally bound to report such a potential accident. My chief thought that I was bloody-minded. Perhaps he was right, but I did file the report. We continued to use the airport for many years without any noticeable repercussions.

Another air miss was rather different. One dusky evening, during a training session at the Thurleigh (Bedford) airfield, we were at 1,200 feet on the final approach for landing when two US Phantom jets streaked across our path. One went just over, and one underneath our nose. They were about twenty feet away from us, so close that I heard their engines. They had flown right through the airport traffic zone without prior notice. We returned to Heathrow, and I was amazed to receive a telephone call from a press agency, well-renowned for coverage of events at the airport. I told them that it was company policy that we could not make statements to the press but, despite this, my morning paper had full details. The agency had been monitoring our radio frequency.

The cause of the Phantoms' appearance was investigated, although never entered in the statistics as an official 'air miss'. They had lost radio contact with the controller at their base in Upper Heyford during a recovery procedure, and were 'temporarily unaware of their position,' which is a nice euphemism for being lost. Hit or Miss

Bedford was also the scene where I witnessed a bizarre but fortunately minor collision between a BEA Trident 3 and the only Comet 3, then belonging to the Blind Landing Experimental Unit (BLEU). Two Trident 3s were in the circuit practicing automatic approaches. I was in a 707, on a routine session of check landings. The Trident 3, a three-engined aircraft, had been stretched from the series 2 to accommodate more passengers, and was now the size of the original design which BEA. had initially rejected. The engines did not provide enough power for a maximum weight take-off, and so a fourth small jet engine had been fitted in the tail, close to the existing auxiliary power unit. The effect was very interesting when viewed from the rear, and a sorry testament to the interference of transitory airline requirements with a good basic design. The blind landing capability of this aircraft was superior to any in the industry at the time, being the product of pioneering research by BLEU and BEA. These two aircraft were the first to be delivered to our sister corporation.

When abeam of the runway I heard one of the Tridents cleared by the tower controller for a low go-around, and instructed not to go below 300 feet. This was because the Comet had been cleared onto the runway, to be ready for take-off after the Trident passed. The Trident struck the Comet's tail fin, knocking part of it off and leaving a long mark along the underside of the Trident fuselage. Luckily there was no further damage to either aircraft. The automatic pilot had apparently lost height after initiation of the go-around, although holding to the runway centre line with impressive accuracy.

Risky rudders

On 8 March 1971 one of our Boeing 707-336s was at Prestwick flying a training session. During the take-off roll, and after V2 (take-off safety speed) had been achieved, the training captain reduced the power of number 4 engine to idle thrust. The aircraft began turning to the right. Thrust was immediately reduced on number 1 and restored on number 4 to regain control. The captain, Jack Wickson, recognised the situation and corrected the asymmetry. Take-off was achieved, missing the control tower narrowly. On landing, difficulty was experienced in maintaining directional control. The rudder could only be moved in one direction, to the right.

Unfortunately this near-disastrous experience was not notified widely. On 31 March 1971, just over three weeks later, a Western Airlines Boeing 720-047B, with a similar rudder installation, was on a training flight at the Ontario airport in California, and was completing an ILS approach with number

4 engine reduced to idle power to simulate an engine-out approach. At 100 feet above the runway a missed approach procedure was initiated. The aircraft climbed to about 500 feet while rotating to the right about its roll and yaw axis, with the nose dropping to a near vertical position, they crashed on the airfield about 400 feet off the runway. The five crew members were killed. The rudder hydraulic actuator support fitting had failed from the weakening effects of stress corrosion cracking. Disturbingly, our Prestwick case had been identical.

Investigation by the US National Transportation Safety Board found that there were insufficient cues for the pilots to determine loss of rudder control, and that only about four seconds remained to effect recovery by adjusting engine thrust. Only 13.8 seconds elapsed between the rudder support fitting failure and the crash. Rudder fitting failures had occurred four times before on training flights involving Boeing 707-300s with the right engines at low power.

A total of 28 cracked fittings were reported between May 1969 and 31 March 1971. Warning from the manufacturers did not reach the flight department of Western Airlines in time, although its engineering department had the information. We in BOAC knew nothing of this history despite being engaged in daily exposure to the risks involved. Modifications involved installing a new fitting made from a better alloy, plus some interim modifications and inspections.

The most serious aspect was the failure of the industry as a whole to warn pilots of a known and potentially dangerous problem. The notification procedures on a world wide basis needed to be improved.

We continued to practice outboard engine failures on take-off, but unless well clear of the ground and at higher speeds, avoided reducing the power on number 4 engine. We also limited the thrust reduction to a level where engine response could be guaranteed, as that of the turbofan engine was very sluggish when set at idle thrust. Our airline installed new rudder support fittings as soon as the components could be obtained.

Machrihanish again - after 26 years

We were very crowded in the Prestwick circuit pattern with four training jets and commercial traffic absorbing the airspace. I wanted to find some crosswinds for command training. We had an arrangement with the RAF allowing use of the NATO runway at Machrihanish, at the end of the Kintyre peninsula. The base was now manned only as standby, on a care-and-maintenance status, with a fire crew, and small administrative staff. The wind was strong, blowing at 90° across the runway. The day was sunny with a few clouds — unlike my visit twenty-six years previously. We had the place to ourselves, and were able to land alternately to the west and east, saving fuel and time. Apart from the turbulence created by the wind cascading off the surrounding hills, we had a peaceful and productive session.

This was watched by the station commander from his old Humber car. To the north of the runway there were several large fields before the ground rose abruptly. In one of these were several hundred sheep. After a couple of landings I began to notice that these animals were running to the far corner of the field as we approached to land. The next landing, from the opposite direction, caused them to run in the other direction. At the time, concentrating on the task at hand, I did not consider what was happening. We were probably ensuring early spring births and a collective weight loss which the local farmer would not appreciate.

Another argument against the use of this airfield came in the form of a large bill from the Air Ministry. Although we had company authority to use the place, the landing fees were nearly three times those of Prestwick, where we had a bulk contract. Perhaps the extra expense was balanced by the savings of fuel and time, but if the sheep had been factored in there would have been an imbalance. Machrihanish was soon removed from our list of training airfields.

Command Courses

Retirements and expansion were continuing to create promotion vacancies. These would all occur on the VC10 and

707 fleets, as transfers to the 747 became effective for the more senior captains. Nine years had elapsed since there had been any promotion within the airline. Most co-pilots had little pilot-in-command experience, but had been in the airline for a long time. A command training programme was devised to ensure that they would be adequately prepared to replace the ex-wartime generation. They would also have to deal with the influx of new co-pilots, many of whom were very inexperienced, and recently recruited.

The command course placed emphasis on aircraft handling ability, and invested considerable flight time to this end. We knew that the new captains needed to develop confidence when landing in strong crosswind conditions, and even went as far as Iceland to find them.

A thin dividing line exists between encouragement and assessment, and as a course moved to its conclusion, the assessment phase dominated. Our aim was a zero failure rate. The economics were obvious, but had to be set against the ultimate arbiter, safety. Would you be happy for that man to pilot your wife and family? We had a shock. The first VC10 command course resulted in a 40% failure rate. The reasons included weak candidates, arbitrary attitudes by training captains, stressful environment, weather, bad briefing, and a host of other difficulties. Much attention had to be given by management to reassuring line pilots and BALPA that the applied standards were reasonable, and were being used with understanding and fairness. The cost of a failed command course was considerable to the airline. For the unfortunate co-pilot it was a far-reaching disaster, involving loss of self-respect and economic loss. For some, their command course proved excessively stressful.

Whiskers

On one occasion, as the usual training airports were unavailable, we had taken a 707-436 to Bahrain for command training, using a selection of the Gulf airports for the various exercises in relatively uncluttered airspace.

One co-pilot was unable to apply correct rudder after a simulated engine failure on take-off. This had led to some fairly interesting gyrations, limited by the training captain's foot firmly stopping further wrong rudder input. The rules called for another instructor to confirm, and if possible to eradicate the problem, and this became my responsibility.

Again he was applying the wrong rudder quite energetically but my foot braced on the pedal against his force. Had he been able to complete his input we would have swerved off the runway and dug a wing into the ground. After this I decided to land, and try one more from a standing start, this time telling him which engine was going to fail. Once again he applied the wrong rudder. It seemed that he was now experiencing something new, and could not correctly sense sudden yawing movements when on or near to the ground.

I rang London to discuss with our aviation doctor the possibility of some physical deficiency, perhaps in his balance-sensing system, and advised a medical investigation. We sent him back to London, where a full examination revealed that a hair growth through the ear canal on one side was probably responsible for his difficulty. After a small operation to remove the offending whiskers he was able to join a later course and complete his command upgrading without further trouble.

Another similar but tragic case occurred one day when we were using Shannon for a brief visit from London. The pilot was one of our most able and experienced senior first officers. He had been on the 707 fleet for eight years, with an impeccable record, but on this day, when flying a standard check routine, could not control the aircraft adequately. He seemed to be a different person, slower, and lacking coordination. I recommended that he be examined by the company doctor. He was diagnosed as having a brain tumour, and died only six weeks later.

Concorde initiation

Career options and Concorde

Waiting for Concorde was a game played with patience. The long gestation of the supersonic aircraft made it difficult for many pilots to sustain interest or enthusiasm. After all, the 747 was immensely successful, and flew everywhere. It was popular, good to fly, and very productive, offering pilots the opportunity to increase their income. For the training captains a similar calculation could be made. We knew that the airline was to become an operator of the supersonic jet, but the delivery date — in the early 1970s — kept slipping. A letter from our chief requested choices for future deployment when the VC10 and 707 fleets were phased out. The options were limited. The nature of the work was changing with the use of better simulators and there would be less flight time, but more simulation. Another restriction was that transfer to another aircraft type would have to be made before the age of 50, to justify the high training costs. I was faced with a transfer to the 747, or an open-ended wait for Concorde, something of a gamble at my advancing age. There was no agreement on how salary would be paid for supersonic operations, and thus no comparison with the 747. Furthermore our pension scheme based its calculations on final salary within the last few years of service.

For many years, I had followed supersonic development with interest and fascination, so could not resist the chance to become involved. The nucleus group was to be formed by two management captains, plus the training manager, his deputy, and four training captains. I was chosen as one of the four training captains. I knew that a BALPA supersonic evaluation team had produced a comprehensive and informative assessment document covering most aspects of the design and operation of Concorde. The amount of dedicated and intelligent work that went into this team's report has never been properly recognised. Unfortunately, none of them managed to obtain a posting to fly the aircraft in service, although they were able to obtain some flight time with the prototypes.

A further period of waiting followed as the delivery date slipped backwards. Although still very busy with 707 work I also started to prepare for the Concorde by studying the large file of information prepared by the BALPA evaluation team.

My last 707 passenger-carrying flight was from Nassau to London's Heathrow, on 23 February 1975. This was memorable because we had to circle over southwest England at high altitude for one and a half hours. Fog had slowed the landing rate to a crawl. In our case we had enough fuel to hang around, but many aircraft were forced to divert. While circling around several English counties, and calculating the time when we would have to join the congestion of diverted aircraft in Manchester, I had time to consider the fate of Concorde in similar circumstances. We were lucky to obtain an approach to Heathrow, and avoid the cost and disruption of a diversion.

Concorde training was to begin within a few days, at the British Aircraft Corporation Product Support Centre, situated on the airfield at Filton, near Bristol, close to the hangars where the British-assembled share of the aircraft was being completed. Before we could start the course some difficulties had to be resolved between BALPA and British Airways. They had been unable to agree on the pay and conditions that would apply to Concorde line pilots, and as we four training captains, Chris Morley, John Eames, Tony Meadows, and myself, were not designated as management pilots, BALPA had refused to allow us to start the course. This resulted in a last minute move by the airline to appoint us to somewhat spurious temporary management designations to circumvent the ban. This proved unnecessary, as an agreement was achieved.

Supersonic schooling

This first Concorde course included eight captains, and eight flight engineer officers. Brian Calvert was Flight Superintendent, and deputy to Micky Miles, who had already been associated with the aircraft for some time. Norman Todd was Flight Training Manager, with Pat Allen as his deputy, and apart from the four training captains there was also John Oliver, the CAA inspector nominated to watch Concorde operations. The engineers included Lou Bolton, George Floyd, Dave MacDonald, Terry Quarrey, John Lidiard, Arthur Winstanley, Bill Johnstone, and Shep Shepherd.

Lou Bolton, Arthur Winstanley and I were the only three who had been involved with the original Comet 1, and now Concorde, after a gap of twenty-three years. For myself it presented many parallels: manufacturer's course, visits to the assembly halls, and a new and unique type. We were too busy to have much time for comparison or reflection. Classroom work lasted six weeks, and proceeded at a brisk pace. We were being used as guinea pigs to refine the course content and the length needed to train line crews. Although audio-visual self-teaching aids were in use in Toulouse, where the Air France crews were now starting their training, the BAC course did not use this method, relying more on conventional instruction, backed up by a push-button system fitted to each desk, which allowed the instructor to ensure that we had grasped a particular subject. We were able to visit the hangars, and watch some of our aircraft taking shape in one that was used originally for construction of the Bristol Brabazon, and later for the Britannia.

A revolutionary design

In many important respects Concorde was different from previous civil transport aircraft types. There were no high lift devices such as flaps or slats. The fuel system was used to trim the centre of gravity during all stages of the flight, by transfer between tanks. Control was by means of elevons (combining the functions of ailerons and elevators) on the rear of the delta wing, and it was the first time that a fly-by-wire control system had been used on a production civil aircraft. Auto-stabilization and hydraulic artificial-feel systems were installed. Lifting component was obtained by a combination of wing, vortex, and engine thrust. Drag rose rapidly as the angle of incidence increased when flying at lower airspeed. Lift reduced significantly with bank angle. The engines used afterburners (reheat) to achieve enough thrust for take-off, and for supersonic acceleration. A complex engine intake control system was the main reason why Concorde was able to achieve the range and fuel consumption efficiency to make it practicable across the Atlantic.

The Anglo-French Supersonic Aircraft Agreement, which had made the programme possible, was signed in November 1962; and Concorde 001 first flew on 2 March 1969 from Toulouse, piloted by Andre Turcat. Concorde 002, the first British assembled aircraft, G-BSST, lifted off from Filton on 9 April, piloted by Brian Trubshaw. After the longest, most expensive, and most comprehensive development programme in aviation history, BOAC and Air France were about to use the aircraft to carry fare-paying passengers. The production version differed substantially from the prototypes, with a longer fuselage, improved engines, fully transparent windscreen visor, and a 19 foot 3.5 inches (5.88m) increase in the length of the pressurised cabin area. Flight deck instrumentation was revised to correspond more closely to airline requirements and contemporary standards. The automatic approach and landing system, for use in Category 3 weather conditions of very low visibility and cloud base, was an essential part of an operational capability that would try to guarantee arrival in the worst conditions.

While technically advanced in so many ways, the systems of the Concorde are not as advanced as those of glass-cockpit aircraft such as Boeing 747-400, 757/767, 777, or Airbus 320 and 330/340 series. Although complex, and fitted with additional systems to regulate the additional requirements of supersonic flight, the status of flight deck instrumentation compares more closely to a first generation 747, circa 1969. The Automatic Flight Control System (AFCS) needs regular pilot input and programming. There are no flight-management-system computer units. Many functions are set up and controlled by direct crew input through the AFCS and the flight engineering station. Navigation is achieved by the use of triple inertial platform sensor units, which refer to each other, and provide accurate guidance. This accuracy is updated by correction data from distance-measuring equipment when within range of ground based stations.

The Olympus

The Rolls-Royce (former Bristol-Siddeley) Olympus twin spool axial flow turbojet which had powered the Vulcan bomber produced only 11,000lb of thrust. This was then developed for the Vulcan B.2 to produce 20,000 pounds (90kN) thrust. The basic engine is used to power the *Invincible* class of through-deck-cruisers carrying Royal Navy Harriers, and is also used by many industrial power stations. One version flew briefly during 1965 in the cancelled TSR2, producing 31,000 pounds (139kN) of thrust.

Peter Duffey became one of British Airways' first four Concorde training captains in 1975.

Concorde's variant, the Olympus 593, began flight testing in September 1966 under the bomb bay of an Avro Vulcan BlA. More than two years elapsed to convert this Vulcan to a new configuration for this task. The Olympus fitted to the Concorde prototypes was the 593B rated at 34,370 pounds (154kN) of thrust. These engines proved to be extremely smoky, causing much criticism from many sources, and threatening the acceptability of the aircraft. Production Concordes were fitted with the Olympus 593 Mk.610. This included an annular combustion chamber design coupled with a new vaporising fuel injection system which resulted in an almost smoke-free exhaust. This engine produces 38,050 pounds (l 70kN) of thrust with 17 per cent after burning, and includes thrust reversers. From 11,000 pounds to 38,050 pounds thrust, Olympus engine development had been a remarkable achievement.

World's first supersonic airliner course

No crew training simulator was yet available at Filton. To practise our drills and establish location of equipment we used a nose section in one of the hangars that had been fitted with dummy instruments and originally used as a cockpit lighting rig. One problem which had nagged the designers became evident. Reflections from instruments interfered with night vision through the side windows. These have never been eradicated but proved to be tolerable in service. Various rigs and devices allowed us to achieve hands-on dexterity with the many controls.

Our daily routine brought us into contact with many BAC employees, and we were able to build a confident relationship which would provide much-needed information during our initial operational period. The motivation of so many dedicated people added to our feeling of full involvement in this important enterprise.

Jimmy Andrew, one of the original BSAA captains, had been appointed as development manager to watch over the Concorde project during the flight testing period. He devised many of the procedures that would be used in service. Using our old Comet 4 simulator, speeded up to Mach 2, he flew many trial hours with various crews to investigate navigational and control problems. Unfortunately, a short time before we were to take delivery, Jimmy lost his pilot's licence because of medical problems, and his place was taken by Micky Miles, the erstwhile flight manager of our 707 fleet, and a qualified barrister, whom I first met when he was a co-pilot on the Stratocruisers in 1949.

We were given briefings by several Concorde test pilots, including BAC Chief Test Pilot Brian Trubshaw, Deputy John Cochrane, and Assistant Peter Baker. Much of the British area of responsibility was in the development of the engine. The nearly seven-year flight test programme involved 2,480 flights and 5,540 hours in the air, so plenty of information was available. Our workload was considerable, and I was beginning to feel a sense of personal involvement and excitement. We used the BAC board dining room for our lunches, and this helped to cement contact with many of those close to the project.

We were looking forward to flying, and welcomed the end of ground school, much was accompanied by the usual Civil Aviation Authority examination. The CAA, with a heavy responsibility on its hands that involved politics as well as its normal functions, was leaving nothing to chance, and could not leave any record of inadequacy uncorrected. The publicity surrounding Concorde was a major factor in our lives, and would have many ramifications in the coming months. After a very pleasant send-off from the BAC instructors, we were each presented with a model Concorde, suitably inscribed, to commemorate completing BAC's first SST course.

Toulouse

The only Concorde simulator suitable for our training purposes was situated at Toulouse-Blagnac airport, where the French assembly line was based, together with the headquarters of Sud Aviation (later Aérospatiale). This meant a visit to the delights of the Haute-Garonne. We would become quite familiar with the rather tortuous journey from London until the BAC Concorde simulator became operational in August 1976. Toulouse was reached by Air France Caravelle via Bordeaux, or via Paris and transfer to an Air Inter Dassault Mercure. I had two BAC instructors during the 20-hour simulator course. Eddie MacNamara was one of the test pilots, and Al Smith was a production pilot. The extensive syllabus covered subsonic handling and use of equipment and emergency procedures. The supersonic high-level portion was new for us, and involved considerations of trim changes, airframe heating, navigation, engine failure, and trans-sonic flight, where aerodynamic drag increased dramatically. The controls were well designed, with the rams-horn control wheel allowing a good view of the many instruments. There was no outside visual simulation or representative motion. Nevertheless, we came away with a good knowledge and familiarity of procedures and drills.

Cooperation between French and British technical and operational staff was very friendly. I was surprised by the way we were accepted within the Sud-Aviation community and supposed that they'd had plenty of time to rub off any rough edges long before we arrived. The provision of a bilingual dictionary of technical terms, two inches thick, and containing thousands of specialised words, contributed significantly towards this understanding.

On one occasion we had completed our evening meal in a restaurant close to the centre of town, and on leaving, walked round the street corner to find our car attended by a gendarme. I had parked it in a bus lane. The policeman volunteered a long and involved statement which left us feeling uninformed but conscious of impending trouble. We instinctively decided to play dumb, ignorant tourists, shrugging our shoulders. After showing him my UK driving licence he suddenly beamed and waved us off with a nasty looking baton. Concorde was apparently alive and well in Toulouse in spirit as well as in name, and our joint aeroplane adventure was, perhaps, serving to revive the *Entente Cordiale*.

Waiting

There was more delay before we could start our flight training at Fairford, where the BAC Flight Test Centre was established.

Concorde 202, G-BBDG, had first flown in February 1974, and was full of test equipment. It was the first British production aircraft, never put into airline service, and was retired in 1981. Concorde 204, G-BOAC, was completed in 1975. Both aircraft were planned to be used for our training programme, but were unavailable for us until July of that year.

Many tasks occupied our time, including training in pressure breathing. With the possibility of a cabin pressure loss at supersonic cruise heights reaching to 60,000 feet, survival depended on obtaining an oxygen supply within a few seconds. The special masks developed for this purpose used oxygen pressure to clamp the thing firmly to the face. The technique required practice, as it was possible to wallop face and nose. As the atmospheric pressure is so low at these heights it is necessary for oxygen to be supplied at a positive pressure. This involves learning how to avoid pressurising the lungs, and controlling the flow of oxygen while at the same time mastering the art of communicating through clenched teeth.

Among the various new subjects to consider was noise, which would be one of our major concerns. Concorde is very noisy on take-off, and needs to be flown carefully to avoid being banned from many airports. Also the boom created by the shock waves at supersonic speed (quite different from sheer noise) needed to be minimised and understood. BAC had a department, headed by Gordon Styles, which was dedicated to the research and evaluation of noise, and they provided us with valuable information. We were to spend many months preparing and revising techniques and procedures.

First Concorde flights

The planned date for our flying was deferred yet again, and to keep my flying licence valid I had to fly a refresher 707 session. A trip from London to Prestwick and back early in July 1975, plus a few landings, unexpectedly brought me back into touch with the old 436. One side of my brain was full of new information fighting the old, but it was a pleasure to handle the responsive Rolls-powered 400 series for one last time. Within a week we were on our way down to Fairford, where we would begin our association with another magnificent aircraft.

Concorde 202, G-BBDG, stood gleaming in the morning sun outside the huts that served as accommodation for the test centre. My first session of landings was with test pilot Johnnie Walker, but apart from a high altitude supersonic session over the Bay of Biscay with Roy Radford, I was under the care of Eddie MacNamara. The test pilots were helpful, if a little diffident with our group. We were able to experience the effect of engine failure at Mach 2.02 (i.e. more than twice the speed of sound) when spilled air from the intake caused an opposite reaction to that expected, and also to handle the aircraft without auto-stabilisation, demonstrating the excellent basic stability. The test pilots had discovered how easy it was to lose height when circling an airfield. The auto-throttles, set to control a specific airspeed, did an accurate job, but a small nose down pitch could result in descent without any physical cue. We soon learned to be alert to this effect. The droop nose provided excellent visibility when on final approach, and had an intermediate setting for take-off. When raised after take-off the wind noise reduced dramatically. At higher speed the visor was raised to fully streamline the nose profile, and silence reigned. The prototype aircraft were fitted with a visor that obscured forward vision, but production Concordes had a fully transparent visor that gave us the ability to see ahead.

The achievement of a smooth landing, always a mark of confidence and satisfaction to a pilot, was possible through a simple technique. The delta wing produced considerable ground effect, and as the runway approached this could be sensed as a cushioning feeling, provided that the descent rate was moderate. The pilot's eye height, similar to that in the 747, is about 35 feet above the runway at touchdown. With a steady approach speed over the last part of descent, the auto-throttles are disengaged at about 50 feet wheel height above the runway, and the power smoothly reduced at about 20 feet with the nose held steady in pitch to counteract nose-down trim forces. Any relaxation of back pressure on the controls allows the aircraft to land immediately, and with a bang. Care has to be taken to avoid over-rotating the nose, as a tailwheel strike can result, and if this is accompanied by a small bank angle this can mean contact with the runway by the thrust-reverser buckets as they are deployed after touchdown. The lack of side fuselage area, and the short wingspan helps to produce very good crosswind performance. The use of roll input into wind for take-off in strong crosswinds is avoided.

We soon became used to the high drag on approach at low speeds. Power had to be increased as we slowed. To reduce noise the initial approach was flown at higher speeds, if weather conditions allowed. A deceleration of about 30 knots between 800 and 500 feet above the runway helped to keep the decibels down. Despite fears to the contrary we found that handling with the auto throttles disengaged was simple, provided that speed was carefully controlled.

Need for speed

With no other civil aircraft is it necessary to fly as fast as possible when ever practicable. The fuel penalty on the Concorde for being too slow is considerable. This is especially the case when having to follow a slower aircraft on a long approach path. The economic and range penalties involved when arbitrary speed restrictions are imposed can be very costly. Prolonged low speed flight after take-off stops the aircraft from climbing rapidly. The effect is to spread more noise over a greater area in an attempt to reduce noise close to the departure point. The US rule limiting speed to 250 knots below 10,000 feet is demanding, as are the height restrictions included in standard departure routings from so many airports.

Another new concept for us was the 'zero rate of climb speed,' which now formed a basic factor in performance certification. For any aircraft weight there is a situation when the thrust available is not enough to provide a climb. With Concorde this is also related to speed. Slowing up increases the drag, so the climb rate is reduced even further. When considering engine failure cases the performance calculations have to make provision for this effect. The aircraft should never be allowed to fly too slowly.

One similarity between the 707 and Concorde was the need to counter, with the use of rudder, the swing caused by an engine failure during take-off. A bonus was the provision of a slip indicator, allowing accurate adjustment of the controls to achieve the best climb rate. This involved a small bank angle away from the failed engine, to achieve zero slip, a procedure which any budding twin-engined pilot trainee would recognise. A small complication when landing on three engines was the continued use of the auto-throttles, which caused small changes of heading as they maintained the selected speed. The emergency case of a double engine failure on one side was the subject of much investigation during the development years. Such an event was thought to be more likely than on many other aircraft because the engines were mounted in pairs under the wings, and there was a possibility that, in the event of engine break-up, pieces could be passed into the adjacent engine. Many drills and procedures were written around this eventuality.

A landing with two engines failed on one side produced an interesting situation. The power available to conquer low speed drag was halved. The auto-throttles could not be used, and manual throttle input was required. Speed was increased to provide a margin above the increased zero rate of climb speed, and the approach was flown using zero slip to preserve performance. Low speed had to be avoided. Temporary use of afterburner could provide power for speed recovery, but the rudder force available was then marginal. At low altitude a commitment to land would be made and speed reduced progressively to cross the runway threshold. This speed reduction required the nose to be raised to keep on the approach path, and avoid landing short of the runway. I was quite used to this procedure, as the Boeing 707's two-engined approach was similar in concept and execution.

This sort of approach is best practised on a good simulator. When done during flight training it is not, of course, safe to actually stop two engines. We simulated the two-engine failure case by throttling two engines on one side to minimum thrust, but they were still producing power, making the exercise unrepresentative. Despite the availability of this power from the 'dead' engines I found that we had to very careful to avoid low speed occurring, and always felt that it could be dangerous.

Stopping short at Bahrain

Concorde 204, G-BOAC, was involved in the 'endurance' flying programme, on a planned series of flights from Bahrain to Singapore and Kuala Lumpur. This aircraft was to be used by the airline, and had a full seating configuration, modified by the provision of a flight-test observer's station at the first row of seats. After some right-hand seat landings from Fairford with Roy Radford, the next day found me on a 747 bound for Bahrain, where I would complete the flying training syllabus.

The first flight involved conversion to Concorde G-BOAC, which had a different inertial navigator installation and other changes to bring it to the delivery standard. We climbed to the certificated ceiling of 60,000 feet to complete a few exercises.

The next flight was to investigate the effects of high incidence. Concorde does not stall when the nose is raised and speed is reduced. Eventually control is lost, and an unrecoverable sideways yaw and tail slide will develop as the incidence increases beyond safe limits. There are several protection systems that cut in to warn the pilot, and help to avoid such a situation. These include application of down elevon to counter sudden pilot up input at low speed, a stick shaker, and a stick wobbler accompanied by a strong down elevon input. Eddie MacNamara took us to 20,000 feet for a demonstration, and reduced to approach speed, asking me to pull hard back on the controls to activate the shaker and wobbler. The air data system on Concorde provides dual indication of incidence which is very valuable for a number of reasons. I am quite strong, and pulled hard as instructed, watching the incidence increase rapidly. The warnings operated, but I was able to over power the wobbler control input and start to go towards a higher incidence. Eddie was obviously surprised by this, and asked me to lower the nose. I think we reached about 17° or 18° of incidence. Nominally 23° is the incidence when control is lost.

When we returned to Bahrain and took the aircraft to a parking area for the night we were instrumental in holding up the programme for a few days. A ground marshaller, naturally inexperienced at this delicate task, signalled us into a tight turn, and just before the turn was completed, waved us to an urgent stop. I had no time to roll forward, and applied the brakes immediately. This twisted a hydraulic seal in the right side main undercarriage oleo cylinder, starting a hydraulic seep. This event demonstrated the need for care in handling parking manoeuvres by rolling forward to relieve any undercarriage stress. A spare oleo was flown from England, and I was presented with a photograph of the wheel tracks as evidence of the crime.

Singapore bumps

Flights out of Singapore and Athens had revealed a problem that was still present during the introductory service period. We were aware of the fuselage flexibility. At Fairford during a refuelling period between training sessions I had stood on the steps outside G-BBDG's front door, and pushed on the fuselage, which moved perceptibly, and continued to oscillate visibly for some seconds. When taxiing the aircraft, ground speed was indicated on the INS (Inertial Navigational System) readout. We avoided 9 knots, because the nose would bob with a small divergent motion when we ran over any bumps. I called it the 'nine-knot nod.'

Take-off at Singapore had to cross a significant bump about a third of the distance down the runway. This started a pitch oscillation which grew to such dimensions that instrument reading was difficult, and crew heads were occasionally hitting the ceiling. The bump compressed the nose gear oleo, which then unloaded, by which time the main gear oleos had been compressed. The excitation was exactly at the rate to produce a divergent and increasing flight deck movement. This raised the question of other airports where this effect might be met. Reducing the take-off weight altered the excitation characteristics to eliminate the problem, but it was some time before the final fix was discovered. Meanwhile we had a list of runways with known bumps where weight would have to be severely restricted. Some runways were unknown quantities, including 31L at New York

JFK. The problem was finally solved by modifying the main gear oleo struts, thus changing the excitation characteristics.

After another couple of sessions, including one with Brian Trubshaw, my training syllabus was complete, and I caught the next 747 home. Three days later I was on another 747 on the way to Singapore, where the endurance programme was now based, to fly some trips to Melbourne. The large group of BAC personnel accommodated in the Marco Polo Hotel included Brian Trubshaw, John Cochrane, Pete Holding, Brian Watts, and Bob McKinlay, the project manager. Also evident were high level BAC Board members including Sir Geoffrey Tuttle, and some of the design team from Filton. One interesting person from the UK Department of Trade and Industry was Mr J Hayhurst, who usually appeared with a small case chained to his arm, in which reputedly there were funds to defray our ever-mounting expenses.

We training captains were to be exposed to en route operation of Concorde prior to our checkout, and also to act as guinea pigs to test our reaction and adaptability to the aircraft and procedures. The initial intention was to keep us out of the decision-making loop, which would be confined to our management pilots. We found that the lack of information produced by this policy was rather unfortunate, and it did produce some perplexity in the BAC ranks, initially denying us some valuable background information. In the midst of our stay in Singapore we were disturbed to discover that Micky Miles had left our ranks, and gone home. Apparently he had managed to scrape thrust reversers on the runway when landing with the nose high and bank applied. Brian Trubshaw had decided that he could not approve his qualification on Concorde. This was a great disappointment for Micky of course, as he had put in years of work preparing manuals, procedures, and many other arrangements, most of which proved to be invaluable. Seven pilots would have to do the work of eight. Brian Calvert took over as Flight Manager Technical. The flow of information was improved, perhaps as it may have been realised that we would need to take on additional tasks, and that we needed a fuller understanding of the aircraft to be effective in our training function.

Melbourne races

The distance from Singapore to Melbourne is 3,375 nautical miles, slightly more than the maximum commercial range for a fully loaded Concorde when allowed to climb out without delay. The time taken for this was just under four hours. The route took us very close to Bali as we flew across the Indonesian archipelago, and I wondered if we had gone close enough to drop a sonic boom there. At cruise levels the boom carpet spreads 20 nautical miles on each side of the aircraft track.

Tropical air at cruise level is colder than in temperate climates, as the tropopause is much higher at equatorial latitudes, and is one reason why heavy cloud builds to extreme height in the tropics. The colder air allows the aircraft to climb above 56,000 feet during the initial cruise climb. Areas of active thunderstorm clouds reached up to that level and above. As we flew across one large area of disturbed cloud I noticed that the indicated outside air temperature was dropping rapidly. The autopilot was set to control us at Mach 2.02. The colder air caused the indicated Mach number to increase with the result that the autopilot raised the nose to keep below the 2.02 limit. We started to climb rapidly, and as we went up the Mach number increased further. Soon the climb rate was approaching 8,000 feet per minute, and we were approaching the 60,000 feet ceiling limit. Although Concorde had been flown to higher altitudes during the test programme we were supposed to be operating a representative commercial flight.

The only way to avoid exceeding our permitted limit was to reduce engine power. During supersonic cruise, as previously explained, the intake system is controlled by a sensitive arrangement so that the engine is supplied subsonic air. The engine demand for air is matched by air volume and pressure. The system controls the dimension of the intake, and positions the intake shock wave by adjusting hydraulically-operated and electrically-controlled ramps. Power reduction had to be made carefully to allow this system to operate. Sudden reduction could result in engine choking, backflow, and surge, causing power loss and severe vibration. We managed to reduce power carefully, to control the speed and height increase. Then, suddenly, the outside temperature started to rise again. The aircraft began to descend rapidly and we were faced with the difficult task of choosing when to restore the power. Inevitably we lost height and speed, causing a longish delay before climbing back to the normal cruise.

This event was repeated, and took my attention away from the operational and tactical aspects of the flight. I suggested that we use the auto-throttles to control the speed and was advised that there was a risk of engine surge.

We did use them, however, keeping an alert watch on engine-power changes. This settled things down somewhat, but autopilot speed control in the disturbed tropical air had proved inadequate, causing excessive pilot distraction and workload.

An interim procedure was written into the flight manual. Until a modified autopilot control-mode could be designed and tested we restricted handling to the initial group of pilots. The eventual fix, devised by Aérospatiale, was excellent, although taking some months to appear. It involved use of the auto-throttles in a standby mode, sensing acceleration in time to control speed. The North Atlantic route did not have any problem, as we flew lower, but the route from London to Bahrain was occasionally affected during the summer, as was the segment from Bahrain to Singapore.

Popularity and politics

After landing at Melbourne we were handed a telex message from Brian Trubshaw advising that there had been a complaint from Bali about a sonic boom and recommending an amended route for the return. This reinforced the extreme sensitivity of our routeing choices, and the need for navigational accuracy.

Our endurance programme flights into Melbourne were the catalyst for a large public demonstration at the airport, protesting against the operation of a supersonic transport over the Australian land mass. The supersonic corridor from Singapore crossed the north-west coast above the Great Sandy Desert, over unpopulated desert for 900 nautical miles, to the Nullarbor Plain and the Great Australian Bight, before

paralleling the coast towards Melbourne. After arrival we were smuggled from the airport out of sight of the crowds.

The next day, relatively unnoticed, we were able to depart, but knew that a special monitoring station had been set up below our route over the Nullarbor Plain. The Australian Minister of Transport, Mr Charles Jones, had decided to be present at the site. We had a special radio channel to talk to him, and the monitoring station. When we passed overhead they could not detect any significant boom. His reaction was reported as: 'Quite frankly the sonic boom would not have satisfied your kids or my grandchildren on cracker night. As far as the sonic boom is concerned this is a non-event.'

My guess was that they were, accidentally no doubt, in the wrong place. The environmental lobby subsided after our visits had passed without any significant recorded noise, but for many reasons we did not extend our commercial operation through to Australia as originally planned, although permission was granted. This event showed that, wherever we went, Concorde would be subject to local politics and pressure. We would have to be very careful.

Finding out

After each trip there was a post-flight discussion with the test pilots and programme managers. For us this involved a double session because of the twin establishments, run by Brian Trubshaw and John Cochrane. One was on the top floor of the hotel, and one on the bottom. Both were spacious, and provided with the usual elements of hospitality, including well-stocked refrigerators. A similar and separate arrangement existed at Fairford. The apparent chasm between chief and deputy chief test Pilots was interesting, but we were far too busy for involvement in such a diversion. We did have to debrief in each location, and this had to be endured, although the second call was always more verbose, as the libations seemed stronger.

Checked out

We left Singapore for London on 22 August 1975, and I flew the segments to Bombay and Beirut under the watchful eye of Brian Trubshaw. This was to be my final route trip under supervision, and all went routinely. Because of the Jebel Liban mountains it is usual to arrive over the Mediterranean coastline from the east above 10,000 feet, quite close to the airport. This requires a rapid descent. We had usually managed to avoid delay in previous aircraft by using air brakes in the Comet, or by lowering the gear and flaps on the 707. Concorde has no air brakes or flaps, but the use of reverse engine thrust is permitted below 30,000 feet. I was able to use this procedure to good effect, but used it only once during the next five years. After achieving a reasonable landing on the downward sloping runway at Beirut, avoiding the temptation to prolong the hold-off and risk a tail strike, my day was over. Norman Todd flew the next segment to London while I sampled the food from a passenger seat. We had 100 passengers on board and full holds.

Gander and Beirut

We lost no time in beginning flights to Gander, with full loads of invited and influential passengers, all of whom were naturally curious. These ranged from the Archbishop of Canterbury to radio personalities, captains of industry, other airline executives, and the politicians. Average block time was 2 hours 35 minutes, with an hour's transit before return to London. One of these flights had to turn back because of uncertain weather at Gander. We were unable to receive an updated report in time to justify continuing, and I thought briefly that a DC-7C style teleprinter would have been very useful.

During one of the turn-rounds at Gander I was tapped on the shoulder by the BAC flight test engineer who asked, 'Do you like salmon?' I confirmed this, and so saying, was handed a package wrapped in brown paper to place in my briefcase. There was an arrangement to supply all our passengers with a sample of fresh Canadian Atlantic salmon. This had not extended to the crew, but I imagined that a beneficent public relations department had relented. This was not so, as I discovered subsequently. Later that evening we had the pleasure of consuming the illicit fish, which proved quite delicious. Someone had gone short.

On 9 September we switched to Beirut, flying at subsonic level at Mach 0.93 until past Venice. This was about 90 knots faster than all other traffic, and provided one or two interesting air traffic control conflicts. The supersonic part of this route was over water, approaching Beirut from a route running south of Crete and Cyprus. The descent had to be started in time to ensure that we were subsonic to avoid booming Beirut. One of our pilots and a test pilot had, during a previous proving flight, been discussing descent technique, resulting in a delayed descent. This had boomed Beirut and Damascus, generating the apocryphal tale of President Assad cutting himself when shaving, and of local gunfire starting up between warring factions close to Beirut.

On 12 September we flew a hundred UK Members of Parliament to Beirut, for a night stop. The Bristol Hotel was, as ever, providing good food and service, and occupied by the usual polyglot mixture of people. That afternoon the St George Hotel pool and surrounding area was full of our well-fed passengers, soaking up the sun as they viewed the Mediterranean scene. We had interesting conversations with these people, and I was amazed at their diversity of opinion and lack of knowledge about aviation. Next day we flew them back home. That evening the long war started with artillery and small arms fire over the area we had left. We had escaped just in time, flying back to London and its less onerous inconveniences: heavy cloud, rain, and wind.

The aircraft was immediately taken over by another crew, to complete the endurance programme with a final 3 hour 37 minute flight around the Atlantic. During most of this flying we were unable to use British Airways cabin staff because of an industrial dispute. Our many passengers were served extremely well by crews from Gulf Air, Singapore Airlines, and Air India, all of whom coped very efficiently with the new equipment. 6,500 passengers were carried by G-BOAC, including many high-ranking and influential political and business personalities. Flying time totalled 380 hours of which 208 were supersonic. Of the 125 flights, we crewed 63, sharing another 51 with BAC; 11 flights were shared between BAC and government officials.

Concorde airline service

The planned date for starting commercial service was confirmed as 21 January 1976. The interval of four months was to require us to have some refresher flying and gave time for grappling with a mountain of paperwork. I flew G-BBDG on a couple of occasions, including training in the right seat as instructor. A week in Toulouse using the new Aer Formation simulator brought us up-to-date on the latest procedures. This machine had a reasonable visual attachment, allowing good practice of low visibility autolands. It was shared with an adjacent Airbus simulator, and it was necessary to negotiate its use. Once taken over, the other instructor could not obtain control without agreement. This amicable arrangement was never abused.

My tasks included drafting the instructors' guidance notes for our simulator course, which consisted of 19 four-hour sessions, and preparing the autoland section of our operational manual. These kept me fully occupied, with no spare time, as the tasks had to be squeezed in-between visits to Filton, Fairford, and Toulouse. The other six members of our pilot team were also engaged in various projects.

Take-off noise

Concorde produces a lot of noise. It is unwise to stand close to the aircraft when full power and reheat is applied. Vibration is considerable, and the perceived noise decibels reach upper limits. BAC had produced a take-off technique which we used during the endurance flying out of London. The results were unsatisfactory. We made more noise than theoretically

271

expected. A revised technique of airspeed control, immediately after becoming airborne, was devised by Tony Meadows, and this gave much better readings from the monitoring stations. We also introduced a method of minimising noise over areas under our initial climb-out by limiting power increases. Opposition to the aircraft by environmental groups had been intense, and became a political and operational consideration of vital importance if we were to obtain permission for regular commercial operation, especially to the United States.

Our group was very concerned that the reputation and viability of the aircraft might rest on the way we flew. New York was a particularly sensitive case, where the proximity of housing around JFK airport made departure routeings ultra-sensitive. The background to how techniques and procedures were developed to achieve acceptable results is a story in itself. We used the various simulators to devise and practice sustainable and safe methods. These were the subject of close inspection, and even suspicion, by BALPA and other pilot groups. Air France used a different crew drill for take-off noise abatement, and the two airlines needed to coordinate results. BAC had its own monitoring team in the New York and Washington areas, and its noise department produced graphic diagrams for each runway to show the maximum weight for any combination of wind and temperature which would allow us to stay below the permitted noise level.

We then found time to take accumulated leave, and managed to visit friends in Auckland before touring New Zealand's beautiful South Island. We did some fishing and painting, and the peaceful and uncrowded environment was in contrast to the pressures of recent months. I returned with renewed vigour and expectation to begin the Concorde era.

The big day

On 19 January 1976 Norman Todd and I flew Concorde G-BOAA, our initial British Airways aircraft, to Fairford. John Cochrane gave us renewal base checks, revalidating our licences for another six months. Norman was nominated to command the first commercial service on 21 January, with Brian Calvert as co-pilot. Lou Bolton and John Lidiard were the flight engineers. I was to be the standby captain, and at the same time to anchor a special internal television commentary arranged through the BBC and the airline. This meant having my bag packed and wearing uniform in case of need.

On 21 January 1976 synchronised departures by Air France to Rio de Janeiro via Dakar, and British Airways to Bahrain, successfully introduced supersonic travel to the world. Our crewing was limited by the availability of just seven qualified captains. We shared the flying, taking turns, and it was arranged that the inbound co-pilot would command the next outbound service. This helped to maintain continuity for the first few services. Thus I found myself crewed with Brian Calvert for the second service on 26 January. We had a load of 79 passengers who must have been a little disappointed when we were delayed to rectify a flight control snag. The ensuing flight to Bahrain registered a block time of 4 hours 15 minutes for the 3,250 mile flight.

Next morning it was my turn to command. After collecting the usual paperwork in the operations office we walked across the hard-standing towards the aircraft. I was surprised to see that a steel hawser was wrapped round the nose wheel assembly, securing it to a large tractor. There had been a problem on the first service. Before Concorde tanks are filled the aircraft can tip onto its tail if baggage or people are prematurely concentrated in the rear fuselage. The operations manual advises that a maximum of four people should occupy the rear cabin area until refuelling has been completed. The aircraft had reared its nose up on the morning of 22 January, and they were not going to let it happen again. I was able to reassure the local staff, and to warn them to stay out of the rear cabin. Everyone wanted to have a look. We did think of a new check list item, ' Remove any tie-down hawsers.'

The flight back carried only 31 passengers, following a path over the northern Arabian desert, across Saudi Arabia,

Jordan, Syria, and Lebanon to join the route south of Cyprus, Crete, Greece, and up the Adriatic descending to cross Venice at 35,000 feet in subsonic flight. Block time was 4 hours 33 minutes. The subsonic portion of flight had been planned at Mach 0.93, but we soon discovered that the aircraft flew well at Mach 0.95 (about 655 mph) without any fuel penalty, and this was adopted as standard policy.

Another flexibility involved the initial level when climbing south from Heathrow. This was nominated as flight level 250, (25,000 feet). We soon found that it was quite practicable to reach flight level 290. This was often more favourable, collecting a good tailwind. There was usually a shortage of available cruise flight levels across Europe so this added choice was important.

The aircraft was proving predictable and pleasant. We were learning some new techniques. On arrival from Bahrain we often had to hold for a few minutes at low altitude before we could be offered an approach. Fuel consumption was dramatically increased if speed was reduced to comply with the usual holding area limits. The air traffic controllers were most helpful in allowing us to keep the speed high. I found

that if two engines were throttled to idle, and speed held above 250 knots, consumption could be then reduced to about 200 kilograms per minute.

For practical purposes, despite the distance travelled, Concorde is a relatively short haul aircraft in terms of time. The fuel reserves can be equated to those carried by most aircraft leaving Paris, Amsterdam, or Brussels for London. The real difference is that a diversion to an alternate airport, if started before descending below 20,000 feet, can confer a much greater range. Once low-down, the aircraft is usually committed to close alternates, and is vulnerable to traffic congestion causing slow airspeed. Accurate and timely information is therefore needed to allow correct decisions to be made. Concorde operation makes a strong case for flight deck data-link. We had to rely on a system geared to the previous generation of subsonic aircraft, and augmented by help from our company flight watch system, who provided updated information.

Media watch

Concorde has always been in the media spotlight. The initial period of our commercial operation was predictably one of the peak periods. We had many examples of this intense interest, and soon developed a combination of caution and cooperation to deal with the wide range of television and journalistic contact.

Aviation disasters have been big news for the press, which has been helpful in searching for causes, creating a positive situation in which most information can be revealed for public scrutiny. When we started our services the media had just been dealing with a catastrophic Turkish Airlines DC-10 crash that had been caused by a baggage bay door opening in flight after take-off from Paris. The *Sunday Times* Insight team of investigative reporters had been able to piece together much information, writing a series of articles that revealed many but not all the details of this unfortunate event. Not surprisingly this same team had arranged to accompany us on a round trip to Bahrain. Norman Todd and I shared the flying on this, the seventh service to the Gulf sheikdom. The trip outbound was without any problem, arriving early just before 6 pm local time. We arranged to meet the journalists after dinner, finding a large table in the ante-room, close to the hotel's restaurant. Norman leant over to me in confidential and conspiratorial manner, 'Do you like Remy Chambertin?' he whispered.

Knowing this to be a most expensive wine I wondered who was paying, but signified approval by a nod, reasoning that the newspaper would probably foot any bill. Norman oiled the conversation with the serving of many such bottles during the next hours. Our party included the airline's local manager, who was keeping a watching brief on things, and perhaps ensuring that they did not get out of hand. He need not have worried, although it soon became apparent that the reporters were more interested in identifying some deficiencies in our aircraft or the operation. We were able to assure them that we had the privilege of flying a truly remarkable piece of engineering that performed magnificently. Pressed to expound on any problems I was able to steer the conversation round to some inadequacies in their DC-10 story. Eventually they gave up, and on the return flight next day were not very visible. This was just as well, for we had to stop an engine because of a nacelle wing overheat warning (an indication of excess heat in an air duct).

Whites of the eyes

Another and rather different media event occurred when I was approached by an Australian television producer after we arrived in Bahrain. They had a film crew making a Concorde documentary programme, and wished to film the take-off. 'How far along the runway do you run until becoming airborne ?'

I said that this depended on the wind, temperature, and the aircraft weight, so that a more accurate estimate might be available close to departure on the morrow. From the conversation they had every intention of filming our take-off from a very vulnerable, almost dangerous, position. They were going to have a camera team standing in the middle of the runway so that the approaching Concorde could be filmed through the complete take-off sequence. Permission had been granted by the airport authority. Liability, insurance, and other considerations had been cleared with the airline. It only remained for me to convince the upbeat Australian director of the risks.

Next morning, with the relevant information, I consulted the basic flight manual to find out where we could expect to become airborne. We were used to calculating the limiting weight for take-off, but this was never associated with the exact length of ground run before flight. My assessment was imprecise, and I said to the director: 'There are so many variables which could change and thus modify my guess so you should be ready to leave the runway quickly. We'll arrange for you to have a walkie-talkie to contact the tower in case of any last minute problems. You must have ear defenders of some type. Just remember that it is possible for the take-off to be abandoned, and you would have to clear out of the way smartly.'

This was all received with a grin of acceptance. We were cleared to the take-off point on the runway, and informed by the control tower that the team was in position. As we accelerated

with full power and reheats lit I could see them in the distance. They stood in the centre of the runway and it was hard to judge if we would clear them. Concorde becomes airborne in less than half the time that a 747 takes when fully loaded. The last sight of the team was when I raised the nose to fly off; they stood resolutely ahead, and we passed well above them. The result of this exercise was a spectacular publicity scoop. The film was used many times, although we never did start an Australian service.

Tribulations

BAC had contracted with our airline to train the first group of line captains who had bid for the aircraft. This 'contractual' course was to prove contentious for a number of reasons. Ground school was conducted at Filton by the BAC product support team, which had cut its teeth on us eight months previously. The course was intensive, requiring considerable after-hours work. Some course members found this onerous, and had problems with the ARB examination. This obliged them to resit the examination, and pay additional fees. The airline refused to pay the extra charges, and this created bad feeling and stress within the group. No time off was granted between the ground school and the next stage.

The simulator course was split between Toulouse, using the Aer Formation simulator, and Filton, where the new BAC-owned simulator had just become available. The long sessions required many rather disjointed demonstrations of performance and drills. This often meant re-initialising the simulator location, height, speed, and many other factors. Each four-hour session could involve the demonstration of performance, mixed with drills in both supersonic and subsonic flight. Like most conversion courses, the syllabus was devised to cover the ground twice, once for each pilot. Sometimes, unfortunately, no time was left for a repeat because of the excessive content. This was caused mainly by the insistence of our Civil Aviation Authority that every one of the many drills should be practised in the simulator. Our instructor group was able to observe this process from the jump seat. I spent a week in Toulouse, and another week in Filton, silently watching these problems develop. We had no input to the contractual course but were taking note of what we might need to do for our own training. We saw that a few course members were becoming worried by their progress, and that the BAC instructional technique, although knowledgeable and punctilious, seemed trapped in the complexities and constraints of the syllabus. We were not far from the days when it had been thought that pilots who were chosen to fly a supersonic airline aircraft would need to be young and exceptionally qualified. In the eyes of BAC and the airline there could be absolutely no doubt about the capability of any captain who would be in command of a new Concorde. The test pilots, understandably, did not wish their carefully developed project to be threatened by any possible incompetency.

Problems began to culminate when flying began. We were able to observe some of the sessions, and attend the briefings. A general atmosphere of resentment prevailed because of the pressure of time and content. I thought that an interval for revision and regrouping would have avoided what was to come. The flying performance of a few pilots did not meet essential criteria. A couple of captains decided to resign from the course. The cost of this decision was substantial, and would also reduce our crewing complement, and affect our build-up of services. Some of the test pilots used an instructional technique that was different from those current in our airline. This appeared to provide less encouragement and analysis during flight, and was sometimes less informative afterwards. The more sensitive captains felt that they were being assessed, not trained. The contractual course failed to produce desired results.

For the first time in our airline it had been decided that there would be no separate establishment of route supervisory captains on the Concorde fleet. The training captains would extend their conversion function to full route training and check-out of converted pilots. No doubt this was inevitable because of the small numbers involved, and our limited experience on the aircraft. We hoped that we could reduce the failure rate.

Washington

At the end of May 1976 we began the route phase for the contractual course. We had just received approval to begin the Washington (Dulles) service on 24 May, and here we were, showing the way to the new group. Although we were more knowledgeable after a year of flying Concorde, the new route required further extension of our competency and understanding. Operation to the US involved grappling with the large environmental lobby. Flying into New York (JFK) depended on giving a good account of ourselves at Dulles. Standards of handling on take-off would be critical to achieve an acceptable noise level. A special problem was our need to slow down to subsonic flight on arrival at least 35 nautical miles before the US coast, close to Atlantic City, to avoid dropping a sonic boom on New Jersey. Unfortunately, we could not start the descent at the correct distance point, as a restricted military area required us to stay at 52,000 feet until only 79 nautical miles from the coast. We developed a technique that started deceleration and descent from a final cruising level of about 58,000 feet, calculated to cross the edge of the restricted area at 52,000 feet and with a lower airspeed than usual. The final 13,000 feet of descent was flown rapidly to reach subsonic cruise at 39,000 feet. The wind and temperature had to be watched carefully to ensure that we could descend in time. A fall in the temperature slowed the descent rate, and an increased tailwind could cause us to arrive early. We named this procedure as the 'Fall off the Wall' and when first introduced it enthralled the New York controllers, some of whom were sceptical about our ability to level off smoothly to capture the allocated altitude. The passengers hardly knew that this was happening. The automatic flight control system was most efficient in levelling off from the rapid descent without any noticeable change in cabin conditions.

On one of my early flights to Dulles we had just reached 39,000 feet when I was faced with an amusing question. The jump seat was occupied by the Mayor of New York, and we could see Manhattan and Long Island clearly about forty miles away to the north.

'When are we going to be on the ground?' he asked. I replied that we had about another 35 minutes to go. We had to follow a rather tortuous airways routeing towards Washington.

'Does it take all that time to get down there?' he said, pointing to New York. I reminded him that we were on our way to Dulles, and that as yet the Port of New York Authority and the US government had not yet approved our operations into JFK airport. Like a true politician he smiled, and riposted. 'It's all politics you know my boy. Don't worry.'

We had to wait for another seventeen months before permission was granted.

San Juan charter

The first G7 (Group of Seven leading industrialised nations) economic summit meeting was convened for 27 June 1976 in San Juan, Puerto Rico. The Prime Minister, James Callaghan, wished to arrive in style. We were advised by HM Government that there would be a Concorde charter. This was the first of many. I was nominated to command this, and became involved in the detailed planning, along with Brian Calvert, who was now our Flight Technical Manager. There was some doubt as to the payload that we could safely carry on this longer sector. The choice of an alternate airfield was difficult. We could use a couple of Caribbean airports provided that we diverted at higher altitude, but once low down we would be committed to use a local field called Roosevelt Roads, at the other end of Puerto Rico.

The Foreign Office pressed us to firm up on the passenger load. They wanted to send about sixty people, and some heavy items of equipment. Brian went on leave so I was left to decide what we could offer, settling for a maximum of thirty with normal baggage. This was accepted, and the usual complex planning for a VIP flight rolled into action. British Airways, and its predecessor BOAC have always had great experience in organising such flights.

On 26 June the day was a scorcher. We were parked in a special area at Heathrow, with marquees close by to cover the departing dignitaries. Security was intense. The aircraft was G-BOAC, gleaming white in the evening sunshine. At the flight planning stage, an hour and a half before departure, we had been confounded by the forecast temperature for take-off, which was two degrees higher than the maximum shown on our performance charts. The exceptional temperature had not been expected. We were close to the maximum weight. I managed to make contact with the performance specialists in BAC and the airline. They agreed that we could prorate the data to determine the performance limit. This was fortunate, for a late arrival would have not been popular. Many arrangements hinged on our punctuality. Apart from the PM we were carrying cabinet members Denis Healey and Anthony Crosland, accompanied by a retinue of civil servants.

The aircraft lifted off from Heathrow on schedule without any concern, and we were soon climbing through Mach 1 over the Atlantic, having passed several slower aircraft during the initial acceleration. A smooth flight was punctuated by a continual assessment of possible alternate destinations en route in the event that we should experience an engine shutdown, or any other reason that could oblige us to descend and establish subsonic cruise. This would reduce our range substantially, making it impossible to reach San Juan with adequate fuel.

We managed to improve on the flight plan, however, so that it appeared that we would arrive 5 minutes too early. The concept of a 'linear hold' had been suggested, which involved losing time by descending early rather than flying in circles. This saved fuel, so we decided to experiment, using a tabulated set of BAC data. After reaching 35,000 feet and looking at the indicated ground-speed displayed on the INS, I was dismayed to see that we now had a headwind, and were going to be four minutes late. This mistake was eventually corrected by a high speed descent, and a close turn into final approach. The airport was surrounded by many thousands of interested spectators who had come to see Concorde, not the politicians. We managed to arrive exactly at the scheduled time.

After our VIP passengers had disembarked, and we were closing down the aircraft preparatory to its transfer to a secure parking area, I noticed a long line of people waiting at the foot of the boarding steps. Apparently they were the family and friends of the Governor of Puerto Rico, and wanted to see inside the aircraft. A burly man standing inside our front door introduced himself as a CIA security officer.

'I would send them away captain.'

I was amazed at the apparent lack of consideration for the Governor, who was a local personality, but compromised by settling for a visit by six people, including the Governor and his wife. At about this time the French President, Valéry Giscard d'Estaing, arrived in a rather tatty 707, to be met by a guard of honour in very colourful uniforms. After a brief visit to the approach control room we departed for our hotel, and a two-night stopover while the G7 economic summit meeting progressed.

An invitation to attend a social gathering at the British Consulate trickled down from a third secretary, and we duly attended in the early evening, to be greeted with tepid drinks in paper cups, and rather mundane conversation. I was again disconcerted by the complete lack of information that our country's representatives possessed about aviation and Concorde, in direct contrast with that shown by the local population, who thronged the airport and surrounding roads to witness our departure on 28 June.

The return journey presented some difficulties, as the San Juan runway was not long enough for a heavy take-off with enough fuel to reach London non-stop. There was a potential strike of air traffic controllers which could sterilise most of the North Atlantic routes. We had intended to fly via Washington to London, but this would be impossible if the strike occurred.

There was another option: a route via Dakar, Senegal, where Air France could handle our transit. The flying time to London was almost identical for each of these options. I decided to uplift a fuel load which would allow a last-minute decision to be made for either destination, and we armed ourselves with flight plans and clearance documents for either eventuality. One complication was the transit of the British Prime Minister and some of the Cabinet at these places. The diplomatic necessities of protocol had to be assembled and provisional warning sent ahead so that local arrangements could be made.

We did not know our destination until 30 minutes before the scheduled departure at 4.30 pm. The strike had been called off, and we could go via Washington-Dulles. This decision was not relayed to Dakar for some reason and a full military guard and brass band turned up to meet our non-arrival. I later discovered that this had led to a diplomatic brouhaha.

Immediately after departure, and before going super sonic, John Lidiard, the flight engineer, revealed that one of the secondary air doors in one engine intake had stuck in the

subsonic position. Unless we could move it to the correct position we could not accelerate to Mach 2, which would mean losing time and consuming more fuel. After I zoomed up to slow the speed, with John carrying out the recommended drill, we were able to get the door to move. On arrival at Dulles we decided to have some components replaced to avoid a recurrence. This caused an extra 45 minutes of transit time above the planned 45 minutes. A query was passed through to us from the PM, but I was able to assure him that we would still arrive in London just after 6 am, which was the earliest permitted arrival time. Some time after this charter I was presented with a signed photograph of Jim Callaghan, a pleasant courtesy.

Training begins for the line pilots — eventually

The BAC Concorde simulator became available in August, and after a final visit to Toulouse with Chris Morley for a mutual refresher routine, we were able to concentrate the training effort at Filton. The first course of line pilots was in ground school. We spent considerable time flying out the conversion course on the simulator to make it more efficient. Unfortunately there was a further delay of three months before we could begin our training task. Agreement between BALPA and the airline had not been finally concluded to cover Concorde operation in all its aspects. One contentious item was the use of our private cars for the many visits to Fairford and Filton. The airline was reluctant to recognise any need to offer recompense for the rapid deterioration of vehicles, and large mileages amassed, maintaining that the usual mileage allowances would suffice. An impasse developed. We continued to fly the services, but training was halted by BALPA until a comprehensive agreement settled all the outstanding matters. This delayed the build-up of crew strength on the fleet but not the service frequency. We still waited for permission to serve New York, which was not to be granted until November 1977.

The new BAC simulator was fitted with a television-type visual attachment, using a model runway and surrounding countryside to provide a semblance of reality. This has now been replaced by a digitally-generated display of impressive accuracy, but although suitable for the practice of Category 2 and 3 low visibility approaches and landings, it was not then possible to reproduce Concorde handling characteristics near to the ground. We would have to spend much time and money making a lot of noise around an airport to complete the pilot conversions. I had received Concorde type-rating examiner authorisation from the Ministry in July 1976 after John Oliver observed a Toulouse simulator session and an aircraft session from Fairford; but it was early December before we started to convert the first group of line captains and co-pilots.

We had success with the long simulator course, finding that a relaxed attitude and revised content produced good results. The weeks were extremely busy, as we were also involved in keeping the services going. Only three of the contractual course members had become operational. Route training had revealed some problems with the others. The need to retain enough spare capacity to deal with tactical and operational problems while handling the routine operation had produced difficulties. and we were involved in learning more about the aircraft. BAC had developed the thin-lip engine intake modification which improved the range performance. The intake sensing and control were subject to continual improvement, with the amplifier control units reaching impressive modification serial numbers as the software laws were modified. We were also gaining an insight into the many other ramifications of our pioneering operation.

Booms and rumbles

A series of loud bangs began to be heard over a large portion of southern England on several evenings each week during the autumn and winter of 1976. There was a 'ten-past-nine bang' heard along the South Coast from the West Country to East Sussex, and as far inland as Berkshire. This seemed to coincide with our arrival from Washington. Another peak coincided with the Air France arrival from Caracas. These noises caused questions to be raised in the House of Commons, and a government investigation concluded that these 'mini-booms' were unrelated to the primary sonic boom, being caused by the refraction of sound waves in the upper atmosphere from layers of air influenced by wind and temperature which varied on a seasonal basis.

We lived in the area where these noises could be heard, and I conducted my own small research project to determine which flights were associated with them. Although this was denied vehemently, it did seem that the late departure from Paris Charles de Gaulle was involved. A turn was required at point 'Delta' in mid-Channel for both inbound and outbound French Concordes. The outbound turn was made at low supersonic speed, when noise generation would be at its peak, further accentuated by the bank angle in the turn. We also shared responsibility, as I discovered one night on arrival from Washington.

We began our deceleration from Mach 2 at the correct distance from the coast, and began to check the descent profile carefully. This was by relating distance-to-go with height and speed, using the INS. A vertical navigation capability, as now provided in modern aircraft, would have been helpful. The fuel and time penalty for an early descent is more penalising with Concorde and is to be avoided if possible. The aircraft is very sensitive to temperature changes during the supersonic phase of a descent. A warm air mass causes the descent rate to increase. I noticed that we were likely to be down to subsonic level too soon, and so increased the engine power a few per cent. This raised the aircraft pitch attitude slightly. When we had recovered the correct descent profile, I reduced the power to the previous setting, and the pitch attitude then reduced. We later discovered this had caused a mini-boom reaching well across southern England, and that it had nothing to do with atmospheric conditions. We had been following another company Concorde which had flown the same route only shortly beforehand without generating any boom. Analysis revealed that the reduction in pitch attitude had probably generated a focussed batch of sonic pressure waves.

This revealed the importance of our flight technique, and emphasised the benefit of having such analysis from the BAC noise department.

Observers

There are two spare seats on the Concorde flight deck. One is a traditional type jump-seat behind the captain, and the other is a fold-down seat across the tunnel leading into the deck. These seats were often occupied by people from the industry, finding out for themselves what supersonic aviation was like in real life, after so many years of planning. Pilots, designers, managers, astronauts, and politicians managed to obtain permission for this. We were inevitably acting as public relations personnel for much of the time. The aircraft was so uniquely interesting, and performing so well, that we were soon able to establish a good acceptance of our operation within the industry. Then there were the visits from passengers, who included many industrial leaders and media barons. Film stars seemed to value the speed but became bewildered by any technical information. On one occasion both Carol Channing and Bette Davis were crowding the flight engineer so much that we had to ask them politely to retire to the rear. Another event was when a well known television commentator was attempting to tape a description of her experience as we raced towards our deceleration point. She had her power pack strapped over her side, and held the mike close to her lips. Apparently her recording effort was unsuccessful — she started her spiel no fewer than four times, only to find that we had to usher her off as we went into our descent drills. The speed was more than 20 nautical miles per minute and she was one very frustrated media person. Frank Borman, the astronaut, then chairman of Eastern Air Lines, also visited us. I think he found it all a bit tame, particularly when we were served tea and sandwiches at 57,000 feet with a ground speed of 1,200 knots.

Flying training

In February 1977 we began our local flight training of line pilots using the RAF station at Brize Norton in Oxfordshire. This was the base for Transport Command VC10s. It is very close to Fairford and we used both airfields. I was used to a four-hour training session with the 707, including about sixteen landings and some airwork. Concorde used fuel so rapidly around the low-level circuit that we needed to refuel after about one-and-a-half hours. It was possible to obtain about seven landings during each session, plus a go-around. The touch-and-go landings involved fewer configuration changes than the 707, for there were no flaps to reset. After flying the nose wheels onto the runway we would bring up the power and get airborne once more. I was pleasantly surprised to find that the aircraft took the wear and tear of our training routines without developing many idiosyncrasies or snags. In fact we used fewer tyres than expected, averaging a longer life than when using the 707.

Academic protest

Local residents living close to Fairford and Brize Norton had been familiar with large noisy aircraft around these airfields for many years. Although Concorde had been around on test work since the 1960s, our concentration of regular training triggered concern. We had to host an open day, and help the communities to understand what we were doing. In particular we had to satisfy the City of Dreaming Spires, Oxford, with a large population and many colleges, only a few miles to the east of Brize Norton.

Our flying was interspersed with regular RAF traffic, some of which was also in the low-level circuit on routine training. Although we were much faster in the pattern than the RAF VC10s, we found it practicable to share the air with them, and to carry on our work in the prevailing cloudy and rainy conditions. It was essential to confirm that we had passed abeam of a VCl0 on its approach before starting our turn towards the runway. This was easy to do when visibility and cloud allowed, but otherwise we relied on confirmation of relative positions by Brize approach control, using their radar.

One afternoon we were nicely spaced with a VCl0, and flying eastwards at 250 knots, preparatory to turning onto final approach. I could not see the other aircraft, as we were in and out of cloud and rain. To start the turn-in before long was essential, as otherwise we would be committed to fly over Oxford. Unfortunately Brize's radar became unserviceable at that very moment. Without confirmation of the other aircraft's position. I had to delay our turn-in while querying its distance from the runway, and this committed us to fly over Oxford at 2,500 feet. A week later I received a call from Norman Todd, our flight training manager. One of the College Masters had complained to the local MP, and a question had been asked in Parliament. Such is the pull of academia.

Norman asked me for a full written report, which was provided, citing the old radar equipment provided for the RAF as cause. We never heard any more, but this was one more instance of how the world was divided into anti-and pro-Concorde factions. The extra time flown in an eastwards direction was less than a minute, but we had noisily disrupted the university peace. *Pax vobiscum.*

Prestwick again

On 26 May I took the aircraft from Brize Norton to Prestwick, where the weather was more suitable. We were still using the Scottish airfield for training. Many memories of the past thirty years passed through my mind as we began a full day of entertaining the local population with sixteen landings. The traffic jams were so bad that the police called to request advance notice of any future plans to use the field. During one of the refuelling breaks, a US C-5A military transport arrived and parked beside the Concorde, contrasting its huge bulk in its drab and purposeful camouflage with our gleaming elegance. The crew visited us, and we were interested to meet their crew chief, a woman in her mid-twenties, responsible for the daily routine maintenance of the huge aircraft.

When the day's work was finished and we were about to leave, the tower controller asked us what height we could reach before the first check point to the south, as nothing was known about our lightweight climb performance. We exceeded the minimum crossing level specified in the air traffic clearance by ten thousand feet.

Radiation

Solar radiation is a threat to crews of aircraft that reach very high altitude. The sunspot cycle varies over a ten-to-twelve year period. A solar disturbance can reach the earth's atmosphere in a few hours. Avoidance of danger is achieved by descent to a safer level. Concorde has a warning system, should notification not be received from the agencies that monitor the sun. A recording of received radiation is made, and this allows study of both cumulative and spot effects. When we began to fly regular services there was some concern that crews could build up exposure to harmful radiation, and might accumulate levels that could be significant. Research concluded that the cumulative effect was similar to that for crews flying subsonic aircraft at lower levels because of the much shorter flight times en route. Most exposure is experienced over or close to the poles, where the atmosphere provides less depth for protection. I know of only one reported warning experienced in flight, and this may well be apocryphal. When Concorde flew Margaret Thatcher to Vancouver in the mid-1980s a red warning was recorded by flight deck equipment while flying over the northern Canadian shield.

In July 1977 another source of radiation arrived in the aircraft for rapid transport to Washington, confirming the advantageous use of supersonic travel for medical purposes. We were used to carrying human organs, but this time a canister containing radio-active isotopes consigned from Hammersmith Hospital to Johns Hopkins Hospital in Baltimore, was loaded on our aircraft. On arrival at Dulles a special car drew up beside the aircraft and whisked the precious box off without delay.

Navigational nuances

Our route to Bahrain crossed Lebanon, Syria, and Jordan before entering Saudi Arabian airspace. This was a highly political and sensitive area, as we were flying over land and causing sonic booms close to many small villages and desert encampments. The best route was subject to many revisions, and careful negotiation. The birth or demise of many a camel or tent was ascribed to our effect. Damage claims were made, and compensation paid in some cases. Our three INS sets allowed the route to be programmed precisely, using way points chosen to take the Concorde round and away from most sensitive areas. After crossing the Lebanese coast close to the port of Tripoli, usually above 57,000 feet, the path taken was curved, with the aircraft in a continuous turn for the next 250 nautical miles. This was achieved by selecting the turning points to cause a change of heading, generating a turn with a huge radius. The bank angle averaged less than 5° but the change of heading was eventually 60°.

Another use of the INS was to control the approach path to New York JFK when close to runways 13L and 13R. The use of 'false' way points ensured that a curved approach path could be flown with precision by the autopilot before completing the final alignment visually. At London we used a 'Stand and Approach' based on the INS to align us to intercept the final instrument landing system. This also allowed us to fly the profile at high speed. Today most modern aircraft can use both INS and GPS (Global Positioning System — from satellites) to achieve these results, but we needed repeatable precision to guarantee our acceptability. Concorde can be very noisy on approach if slowed prematurely.

Pilots who may read this book will probably know that Concorde does not receive any priority or special privileges from air traffic control, although the different performance and characteristics of the aircraft require controllers to obtain knowledge of the its capabilities in special circumstances.

On one of his first flights to New York, during the descent from supersonic height, a captain was faced with the request from a controller to turn 40° to the right and level off at flight level 420 (42,000 feet). This was to avoid military traffic. Had he obeyed this instruction, reheat would have been needed to stay level, because of the trans-sonic drag, as they were still at Mach 1.2. The turn would have pointed a focussed boom at the US coastline, and probably caused a political storm. The fuel used would have depleted the reserves for diversion

to an alternate. The situation was immediately explained to the controller, who then diverted the military aircraft. We made visits to various control centres to explain this period of inflexibility during the descent from supersonic altitude.

Surprises

I often wondered if our sonic boom could be heard in another aircraft, or if the accompanying pressure wave would be felt. This was answered one afternoon as we flew south of Crete on our way to London. We were in contact with the Greek air traffic control centre when a Gulfstream executive jet, flying at 39,000 feet, called us to report that they had felt our shock wave, which had rocked their aircraft, and caused various instruments to fluctuate. This had quite alarmed them. I was able to reassure them that research had found that the effect was harmless, and posed no threat to safety; but this did not silence their concern.

Another, and regular, event was the encounter with a scheduled inbound 747 as we were accelerating in supersonic flight when departing from Washington. We crossed an active airway, and were so positioned to fly above the jumbo at just the right distance for them to feel quite a jolt. This was reported to be similar to the experience of flying through a portion of cumulus cloud. On several departures I was able to warn the TWA aircraft to expect a bump. Flying south of Crete one day we were surprised to find that we had entered an area of rapidly rising air, probably associated with a very strong wind from the north, and a standing wave. The speed increased, and we climbed rapidly, with the newly modified auto-pilot/auto-throttle control clutching in to reduce engine power. We seemed to glide along in the lee of Crete at about 58,000 feet without visible means of support. After about three minutes there was a lurch and we left the wave, decelerating.

Tyres and wheels

Tyre design and technology were stretched to the limit when Concorde was designed. For a take-off at maximum weight, the ground speed at lift-off, close to 220 mph, is near to the maximum which the tread carcass can stand. Should the aircraft be allowed to overspeed on the runway one or more tyres may be 'cooked', weakening them for subsequent take-offs. Conversely, however, if the pilot pulls the aircraft off the ground at too low a speed, the climb performance can be significantly reduced.

An example of the tyre problem occurred to an Air France Concorde on take off from Washington (Dulles). A tyre tread detached, and hit the adjacent tyre and wheel. Pieces flew upwards to create a large hole in the wing structure, luckily penetrating the only bay that contained no fuel. Bits were sucked into two engine intakes, and also damaged the hydraulic pipelines in the wheel well, putting two of the three fluid systems out of action. With engine power reduced, and various systems inoperative, the crew flew around for nearly an hour, preparing for a difficult landing back at Dulles. This was achieved without further damage, and was a fine example of crew handling. I saw this aircraft shortly after the occurrence and was surprised at the extensive damage that one tyre tread could cause.[1]

After this event many steps were taken to protect against any recurrence, including strengthened wheels, better protection and re-routeing of hydraulic pipelines, a re-examination of tyre quality control, and re-emphasis on the need to observe correct speed on the runway during take-off by using the correct rate of rotation to become airborne.

Contributory evidence for the need to realign and otherwise protect hydraulic pipes from damage was provided as I was taxiing in at Heathrow after arrival from Bahrain. As we began a final turn to align with the parking spot, a marshaller ran out and urgently waved me to stop and to cut the engines. After applying the brakes we had indications of total hydraulic contents loss in two systems, leaving us without any brake pressure. A tyre had burst on landing, and had damaged the hydraulic pipes that ran down the oleo leg. Lockout valves

---

1   Detachment of a tyre tread played a significant role in the fatal accident which occurred to an Air France Concorde at Paris in 2000.

should have isolated fluid loss to the oleo region but we lost full system pressure, and had been making a tell-tale trail of leaked fluid as we approached the terminal. An astute member of the maintenance crew awaiting our arrival had seen this.

This was an unusual example of an airport-located near-miss. The sharp-eyed maintenance man was luckily in the right spot. We were within a few moments of making a very sharp-nosed entrance past the gate right into the main terminal building. Apart from notification by traffic controllers in an airport tower, it is difficult for the pilot of a multi-wheeled aircraft to discover that a tyre has burst, although initiation of a heavyweight take-off with a deflated tyre could have serious consequences. Concorde has brake temperature indicators which do provide some element of warning, showing the overheating that should accompany a deflation.

This raises the subject of the crews' ability to inspect the outside condition of an aircraft on the ground or in flight, which is desirable because of the danger, for example, of ice accumulation, leaks, engine condition, or fire. I would have welcomed some investment to provide a couple of remote television cameras positioned to view vital areas.

New York

The struggle to obtain landing rights at New York JFK has been a story worthy of separate books. The Port of New York Authority (PNYA) was finally persuaded to allow a proving flight by the first French production Concorde, F-WTSB. Jointly crewed by British Aerospace and Aérospatiale, this flew into JFK on 19 October 1977, and was subjected to intense noise measuring. The take-off followed the carefully developed procedure that we had been practising for more than two years, and which had caused concern to many non-Concorde pilots. This proved to be safe, effective, and predictably simple to fly.

The basic premise of a quieter departure was a take-off from runway 31L turning as soon as possible to cross Jamaica Bay and avoid populated areas. This required a left turn to be started soon after becoming airborne. A bank angle of 25° was needed to produce the necessary turn radius. The idea of winding on this amount of 'wing down' at a low height produced misgivings in many conservative minds. The procedure calls for a double check of radio and pressure height indications before a turn is started. The bank angle reduces lift and climb performance, and also helps to stabilise the increasing speed to achieve the desired radius of turn. A reduction in engine power after cancelling the reheat/afterburner selection allows a slow climbout towards the coast, where speed and power can be increased.

The proving flight went well, and satisfied all but the most diehard environmentalists. Regular services to New York began on 22 November 1977. At the time I was at Filton, training the second group of line pilots on the simulator. My first trip to JFK was on 6 December, and on the returning departure, next day, we recorded only 89 PNDB (Perceived Noise Decibel Level) while carrying a full load of 100 passengers, achieving a block time of 3 hours 45 minutes to Heathrow. All went smoothly; we were the subject of spectator sports, with aircraft giving up their take-off clearance to watch us depart, and many boats crowded into Jamaica Bay to catch a glimpse.

Decisions, noise, and reputation

Departing from Washington-Dulles usually involved a slow climb to the north before turning towards the coast. On one occasion we were cleared for take off, and as we turned onto the runway I looked at the weather radar to discover a line of very solid thunderstorm-type contacts painted right across our initial departure route. We had been informed that an active weather front was due to arrive later in the day, but here it was in full force. I advised the tower controller that we required a re-routeing to avoid the area north of the field. He advised us to taxi off the runway, and to hold clear. Meanwhile our idling engines used fuel at about 100 kilograms per minute. After several minutes we were advised that the only clearance available would take us close to the White House, at 5,000 feet, until joining our usual route over Baltimore. We had now used some of the flight contingency fuel, and a further delay would soon mean a return to the ramp. The heavy cloud was only ten miles to the north. With some trepidation I accepted the new routeing. We turned right after take-off and approached central Washington, passing quite close to the Smithsonian Museum, which I had visited the previous day. I had increased the speed temporarily to the upper tolerance of 260 knots, hoping that a slight deceleration as we flew over the city would reduce noise. We were soon past and into our normal routines. We never received any complaints, and wonder if this was because of the prevailing weather, Perhaps the President was not in residence. One interesting operational aspect was apparent as we went on our way to London. The delay had cost about 1,000 kilograms in fuel, but the lighter aircraft reached a higher level sooner, and by the time we arrived our shortfall had been reduced to only 500 kilograms. Yet another ghost was laid to rest. Many had forecast that long ground delays before take-off would cause an SST to need refuelling, but the better performance of a lightened aircraft markedly reduced this effect.

Departure weights from New York were mostly governed by noise limits. Permissible take-off weight was defined by a series of special charts that took into account the wind, temperature, and runway length, to arrive at the best option for the conditions. This could occasionally mean that we would depart with a tailwind and against the traffic flow. In the summer months, with high temperatures, we sometimes had to depart with fuel for Shannon, with London as the alternate, with the initially surprising result that the fuel requirement for London would soon be met, once established in the cruise. Very occasionally, because of runway maintenance, or wind direction, we were forced to use a take-off direction that took us over sensitive areas.

Concorde's departure record at JFK was soon better than that of many other aircraft. Our careful crew training, and the efforts of BAC, British Airways, and Air France planners were brought to fruition by the ability of the line crews, who were required to evaluate and fly complex procedures with accuracy and understanding.

Occasionally things did not go quite as well as intended. We usually listened out on our company radio frequency to obtain the noise result recorded by our departure. I was disturbed to hear that we had broken the permitted level one day when departing from JFK. This was caused by one of the flight engineer's fingers slipping off a reheat selector as he was supposed to switch them all off. One engine stayed with full reheat/afterburner selected, and although the error was rectified a few seconds later, it 'rang the bell.'

Once offshore and outside US domestic airspace we could accelerate to maximum speed, which at lower subsonic levels was 400 knots indicated. Such was the reserve of power and climb performance that it conferred extraordinary flexibility when needed. Our route eastbound from JFK paralleled the coastline in subsonic flight until close to Nantucket Island after which we started the climb to supersonic level. On one occasion we were held at 9,000 feet while waiting for inbound traffic to pass. The weather ahead could be seen as a solid mass of dark cloud containing many radar returns. The airways controllers replied to our request for an immediate climb to top the bad weather by querying how long it would take us to reach 29,000 feet. This was because of possible conflict with various other aircraft. I estimated six minutes as a conservative reply, and we were then cleared to climb. Zooming to reduce the speed, and using normal climb power, we reached 29,000 feet in half that time.

The route past Nantucket was changed. Originally we passed over the island, starting to accelerate to supersonic flight when overhead, although not reaching Mach 1 until well past. There were complaints, and our route was moved to pass about 20 nautical miles to the south, which allowed an earlier acceleration and avoided the overflight problem.

On Sunday 3 February 1980 two Concordes were outbound from New York following this revised route. The first aircraft boomed parts of Nantucket Island, causing many complaints. The boom wave took 282 seconds to reach the southern part of the island. The aircraft was climbing through 37,000 feet at a speed of Mach 1.29. The second aircraft passed by without causing any boom 83 minutes later. The booming aircraft was closer to Nantucket, about 18 miles away. The second Concorde was only two more miles away. The presence of a very cold atmosphere and large inversion of temperature produced an unusually wide boom carpet. The incident illustrated the need to stay well clear of sensitive areas, and to be very sure that we stayed right on the pre cleared track.

Middle East problem

After four years of our services to Bahrain, crossing the Mediterranean coastline near the port of Tripoli, the Lebanese government banned supersonic flight over its territory. A joint BA/CAA team went to Cairo and Jeddah to negotiate a new route across Egypt and Saudi Arabia. A visit to Damascus to amend our route resulted in a ban of flight over Syria. A temporary procedure was devised to fly subsonically from south of Cyprus to Bahrain, with the acceleration and deceleration flown under the watch of Olympus Radar (RAF) in Cyprus.

The impasse was solved when we were granted a route over Egypt and across Saudi Arabia on a trial basis. The initial route went close to Alexandria, and to the west of Cairo. I flew this on a clear day, and looked down on the Egyptian capital from 58,000 feet as we described a gentle turn over the western desert towards the Red Sea, turning east to enter Saudi airspace, and enjoying a magnificent panorama. Such changes, however, produced commercial uncertainty for advanced ticket sales. A magnificent aircraft was severely limited by the sonic boom to over-water or over-desert flight. The overland flying restriction destroyed all hopes of a commercial sales market for Concorde.

Shared ventures

In May 1976 the Australian government had given approval for British Airways to fly three services a week to Melbourne. These would have called at Bahrain and Singapore. For a variety of reasons this never came to fruition, although an extension to Singapore began in December 1977 in association with Singapore Airlines. Concorde G-BOAD was repainted with the SIA colours on the left side. Cabin crews were drawn from each airline, although BA flight crews were used throughout. This service was curtailed after only three flights because the Malaysian government deferred permission for us to fly along the Straits of Malacca, and did not relent until January 1979, after much political persuasion. Meanwhile, we had a Concorde going everywhere with a free advertisement for SIA on one side. This led to some fairly ribald comments, and occasional confusion.

The Singapore venture was terminated in November 1980 as the westbound load factors were very low. Some crews had been temporarily based in Singapore. The Singapore-Bahrain segment was fairly critical for payload at times when the ground temperature limited take-off weight, but this was compensated for by the delay-free and speed-free transition to supersonic flight at both ends.

Simultaneous with our 1979 pooled operation with SIA was an arrangement with Braniff International of Dallas, Texas. This covered a through route to London with us, and a parallel route to Paris with Air France. This time their flight deck crews were trained to fly our Concordes, and those of Air France, between Washington Dulles and Dallas. We were involved in training half their crews, and Aer Formation in Toulouse (Flight Safety International) was responsible for the other half, using the French aircraft. The main difference between the two airlines' Concordes was the INS sets, and the radio/intercommunication boxes. The latter had switches that operated in the opposite sense to ours. The Braniff crews were experienced, and soon mastered the subsonic characteristics

of the operation, expressing frustration that they would not be checked out for supersonic flight, as the Dulles-Dallas sector was limited to Mach 0.95.

Bureaucracy and insurance concerns

As the time for their initial service approached, and their training was completed, our airline insurers complicated matters by insisting that so long as British Airways owned the aircraft, and half the pilots who flew them were not originally trained by our organisation, we would have to involve ourselves in some sort of confirmation of their competency. I thought that, provided the French had signed them out, that would be good enough, but was not party to the ultimate decision that one of our training captains would witness a Line Oriented Flight Training (LOFT) procedure on the simulator. This would duplicate a flight from Dallas to Dulles, with an engine failure thrown in to ensure that things would go smoothly. This was not to have any status as a check flight, for we were dealing with US airmen and had no jurisdiction. It was merely to discern if perhaps there was any omission in training that might need rectification. I was delegated to conduct this exercise.

The actual LOFT, which was flown using the Filton simulator, went well enough until the crew decided to jettison fuel to reach landing weight after an engine failed en route. Instead of calculating the amount of fuel being jettisoned by timing (as was our procedure) they decided to dump down to the stack pipes. Normally this would have allowed sufficient reserve fuel for their landing but the Filton simulator had not been modified to the aircraft standard in this respect, and allowed most of the fuel contents to be lost. The effect was that a major emergency developed, and they landed with only ten minutes of fuel remaining. My decision to have another practice session was met with disaffection, though supported by our management. There appeared to be no effect on the pilots, or the start of services, but some words were exchanged between the two airlines which had the effect of bringing our simulator up to aircraft standard.

The Braniff operation was carried out under the rules and regulations of the US Federal Aviation Agency (FAA), and was a good example of petty bureaucracy. Concorde was issued with a US certificate of airworthiness after nearly eleven years of discussion and negotiation. Our aircraft were re-registered in such a way that it was possible for the initial 'G' to be removed after arrival at Washington. For example G-BOAC became G-N81AC. A separate Flight Manual containing FAA approved procedures became the mandatory operational document. After landing we would throw all our documentation into the forward toilet compartment (but not down the toilet) to be replaced with theirs. The reverse procedure happened after their arrival from Dallas, when the 'G' was reapplied.

One significant operational handicap applied to the Braniff crews. The FAA required each pilot to complete a full autoland training programme on the simulator and on the aircraft before obtaining authorisation to land in Category 3 conditions. For some reasons, probably cost and time, Braniff did not train its pilots to meet this requirement. This meant that in bad weather, which is not unknown at Dulles or Dallas, they might not be able to land. In particular, the arrival of the aircraft from Dallas could be delayed or even cancelled despite our crews being qualified for the conditions. Although this piece of bureaucracy was not as insurmountable as it seemed, it illustrated some of the problems when sharing aircraft with other operators.

Another interesting problem appeared during the US certification process. The British/French standards governing the aircraft structure differed from the US requirements. The US regulations were based on a fail-safe structure and called for containment of any metal crack in the fuselage skin by conventional construction. The British/French requirements allowed either safe-life or fail-safe characteristics. Concorde had entered service before full completion of the test work to substantiate the fail-safe properties of the fuselage, although complying with the safe life requirements. When this fail-safe work was completed, it revealed the need to modify a portion of the fuselage because of the possibility that very small cracks would be difficult to detect in service.

By the time the FAA allowed Concorde on to the US register, a factored safe-life of 5,000 flights had been demonstrated. This was noted by the FAA, although it could not finally certificate on that basis. Had Concorde remained on the US register, the upper fuselage would have had to be extensively modified, or (perhaps more likely) the regulations would have been updated to recognize the construction method. Although this sounds complicated, the end result was sensible. Much of Concorde's upper fuselage is machined from solid alloy, unlike that of many other aircraft that are constructed of frames to which metal alloy sheets are riveted or bonded.

My next task was again at the behest of our insurers. As owners of the aircraft, British Airways arranged that they should provide a captain and a flight engineer to ride as supernumerary crew for a number of the Braniff flights. This safety-play did not take into account the very careful training, or the competency and experience of the excellent Braniff crews, but was similar to the route endurance programme before delivery when we did the flying and BAC test pilots were observing We shared the embarrassing task between several training captains and engineers. The way in which our aircraft was used by our American friends was interesting. They developed a very slick operation on the Washington-Dallas segment, which averaged just over 2 hours 10 minutes airborne time. One nice touch by their cabin crew was the deposition of a yellow rose of Texas on each crew seat before our crew took over for the flight to London. Unfortunately the Braniff arrangement ceased in June 1980, because of low load factors and competition brought about by airline deregulation in the United States.

Charters

We soon began to fly charters, which still remain a significant part of Concorde operations. Many of these involved an out-and-back trip lasting an hour or two, reaching supersonic speed and height perhaps over the Bay of Biscay, or en route to land at some European airport. The Concorde Fan Club was formed, and we became adept at showing its members round the aircraft after landing. The constant interest and enjoyment shown by most of these people was matched by the way our crews made every effort to make their trip enjoyable.

On 17 January 1980, on a flight from London to New York, we welcomed our 250,000th passenger, Mr Baus. 98 passengers were on board, and we completed the trip in a block time of 4 hours. My days in the airline were drawing to a close, as our compulsory retirement age of 55 would mean that the day before my birthday I would be a competent, certified Concorde Captain with a type rating /instrument rating examiner authorisation, and after midnight I would be grounded. However I still had another eight months to run, and these produced one or two surprises.

Surges — engine (and heartbeat)

The potential of an engine surge always exists for any jet engine. A subsonic engine can experience choking and reverse flow for a number of causes, although this is usually associated with fuel control, or intake fan problems, and it is a rare occurrence. Concorde relies on subsonic air to feed the core engine. This is achieved in supersonic flight by the positioning of two variable position ramps in the top of each intake box. The effect of these is to adjust the intake size to position shock waves on the front intake lips. Duplicated electrical and hydraulic supplies are used to sense and position the ramps. We had experienced the occasional failure of an automatic intake system, so descent from supersonic flight was made with a fixed intake, involving cautious power adjustments. This was tricky and sensitive, requiring interpretation of a small gauge that indicated a reference point for the pressure balance in the intake. The air mass going into the intake depends on speed, density, and temperature. Should these vary then a new intake ramp position is needed and if not provided there is risk of an engine surge.

On 26 April 1980 we were on our way to New York, with 78 passengers being served their champagne dinner, when the trouble began. Roger Bricknell, the flight engineer, advised that we had problems with the left outboard engine intake system which culminated in a complete failure of that system, and resulted in fixed intake ramps. We were flying at about 57,000 feet over the Atlantic, and had just passed 35° West, about 690 nautical miles from Newfoundland. The weather at the various Canadian maritime airports was very poor, although good in the eastern US. I decided to continue the flight with the intention of completing a fixed-intake descent. However this was not to be, because five minutes later Roger reported identical symptoms affecting the left inboard engine, again culminating in another fixed intake. We now had two engines that were running quite well, but which would need most careful attention until achieving a speed below Mach 1.3. The possibility of engine surges existed. That would mean descent to a subsonic cruise height and a loss of range. I therefore decided to return to London. Shannon was on the way, and would serve as a precautionary alternate. Our tactical chart information indicated that we could easily reach Heathrow at subsonic speed, but not JFK. The weather was a decisive factor.

At Mach 2.0 the turning circle of Concorde is approximately 60 nautical miles wide, a full degree of latitude. The segment was being flown by Senior First Officer Mick Burke, an experienced ex-RAF Vulcan pilot. A bank angle of 25° produced a very slow change of heading. During such a 180° turn more than 2,000 kilograms of fuel is consumed. The loss of lift associated with the bank angle caused us to descend. We encountered changes in temperature and some turbulence during the turn, and the speed increased to produce an overspeed warning. I was sure that a surge or surges would occur and decided to take control. The previous day we had all been at Filton, where I had conducted a regular six-monthly simulator check ride and briefing with Mick and Roger. We had practised the surge drill and I knew that it would be more efficient if we all reverted to our normal duties, also that they would be familiar with the procedures. It was certainly a case when practice made for perfection.

As the overspeed warning continued we either had to climb, or reduce power, to control the speed. A little of both immediately induced a double-engine surge. The noise was loud and the vibration severe: just like the simulator only at double the intensity. We went into the surge procedure. This reduced power to a minimum, beginning a deceleration and descent. The workload was considerable, for, apart from the surge drill, we needed to obtain an air traffic clearance, and North Atlantic airspace normally contains many aircraft at the subsonic levels. I managed to make a palliative announcement to the cabin crew and passengers as the surges ceased. We checked the engine instruments for signs of any consequential problems as we reduced speed through Mach 1.3 — all was well. Clearance to fly back at 39,000 feet was obtained, and we arrived at Heathrow four-and-a-half hours after our departure with plenty of fuel for an alternate diversion. The aircraft was Concorde G-BFKW (later re-registered as G-BOAG), then non-standard in a few respects, having been originally built as a 'whitetail' for sale on the open market, only to be acquired by British Airways when a market did not emerge. Unfortunately, the flight recorder was not serviceable, thus limiting the operational evaluation of this noisy event.

The cause of the intake failures in this instance was water contamination of the hydraulic system and the associated corrosion of components. Somehow, water had been introduced during the regular replenishment of the hydraulic contents. Such was the extent of damage to the system components that this aircraft was not flown again for more than a year. The final cost in lost productivity and repairs exceeded a million pounds. I later met Peter Baker, the pilot responsible for much of the engine test work. He apologised for the absence of a double-engined surge drill. We had drills for almost everything else.

Discussing the incident with Captain Tony Meadows, who had flown this aircraft, Kilo Whiskey, from New York on the previous day, revealed that his crew had also experienced a single intake failure leading to a fixed intake deceleration. The aircraft technical log and history records had provided no information for us about this event, and were blank sheets. After some detective work I discovered that KW had a longish history of developing problems that were obviously related to this very costly happening. Forewarned is forearmed, and ignorance may not be blissful. Anyway, my luck had held again.

On the next trip to New York, Ross Stainton, our Chairman, was sitting in the jump seat for the landing at JFK. During the taxi in I spent some time telling him of the need to convene an independent inquiry to get to the bottom of the incident, and in particular to ensure that aircraft on-board records should reflect currently unsolved problems. This caused me to miss the sign from our terminal marshaller that we should park on a different gate than usual, and I mistakenly aligned the aircraft towards the normal spot. This was accepted by the marshaller, and all went well. When we had disembarked, the BA station manager met me, smiling hugely. They had laid on a special reception for the Chairman at the other gate, and had just managed to panic around to meet him while was I castigating the airline's documentation. It was nice to have friends.

Competition versus cooperation

We were colleagues with Air France, although we served different European and world destinations. Their service experience was of great interest to me during the first year of operation but line crews never received an analysis of how they were faring. No doubt this was available somewhere in the BAC labyrinth, the CAA, or even our operations department; but not to the flight crews. I did manage to secure some information through the French pilot's association and this made fascinating reading. Their problems were not entirely similar, nor were their procedures.

The relations between our two airlines were brought into a more personal focus when we were called to fly a charter for a cruise shipping line, from Paris Charles de Gaulle to Bahrain. A full load of 100 passengers had to be delivered to their ocean liner for a segment of its world cruise. We flew a partly full aircraft to CDG, taking just less than an hour. This was slower than my DC-7C trips when BOAC flew BEA services for a while, 33 years previously. We could not beat the clock despite the use of a special jet letdown procedure that started at 20,000 feet. This was because of less direct routeing, and congested traffic.

During the transit at CDG, Air France staff were responsible for the routine, with an attendant BA representative. Before leaving Heathrow the full through-route air traffic flight plan had been filed by our office. This included the Paris-Bahrain air traffic control flight plan. When the passengers were all seated, we called for our start clearance and traffic clearance only to be told that CDG ground control had 'no flight plan'. After radio and telephone calls to London, which confirmed that the flight plan had been sent and acknowledged, we were again given the same message by the CDG controller. There was no access to the Paris control centre from our satellite terminal at CDG. The impasse was eventually unlocked when we prepared our own flight plan copy, and arranged a messenger to deliver it. We thus spent nearly two hours on the ground instead of what should have been a 45-minute stop.

The routeing out of Paris bore no relation to our filed or planned request, and we were held at low speed on a circuitous journey round the environs of the city before being allowed to climb and accelerate.

On the transatlantic route, our departure time from Washington clashed with Air France's time from JFK so that both aircraft would join the supersonic routeing at the same time. We were vying for the same eastbound supersonic route. The alternate route was displaced to the south and was longer, requiring more fuel and time. Cooperation between the airlines arranged that our expected departure time off the ramp would be exchanged via each company office, so that a clash could be avoided. An extra ten minutes' wait before starting engines was preferable to being penalised once airborne. However this process had a built-in element of imprecision in arriving at the forecast times when each Concorde would become airborne. Random delays were caused by take-off point congestion, air traffic departure control, and even last-minute passenger and baggage loading.

Sunsets, sunrises, and mirages

New York and Washington time is five hours behind London's. Concorde takes less than four hours on the westbound flight, and so gains more than an hour of daylight, as well as arriving an hour before departure, local time. The winter evening schedule was timed so that departure from Heathrow was after dark, and we could then view the sun rising from the west as we crossed the Atlantic.

British Airways Concorde, G-BOAC, is preserved at Manchester.

The eastbound flight can produce spectacular effects, rapidly shortening the onset of twilight and night. This is seen as a blue-black; semi-circular cap that visibly moves towards the aircraft as if to snuff out the light. As the sun sets rapidly behind Concorde a projection of the aircraft shape and its jet trail can be seen thrown onto the sky ahead with remarkable clarity. This looks as if there is another aircraft ahead and above, proceeding at the same speed.

I pointed this out to a passenger who was visiting the flight deck. She absolutely refused to believe that it was not another aircraft, and accused us of trying to fool her. When the next visitor arrived I asked her to look at the aircraft in front, claiming that it was going to Paris, before revealing the truth. Once again there was disbelief. At heights approaching 60,000 feet it is possible to see the curvature of the horizon if the lighting, time of day, and vapour layer refractions are favourable. Vision was so panoramic at times, with so many new perspectives of weather formation, that it could distract from routine flight monitoring. We were able to see a hurricane in mid-Atlantic, showing the characteristic S pattern around a swirling eye, and to view the complete system as we flew across the cloud mass. At night the sight of an array of 'shooting stars' seemed so much closer than when seen from subsonic heights. One of the bonuses throughout my flying career has been the sight of landscapes and cloudscapes of unique beauty. The chance to see our earth in a new perspective is an experience that can be enjoyed by only a few. With so much turmoil below, the chance to spend an hour or two above and away from it all has been a rare privilege. The knowledge of imminent retirement made these opportunities even more poignant.

Gatwick swansong

At the end of August 1980, about three weeks before leaving British Airways, I was asked to fly Concorde to Gatwick. The airport was celebrating its 50-year operational anniversary, and we would take a charter-load of passengers on a special trip around the

Peter Duffey at the controls of Concorde.

Bay of Biscay, to supersonic height and speed, serving a champagne lunch before returning. The occasion was festive, with a brass band playing our passengers on to the aircraft. After the round trip had been completed, we were preparing our return to Heathrow when the airport manager asked me to estimate what height we would reach over the end of the departure runway.

The aircraft was very light, with minimum fuel. I was now familiar with the low weight performance we experienced during training and said that this would be about 4,000 feet, if we used full reheat power for the permitted noise abatement procedure. An alternative was to reduce power when passing 1,000 feet,which would help to control the speed increase. The manager told us that a Cessna 172 would be positioned to photograph our departure, and he had to let the pilot know where to position the little airplane. I succumbed to the temptation for a full power and reheat climbout. We were airborne in less than 15 seconds, climbing out at 250 knots. Cleared by the controllers to 7,000 feet, and then to turn left for Heathrow arrival, we reached that height so quickly that it was possible to turn round close to the Gatwick terminal complex. We gave quite a thrill to the watching crowds, and avoided recording any official noise, although it delivered a resounding crackle to the immediate locality.

Coming in to land

My last flight, from New York to London, on 10 September 1980, was a fast one. We took just 3 hours and 35 minutes block time. The co-pilot, Senior First Officer Chris Norris, and engineer, Senior Engineering Officer George Floyd, together with the cabin crew, had rushed out into Manhattan to find a suitable beer mug, and had it inscribed appropriately. Keith Myers, by then the Flight Training Manager, replacing Norman Todd who had retired, had arranged for my wife and two daughters to meet us on arrival. The dark September evening was punctuated with flash photography. Fittingly our aircraft was G-BOAC, the one used for the initial endurance flying. As we walked away from the elegant shape it was difficult to suppress emotion and regret. To have been associated with so many wonderful people, and to leave on such a high note: this was the culmination of a wonderful and rewarding airline career.

My flying days were not quite over, however, for only a few months later we found ourselves based in Vancouver, in British Columbia. Obtaining the necessary Canadian flying licences had required passing a series of their examinations and flying tests, as there was no reciprocity with the UK. Going back to school and into the books once more, although time-consuming, was a healthy exercise preparatory to new work with a flying school. Conversion to seven types of aircraft, and the acquisition of a floatplane rating, opened up new horizons. This was followed by a period flying another de Havilland design, the twin-jet HS 125, for a large corporation. The development of Jeane's artistic career convinced us to remain here in this beautiful province, where she has found so much inspiration. I have now hung up the headphones, and stored the helmet, with many memories to sustain the passing years.